Action Research in Education

Ernie Stringer
Curtin University of Technology

PEARSON

Merrill
Prentice Hall

Upper Saddle River, New Jersey
Columbus, Ohio

Library of Congress Cataloging-in-Publication Data

Stringer, Ernest T.
  Action research in education / Ernie Stringer.
    p. cm.
  Includes bibliographical references and index.
  ISBN 0-13-097425-0
  1. Action research in education. I. Title.

LB1028.24.S86 2004
  370'.7'2—dc21
                                         2002044490

Vice President and Executive Publisher: Jeffery W. Johnston
Assistant Vice President and Publisher: Kevin M. Davis
Editorial Assistant: Autumn Crisp
Production Editor: Mary Harlan
Production Coordination: Lea Baranowski, Carlisle Publishers Services
Design Coordinator: Diane C. Lorenzo
Cover Designer: Rod Harris
Cover Image: Getty One
Text Design and Illustrations: Carlisle Communications
Production Manager: Laura Messerly
Director of Marketing: Ann Castel Davis
Marketing Manager: Amy June
Marketing Coordinator: Tyra Poole

This book was set in ITC Century Light by Carlisle Communications, Ltd. It was printed and bound by R. R. Donnelley & Sons Company. The cover was printed by Phoenix Color Corp.

Pearson Education Ltd.
Pearson Education Singapore Pte. Ltd.
Pearson Education Canada, Ltd.
Pearson Education—Japan

Pearson Education Australia Pty. Limited
Pearson Education North Asia Ltd.
Pearson Educación de Mexico, S.A. de C.V.
Pearson Education Malaysia Pte. Ltd.

10 9 8 7 6 5 4 3 2 1
ISBN: 0-13-097425-0

Preface

Research—A Personal History

Research has been part of my life since my childhood. At school I "researched" topics for class, carefully gathering material and sorting through it to select the most relevant information with which to formulate papers or presentations. In a high school physics class, I engaged in a small experiment with my teacher and classmates on a sports field. We used an empty can and a stopwatch to estimate the speed of sound. At that time, I also became fascinated by theories and experiments in cosmology and particle physics, which began a life-long fascination with explanations of the nature of the physical universe. As I write this book, I am struggling to read and understand *Fire in the Mind* (Johnson, 1995), which seeks to elucidate the ways scientists try to explain the puzzling phenomena coming to them from the infinitely regressive micro-world of particle physics, and to juxtapose these explanations with theories emerging from their investigations of deep space—the cosmos.

These first forays into the field of research expanded dramatically when I entered university and teacher training. In these contexts, I explored material derived from a wide range of experiments in the behavioral sciences, providing information about intelligence, personality, learning processes, child development, teaching strategies, and a host of related topics. This information helped me to grasp some of the fundamental features of human life—to know how and why people behaved as they did—and enabled me to understand more clearly how I could teach children effectively. This knowledge, sometimes laboriously acquired in education, psychology, and sociology classes, provided a wealth of information that still informs my educational practices. I've learned to understand the varying capabilities, capacities, and behaviors of young children as they grow into adulthood. I understand more clearly the conditions under which learning takes place and the different factors influencing educational achievement. As an experienced educator, I now draw from a considerable stock of knowledge as I organize the teaching/learning processes with the diverse groups of students who enter my classes.

When I entered graduate school, my first research methods classes showed how these experiments were constructed and enacted and showed me how survey research, sometimes called quasi-experimental research, could further extend my

understanding of the very complex problems involved in educating diverse populations. I learned how to perform research investigating the effects of factors like social
class, gender, culture, and language on educational achievement, and to structure investigations exploring their relationship to employment, income, health status, and
so on. Not only were my research skills increasing dramatically, but I was able to link
knowledge available from research studies to theories of education, human behavior,
and the social world.

Research, therefore, has informed my educational practices and made them increasingly sophisticated and effective. I have become aware, however, of the limitations of the often abstract and highly generalized nature of much of the information
I derive from the research literature. Much of it is compelling and makes a great deal
of sense within the sophisticated and complex explanations contained with the theories of the academic disciplines—psychology, sociology, anthropology. But I have
also learned that much of this theory is often irrelevant and lacks meaning or utility
when applied to many of the deep-seated and long-term problems people experience
in classrooms and schools.

Although I became aware of these limitations as a graduate student at the University of Illinois, the full force of this paradox became apparent in the early 1980s
when I started to engage in work in Aboriginal communities in remote regions of Australia. In these contexts, the sophistication and breadth of my academic expertise
proved illusory, and the concepts and theories of behavioral and social theory were
lacking in substance or function. As I helped people in these places come to grips
with the difficult and multifaceted problems they faced in their everyday community
life, I learned a decisive lesson about the nature of knowledge and its application to
everyday life. I learned that the sophisticated knowledge emanating from academic
understandings often had little relevance in these contexts.

Even today, if you visit a remote Aboriginal community you will see the tattered
remnants of community gardens developed with great skill using the best information and technology available from horticultural science. What is not evident is the
place of *gardening* in the life of a desert people still heavily instilled with the cultural perspectives of the hunter-gatherer. You can see their counterparts in schools
in urban and suburban America, where dusty boxes of unused materials remind us
of yet another quick-fix program developed and funded, for a time, to deal superficially with some deep-seated educational issue.

At this time, I also learned how people's own knowledge and wisdom were often
more useful in working toward solutions to the problems they faced. A clear instance
emerged during a visit to a remote community where the people, becoming tired of
the inadequate and damaging education provided for their children, set up a school
themselves. Despite inadequate classroom accommodation and a dearth of books,
materials, and equipment, the community school provided one of the most exciting
educational experiences for children I have witnessed. Although they were assisted
in this process by a non-Aboriginal teacher who lived with them and provided her expertise, the school was structured and operated on the basis of educational processes
and a style of operation that "made sense" to the lifestyle and life-ways of local people—their culture. Though very different, in many respects, from traditional schools,
it was very effective in providing an effective and relevant education for the children
of this community.

At that time, I was unaware that I had witnessed what was, in effect, the outcome of an action research process. The people had started with a problem—providing adequate schooling for their children—and worked toward a solution. They also gained information and expertise as they acquired the understanding necessary to organize their school. Each of the many questions involved in developing a fully functioning school—how to build classrooms, how to hire and pay a teacher, how to develop a curriculum, how to organize a timetable of learning, and more—became subjects of investigation. As they developed their understanding of each of these issues, people were able to map out the actions required to bring this part of the puzzle into operation. They started with a little understanding of what they wished to achieve and worked systematically to acquire the knowledge leading to a solution to their problem—a classical action research process.

That experience has changed the way I now view research and the way I engage in research processes. For me, the process of research central to my professional and community life is participatory action research. It requires me to work with people to assist them in making use of their own understandings and expertise—to use their experience and local wisdom to work systematically through a process of investigation to acquire deeper, broader, and more effective understandings that enable them to develop workable solutions to the problems they investigate.

Although I still appreciate my extensive academic and professional knowledge, I engage it warily, sensitive to the need for people to conceptualize and understand issues in terms that make sense in their everyday lives. I, therefore, provide my professional expertise gently and with humility—always providing opportunities for people to reject or modify ideas I might inject into an investigation. In a recent community-based research project, I provided neighborhood parents with a list of questions to use in interviews. I presented them as examples of the type of questions they might ask and was pleased to see them accept the general approach to interviewing, but to tell me "You can't ask that question like that! You'd have to say . . . ," and then start to formulate questions of their own.

Research has become a much broader set of activities than those I initially learned in my experimental and survey research classes. According to the issue, the context, and the purpose of research I may now choose from a wide array of approaches and methods to satisfy the needs of the project in hand. Since I largely work as a consultant, however, helping people find solutions to particular problems, I rarely engage in experimental or survey research. In school settings, I assist educators and families in improving their educational practices or in evaluating, planning, or implementing educational programs and services. This is the work that informs my educational understandings and forms the basis for the examples and illustrations of action research processes in this book.

The effectiveness of this approach to research is demonstrated by the degree to which teachers in the United States have been able to apply successfully my models of research. Their work extends in range and variety across age groups, grade and school levels, and across regions. Educators from preschool to university graduate classes successfully apply research processes to enhance their educational practices or to find solutions to significant problems. Stories from their experience permeate the pages of this book and illustrate the ways action research has been used in schools.

The stories also include accounts, however, of the way action research has been used in the community to assist educators in making effective links with parents and other neighborhood groups. Stories demonstrate the continuing ways in which I have found action research to be a productive professional set of tools and a means of enhancing and enlivening my professional life and instilling it with joy and vigor as I work collaboratively with people in their schools, offices, homes, and neighborhoods. It keeps me alive, enhances my spirit, and maintains the keen edge of my understanding of people's lives.

The Nature of This Book

The previous narrative suggests how this book sits within the research methods literature. Though there are many approaches to research, each valid for its own purposes, the orientation to research in this book is derived from my history of experience in educational and community settings. It does not represent "best practice" as defined by an objective set of criteria, but it does represent a methodology that has produced highly successful, practical outcomes for those with whom I have worked in the past two decades. The approach to action research described in this book also represents an approach to inquiry derived from a tradition originally ascribed to Kurt Lewin in the United States, but having more recent proponents such as Peter Reason in the United Kingdom, and Stephen Kemmis, Robin McTaggart, and Bob Dick in Australia.

In a recent presentation, management consultant Alistair Mant suggested that it is possible to envisage human systems as either "frog-like" or "bicycle-like." The difference is that when a bicycle is not working properly it can be taken apart, examined, and the faulty part repaired or replaced. You cannot do the same with a frog. It will cease to function. I believe that human systems are frog-like, insofar as investigation that seeks to work mechanistically with people's work and community lives has limited utility. We need to acknowledge the organic nature of human systems and work with them accordingly.

The model of action research thus necessarily focuses largely on qualitative research. It differs from the "bicycle-like," objective and reductionist, clinical approaches to research common to many forms of inquiry, though it may complement or be complemented by clinical studies. Essentially, both researcher and researchee are positioned quite differently and are engaged in meaning-making processes in which both must participate. Though apparently time-consuming, action research works on the basis of long-term economics—that an initial investment will pay off in the longer term—and will provide continuing and increasing dividends as those involved become more skilled and develop a sense of community—a "common unity" of perspective and purpose.

The book, therefore, also has a very practical orientation since it speaks directly to the needs of those involved on a daily basis with classrooms and schools. It seeks to provide tools and skills that enhance the ability of teachers and administrators to engage their demanding work more effectively. More important, however, is the desire to ensure that research becomes a creative and joyful process that taps the life and vitality of the students who enter our schools—that it engenders an approach to educational work that contributes to a truly human education.

Acknowledgments

It is difficult to select from that multitude of people who have made significant contributions to the writing and development of this book. My close colleagues and students at Curtin University of Technology, the University of New Mexico, Texas A&M University, and the University of Houston, by engaging in constant dialogue around the ideas and practices revealed in this book, have provided clarity and energy to the project. Jill Abdullah, Bill Genat, and Fritz Kaser have provided particularly unique and challenging perspectives that have helped frame and elucidate the material encompassed by this book. I am particularly indebted to Maria Hines and Christina Chavez Apodaco, whose dedication to the education of children in their communities provided clear examples of the way parents can engage in effective research.

Thanks are also due to Kevin Davis and members of his staff, April Crisp and Mary Harlan as well as Lea Baranowski at Carlisle Communications, for easing the path toward publication. His efficient and direct approach to our work together has been both encouraging and productive, providing clear direction and a supportive work environment. I'm also indebted to reviewers who provided detailed feedback for each chapter: Blaine C. Ackley, University of Portland; Robert Fallows, Northern Arizona University; Douglas Fisher, San Diego State University; Gonzalo Garcia, Jr., Texas A&M University; Barbara B. Kawulich, Georgia State University and Mercer University; Ochieng' K'Olewe, Western Maryland College; Margaret Malenka, Michigan State University; and Mildred Murray-Ward, California Lutheran University. Their efforts have greatly increased the clarity and utility of the text and enabled me to discard extraneous material and be more precise in my writing.

Finally, writing a text requires long hours of highly focused energy which often detract from family life. My greatest thanks, therefore, go to my dear wife and wonderful partner, Rosalie Dwyer, who continues to provide personal support and professional input to my work.

Brief Contents

Contents

4 Gathering Data: Sources of Information   62

5 Giving Voice: Interpretive and Qualitative Data Analysis   96

6 Representation: Communicating Research Processes and Outcomes   125

9 On-line Resources   228

References   235

NOTE: Every effort has been made to provide accurate and current Internet information in this book. However, the Internet and information posted on it are constantly changing, so it is inevitable that some of the Internet addresses listed in this textbook will change.

The Purposes
of Action Research

Action Research in Classrooms and Schools

A common response from teachers when it is suggested they engage in research in their classrooms is often some combination of surprise, disbelief, and wariness. Their responses are linked to images of research involving highly technical routines of investigation engaging sophisticated research instruments and complex statistical analysis. The teachers cannot imagine that they would have the time or the inclination to engage in such activity, or that it would serve any useful purpose. These images relate to traditional approaches to experimental research that fail to encompass the diverse array of teacher, practitioner, and action research becoming increasingly commonplace in schools and classrooms. Although these relatively new approaches to research have much in common with the traditional approaches engaged by scholars and scientists, they have distinctive qualities that make them more particularly relevant to classroom practitioners. Recent developments in research methodology have therefore spawned a rich variety of approaches for teachers and others involved in schools to engage in systematic inquiry with the intent of improving their educational practices or solving significant problems they experience in their professional life.

Action research now provides a fruitful avenue of investigation for teachers, administrators, and others involved in education. It has spawned a generation of professionals who are sensitive to the value of research and the accompanying need to rethink aspects of traditional classroom and school roles and practices. In a recent research class I asked participants, all experienced practitioners, to tell me how doing research was important for them. They focused on general issues concerning their teaching practices and the ways systematic inquiry might assist them in resolving those issues. One, focusing on the administrative, organizational context of her work, talked of "the need to learn to interpret outside the hierarchy" making the familiar ways of organizing school life "strange." Her words echoed the sentiments of another class member who, speaking as a Hispanic person, realized how damaging research could be when information derived from generalized studies was used inappropriately in particular classroom settings. A fellow class member expressed that idea as "using research as a vehicle of oppression." Other class participants were concerned about the impact on children and teachers of current school practices, many of which they perceived as either damaging or inequitable. They wished to learn an approach to research that enabled them to empower teachers and children, giving them voice and enabling them to be part of the research process rather than being outside looking in.

One member of the class, mindful of ways in which experts and administrators had impinged on his professional life, expressed a concern that he might be guilty of the same crime. "How do I leave my own baggage behind in order to see the world [clearly]?" This was a common sentiment, expressed as the need to "change my mind-sets," be more alert, be more sensitive, and see more clearly what was happening to people and children around them. Others spoke of the need to be sensitive to their position as researchers, expressing a desire to "be a team player with the people I'm working with," or "to sit and talk with children."

All were concerned that their research should have some practical outcome. As one indicated passionately, "I want to do research that will make a difference!" Another concurred, saying "I want to have a positive effect on children." All saw research, therefore, as a way of furthering their professional life, enabling them to improve the educational experience of children in schools, and having an impact on the lives of those with whom they worked. Research, they implied, could provide powerful tools for improving or enhancing their educational work.

Although there are limits on the time and resources available to engage research in everyday classroom and school life, by building their research capabilities, teachers enhance their professional capabilities as they acquire and extend the skills and experience to engage in systematic investigation of significant issues. Action research is designed for practical purposes having direct and effective outcomes in the settings in which it is engaged. At the heart of the process, however, are teachers with the intent to investigate issues that help them more effectively and efficiently engage the complex world of the classroom.

Action research is not just a formal process of inquiry, but may be applied systematically as a tool for learning in classrooms and schools. Sometimes referred to as inquiry learning, action research is particularly relevant to those who engage in constructivist approaches to pedagogy. From an administrator's perspective, it is also a management tool providing the means for developing effective plans, policies, programs, and procedures at classroom, school, or regional levels. Chapter 7 provides specific procedures, with relevant examples, of the ways action research processes assist educators to accomplish these types of activities. Although the application of systematic research processes sometimes requires a significant investment of time and resources, the payoffs are considerable. Improved educational outcomes, highly engaged students, enthusiastic parents, and effective programs emerge that enhance the quality of student achievement and the educational life of all those who inhabit the school.

Research Conceptualized

The Meriam-Webster on-line dictionary (2001) provides the following ways to use the term "research":

1. The collecting of information about a particular subject
2. Careful or diligent search
3. Studious inquiry or examination

4. Investigation or experimentation aimed at the discovery and interpretation of facts
5. Revision of accepted theories or laws in the light of new facts
6. Practical application of such new or revised theories or laws

Thus, when we research a particular topic for a school project, we are doing so in terms indicated by definition one, collecting information in a general sense. Traditionally, research engaged by scientists and scholars related to definitions four and five, though in recent times a broader use includes the more general sense of systematic inquiry implied by definitions two and three. When practitioners engage in *action* research, however, they add another dimension to the definition. They engage in careful, diligent inquiry, not for purposes of discovering new facts or revising accepted laws or theories, but to acquire information having practical application to the solution of specific problems related to their work. This book focuses on the latter use of the term, though its intent is to demonstrate how some of the tools of scientists and scholars may help professionals to solve significant problems and enhance their educational practices.

The deeper purpose of research is to provide people with knowledge and understanding that makes a difference in their lives. Research is a form of transformational learning that increases the "stock of knowledge" that provides people with the means to engage their lives more effectively. This does not necessarily mean fundamental changes in world view or cultural orientation, but includes the small "ah-ha" moments that enable people to see themselves, others, events, and phenomena with greater clarity or in a completely different way.

Transformational understandings derived from research can provide people with new concepts, ideas, explanations, or interpretations that enable them to see the world in a different way and therefore to do things in a different, hopefully better, way. Though any type of learning may provide people with feelings of satisfaction, research may also provide an understanding that truly moves them into a different universe—the effect of a truly "ah-haaa!" experience. Good research, for me, is a truly epiphanic experience. I have seen the excitement and wonder in people's eyes, heard the wonder in their voices, and felt the excitement and even awe that comes with a new way of seeing, and sometimes a new way of being.

Research, more formally, may be defined as a process of systematic investigation leading to increased understanding of a phenomenon or issue of interest. Though research is ultimately a quite ordinary activity, a process for looking again at an existing situation (*re*-searching it) and seeing it in a different way, systematic processes of investigation provide the means for ensuring strong and effective processes of inquiry. Within the academic and professional worlds, however, two major systems of inquiry—paradigms—provide distinctly different ways in which to investigate phenomena in the physical and human universe. **Objective science,** more correctly known as **scientific positivism,** and **naturalistic inquiry,** often referred to as **qualitative research,** provide powerful but different approaches to research. For purposes of clarity, the following chapter explores the differences between the two paradigms to provide researchers a clearer understanding about the nature of investigations in which they are involved in their own classrooms and schools. As the following section indicates, action research has a history and tradition that differs significantly from other forms of research that have been commonly used to investigate educational issues.

Characteristics of Action Research

Action research has a long history that is often associated with the work of Kurt Lewin who viewed action research as a cyclical, dynamic, and collaborative process in which people addressed social issues affecting their lives. Through cycles of planning, acting, observing, and reflecting, participants sought a change in practices leading to social action for improvement. A form of action research was used to address problems of assimilation, segregation, and discrimination, assisting people to resolve issues, initiate change, and study the impact of those changes (Lewin 1938, Lewin and Lewin 1942, Lewin 1946, Lewin 1948). Lewin's approach to action research is reflected in the definition given by Bogden and Biklen (1992); "the systematic collection of information that is designed to bring about social change."

Kemmis and McTaggart (1988) suggest action research is "a form of collective, self-reflective enquiry undertaken by participants in social situations in order to improve the rationality and justice of their own social or educational practices, as well as their understanding of these practices and the situations in which these practices are carried out." For Kemmis and McTaggart, research is carried out by any group with a shared concern and is only action research when it is collaborative.

Reason and Bradbury (2001) extend this vision by describing action research as "a participatory, democratic process concerned with developing practical knowing in the pursuit of worthwhile human purposes, grounded in a participatory worldview which we believe is emerging at this historical moment. It seeks to bring together action and reflection, theory and practice, in participation with others, in the pursuit of practical solutions to issues of pressing concern to people, and more generally the flourishing of individual persons and their communities." For them, action research requires skills and methods that enable researchers to foster an inquiring approach to their own practices, to engage in face-to-face work with others to address issues of mutual concern, and to create a wider community of inquiry involving whole organizations.

Action research, therefore, might be distinguished from *practitioner research* insofar as classroom practitioners may make use of a variety of approaches to research to assist them in their teaching. When they stand back from the class and obtain factual information related to teaching practices, learning strategies, assessment, and so on, they may use a variety of small experiments or surveys, engage in classroom observations, or apply reflective analysis to issues of interest. When they engage others in the process of inquiry, however, with the intent of solving a problem related to their educational work together, they are doing *action research.*

Not all adherents, however, see action research as participatory, and there is continuing debate about what "counts" as action research. Susan Noffke (1997) suggests, "action research is best thought of as a large family, one in which beliefs and relationships vary greatly. More than a set of discrete practices, it is a group of ideas emergent in various contexts. It takes only brief perusal of the action research literature to recognize that the growth and salience of work in this area in recent years have been marked not only by an increase in volume of references but also a proliferation of varied usages of the term" (p. 306). Noffke quotes a generic definition of action research from ERIC (Educational Resources Information Center) as "research designed to yield practical results that are immediately applicable to a specific situation or problem."

The literature on action research in education is now voluminous, but some of the more recent contributions include Arhar, Holly, and Kasten (2000); Atweh, Weeks, and Kemmis (1998); Bell (1994); Berge and Ve (2000); Bray, Lee, Smith, and Yorks (2000); Brown and Dowling (1998); Burns (1999); Burnaford, Fischer, and Hobson (2001); Calhoun (1994); Carr and Kemmis (1986); Carson and Sumara (1997); Christiansen, Goulet, Krentz, and Maeers (1997); Dadas (1995); Fals-Borda and Rahman (1991); Heron (1996); Hollingworth (1997); McClean (1995); McNiff (1995); McNiff, Lomax, and Whitehead (1996); McTaggart (1997); Mills (2000); Noffke and Stevenson (1995); Reason and Bradbury (2001); Schmuck (1997); Stringer (1999); Wallace (1998); and Wells et al (1994). These diverse orientations are based on the different theories used by the writers, the different assumptions that derive from these theories about what should or could be accomplished, and the set of appropriate practices that are therefore entailed. Noffke (1997), for instance, defines differences in action research according to their personal, professional, and political dimensions. On a more pragmatic note, Calhoun (1994) focuses on the possibilities for engaging action research at the level of the individual teacher, as the collaborative practice of a group of teachers, or as a more encompassing process involving a school. Most authors, however, present a naturalistic approach to research, seeking to engage teachers in reflective processes illuminating significant features of their classroom practice and enabling them to understand the experience and perspective of other participants in classroom and school contexts.

The following section, therefore, provides a description of the approach to action research presented in this book. It differs from much of the literature on teacher research or practitioner research in that it does not focus solely on teacher knowledge, though that is an important ingredient. Neither is its primary intent to add to the stock of knowledge available to teachers, though the outcomes of action research projects may indeed act in that way. The action research described herein focuses on:

1. **Change:** Improving practices and behaviors by changing them
2. **Reflection:** People thinking, reflecting, and/or theorizing about their own practices, behaviors, and situations
3. **Participation:** People changing their own practices and behaviors, not those of others
4. **Inclusion:** Starting with the agendas and perspectives of the least powerful, widening the circle to include all those affected by the problem
5. **Sharing:** People sharing their perspectives with others
6. **Understanding:** Achieving clarity of understanding of the different perspectives and experiences of all involved
7. **Repetition:** Repeating cycles of research activity leading toward solution to a problem
8. **Practice:** Testing emerging understandings by using them as the basis for changing practices or constructing new practices
9. **Community:** Works toward the development/building of a learning community

The systematic processes of action research extend teacher professional capacities, providing a set of tools that enhance general classroom planning and school program development. They enable educators to come to grips with significant problems in classrooms and schools that seem impervious to solutions provided by a teacher's regular professional stock of knowledge. The processes of inquiry signaled in action research may therefore be used for general classroom and school purposes, but are particularly relevant when educators face long-term, deep-seated problems indicating a need for significant changes to existing programs and practices, or for new educational strategies or programs. Action research differs quite significantly from the highly objective and generalizable experimental and survey studies that continue to provide significant information about schools and classrooms. It does, however, encapsulate the systematic qualitative research routines now becoming commonplace in the educational arena and increasingly applied by teachers and administrators as part of their work in schools.

Using Action Research

Action research has a wide range of applications in classroom, school, and community contexts. Action research provides the basis for formulating effective solutions to highly significant classroom and school problems—classes that are particularly fractious, exceptionally problematic groups of students, underachieving students, multiple external demands, and so on. Action research also provides a useful tool for day-to-day planning in classrooms such as lesson planning, formulating teaching strategies, and student assessment, or more extensive tasks like syllabus planning, curriculum construction, and evaluation. For the school administrator, action research is also a management tool, providing the means to systematically resolve difficult situations, to engage in program development and evaluation, or to develop strategic initiatives with families and the community.

A small sample of action research projects in schools, universities, and community contexts includes the following:

• A young teacher, concerned by the disciplinary problems she experienced with a group of "at-risk" boys in her classroom, engaged in an action research process that revealed to her a very different understanding of these children. The knowledge she gained changed her view of the problems she was experiencing and lead to dramatic changes in the way she approached her teaching.

• A third-grade teacher, concerned that the district was cutting funds for art in schools, investigated with her students the part art played in their classroom lives. They produced an illustrated booklet and a mural for presentation to the district superintendent.

• A teacher engaged action research processes with his students to construct and implement class syllabi and achieved high levels of student engagement and exciting learning outcomes.

• A neighborhood group engaged in participatory action research with principals, teachers, and parents to investigate ways of increasing parental involvement in local schools. Between them, they produced a highly useful list of actions to be taken by teachers and parents.

• A school hired a consultant to help them evaluate its programs. Using action research, he worked with teachers, administrators, and students to highlight positive features of the school's operation and to reveal issues and challenges needing to be addressed.

• A university department used action research processes to plan the implementation of a large new program to integrate technology into educational programs. The project was highly successful in the levels of engagement of participants and the outcomes achieved.

• A school used action research to resolve racial problems threatening the stability of school life. A teacher assisted a group of students to investigate related issues in their school and community, leading to a new program aimed at ameliorating problems the school had experienced.

• Two middle-school teachers used action research processes to investigate issues of harassment and prejudice with middle-school students. Following processes of exploration, students in both groups identified key features of these issues and used them as the basis for producing and staging highly informative plays.

Case Study: Teacher Action Research

The following story, and the examples contained in subsequent chapters, provides some indication of the potential rewards to be attained as educators become sophisticated researchers in their own right. The stories illustrate how classroom teachers have added to their repertoire of professional skills and in the process made their work more productive, successful, and enjoyable.

Student Apathy: A Teacher Studies Her Classroom

By Lorise Dorry

A month into a new school year, I was puzzled by my inability to engage the students in my sixth-grade elementary class in a poorer suburb of a large city. In my fifth year of teaching, I felt myself to be a competent and experienced teacher, now well able to handle the rigorous daily routines of working with a large group of children. Despite careful creative planning, however, the students seemed to lack the life and vitality I had experienced in other classes. While they were not badly behaved children, they seemed to be merely "going through the motions," were apt to be a little cynical about the work I prescribed, and "smart" comments intruded into their classroom discussions with some degree of regularity. Despite instituting a number of classroom management techniques and attempting to find interesting ways to present the work, I found them decidedly apathetic. Nothing I tried, it seemed, had any impact on the dull listlessness with which they greeted each new learning activity, or enticed them to improve the rather mediocre work they consistently produced.

Six weeks into the semester, experiencing some degree of frustration and increasing levels of anxiety about my capabilities as a teacher, I decided the time had come to investigate the situation more thoroughly. Using an action research routine I had learned in college, I systematically planned how I would seek to gain greater understanding about how and why my students were so apathetic in class. I began to observe my class more carefully, noting the ways different students went about their work, when, where, and how they engaged in the different classroom activities, their responses to different events occurring within the classroom, and the ways in which different individuals and groups interacted. In doing so I gained greater insights into the social dynamics of my classroom, noting those students who tended to "hang" together, individuals who seemed to be the natural leaders, and those who were isolates—the informal social groups and leaders that are part of any social situation. Over the following weeks, I also found opportunities to meet informally with a number of students—leaders and members from the different informal groups—chatting with them in the school yard, corridors, and in "down-times" in the classroom. I gradually accumulated information that enabled me to understand my classroom from the children's perspective and gained much deeper insights into what was affecting my children's classroom life.

Wishing to take advantage of the new insights into my students' experience, I decided to engage the class in a research project as part of the literacy objectives of my class syllabus. I explained to them my concerns about their apparent lack of interest in their schoolwork and my desire to have them help me explore the issue. Using small focus groups, I provided time for students to talk about this issue and list the major features of their experience. As the list of issues emerged, I noticed how negative the comments seemed:

- *The work we do in class is boring.*
- *We don't like the reading we have to do each day.*
- *Math is too difficult.*
- *It's embarrassing when Mrs. Dorry comments on our work.*
- *We hate the comments some students make about us.*

And so on.

A little perturbed by the negative tone of their comments, I asked students to return to their groups to discuss whether there was anything they liked about the class. Feedback sessions revealed a number of aspects of the class experience they enjoyed:

- *The computer lab is cool.*
- *The last social studies project was awesome.*
- *We like it when we can work in groups.*
- *We really like Mrs Dorry.*

And so on.

The following day I returned to the issues with the whole class, asking them to talk about those they considered most important. Gradually, a consensus emerged that "boring class work" was a major issue. Further group discussions identified the areas of work and the type of activities they found boring. In the process, some children started to spontaneously suggest ways they could make their work more interesting. At that stage, I suggested that students form work groups to investigate ways they could make work in those areas more interesting. Different groups focusing on reading and literature, social studies, math, and science worked excitedly as they came up with "bright ideas" drawn from their previous classroom experiences, from ideas they'd heard other students or family talk about, or from their own creative imagination.

Sessions in following days provided opportunities for each group to present their ideas to the whole class and for other students to provide suggestions for extending or enhancing the learning content or activities being presented. The process was not straightforward for all groups. The math group, for instance, required considerable attention, and I discovered I needed to provide a simple explanation of the purposes and content of the math syllabus to the work group. I discovered, however, that this provided them with a much deeper understanding of math as an area of study, an understanding that was passed on to the class in feedback sessions.

In the following weeks, I was able to work with the class, providing simple descriptions of the syllabus of each of the content areas and having the students help me to show how they could attain the objectives though learning activities they were largely able to define themselves. As they engaged the process, I noticed increasing levels of engagement, as students not only became absorbed in the learning activities they had helped devise but excited about their achievements. They also, in the process, dealt with some of the behavioral problems that had been noted in their initial discussions, devising a "code of conduct" that, amongst other things, prohibited "putting down" remarks, or comments likely to embarrass individuals.

Within a few weeks of starting the process, I was able to reflect on what the class had accomplished under my guidance. Most of the students were engaged in their work most of the time, they appeared happy with and interested in the work they were doing, and the quality of their work had risen dramatically. Eventually, I started getting positive comments from parents indicating they were aware of the differences in their children's responses to school. "I don't know what you've done," said one parent with a laugh, "But I have to stop Clyde from coming to school at daybreak!" My principal and fellow teachers also noted the difference. One commented, "That class has been difficult to work with for years. You've certainly made a difference. What are you doing?"

By the end of the year, comparing results on tests from previous years, I was able to take satisfaction in noting the gains accomplished in many areas by many of the students and the excitement and enthusiasm that permeated my class for much of the day. By having the class assist me in systematically investigating the problem I had identified, I was not only able to understand more clearly the nature of the problem, but to engage my students in helping plan solutions to the problems that emerged during our research.

An Action Research Routine: Systematic Processes of Inquiry

Although action research has much in common with the regular problem-solving and planning processes used by educators in the course of their daily classroom and school work, its strength lies in its systematic execution of carefully articulated processes of inquiry. As researchers implement a study, they:

- **Design the study**—carefully refining the issue to be investigated, planning systematic processes of inquiry, and checking the ethics and validity of their work
- **Gather data**—including information from a variety of sources
- **Analyze the data**—to identify key features of the issue investigated
- **Communicate**—the outcomes of the study to relevant audiences
- **Use**—the outcomes of the study to work toward resolution of the issue investigated

These processes may usefully be depicted as shown in Figure 1.1.

As the figure illustrates, action research is distinguished from basic research by an "action" phase of inquiry. While basic research provides information not necessarily used in the research context, action research always has an immediate practical or applied purpose. Action research usually is cyclical in nature, since research participants continuously cycle through processes of investigation as they work towards effective solutions to their research problem. The sequence depicted previously, therefore, is more commonly presented as a cycle, as shown in Figure 1.2.

In some contexts action research is presented as a helix (see Figure 1.3) to indicate that phases of the research are repeated over time.

Working Developmentally: Enlarging the Circle of Inquiry

Although action research works effectively for discrete problems and issues within classrooms, it has the potential for more extended applications across classrooms, within schools, or within a community. As participants cycle through a research process, increasing understandings reveal related issues going beyond the immediate focus of investigation, pointing to productive possibilities that might emerge by increasing the scope and power of inquiry. Investigation of specific problems often reveals the multiple dimensions of the situation requiring attention, and investigation of each of those dimensions further illuminates the situation, revealing further possibilities for action.

<----------------------------------- ACTION RESEARCH ----------------------------------->

<------------------------ BASIC RESEARCH -------------------------->

RESEARCH DESIGN	DATA GATHERING	DATA ANALYSIS	COMMUNICATION	ACTION
INITIATING A STUDY	CAPTURING STAKEHOLDER EXPERIENCES AND PERSPECTIVES	IDENTIFYING KEY FEATURES OF EXPERIENCE	WRITING REPORTS	CREATING SOLUTIONS
Setting the stage			Reports Ethnographies Biographies	Solving problems
Focusing and framing	Interviewing	Analyzing epiphanies and illuminative experiences	PRESENTATIONS AND PERFORMANCES	Classroom practices
Literature review	Observing			Curriculum development
Sources of information	Artifact review	Categorizing and coding	Presentations Drama Poetry	Evaluation
Ethics	Literature review	Enhancing analysis	Song Dance Art	Family and community
Validity		Constructing category systems	Video Multimedia	School plans

Figure 1.1
Action Research Sequence

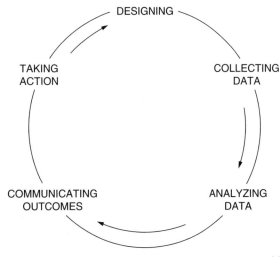

Figure 1.2
Action Research Cycle

11

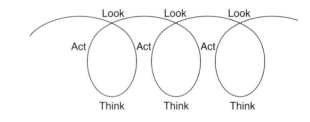

Figure 1.3
Action Research Helix

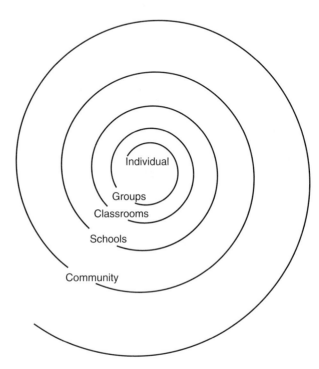

Figure 1.4
Action Research Spiral

The process of "starting small" and increasing the breadth and complexity of activity is what I call "working developmentally." This is very different from the developmental psychology or child development that is an integral part of most education programs, though conceptually there are some similarities. In each, it is important to engage the learner at the level they are capable of comprehending and achieving according to their stage of "development." In participatory action research, a study may start with limited objectives but the scope of the study may be extended as understanding and awareness increase (see Figure 1.4). The potential for positive change and development increases exponentially as increasing numbers of people and issues are included.

When Shelia Baldwin's group (Baldwin, 1997) investigated the problem of racial disharmony in their school, for instance, they discovered the need to increase the scope of their investigation to include their homes and neighborhoods. The understandings emerging from these investigations greatly increased the power of their investigation and provided the basis for school-wide action.

In similar fashion, girls involved in the sexual harassment study (see Chapter 9) first increased the number of girls involved, then discovered the need to include boys as part of the group. Investigation of group members' own experiences eventually revealed the need to communicate with other people, including school administrators and security officers. They were eventually able to take actions that enabled them to inform all people within the school of the outcomes of their investigation and to see quite dramatic outcomes emerge from their efforts.

A key feature of developmental process is to start with limited objectives. Although many problems within schools, such as high drop-out rates or low student achievement, are complex and multidimensional in scope, it is best to focus initial inquiries on some tangible and achievable objectives. Small initial gains provide people with the stimulus of success and inspire them to take further action. By engaging continuous cycles of the "look, think, act" process, they are able to encompass more dimensions of the problem and increase levels of engagement. Eventually, they may be able to incorporate other stakeholders—teachers, administrators, family, and community—thus marshalling increased levels of support and resources that extend the power of actions they take.

Summary

- Action research is a process of systematic inquiry.
- The purpose of action research is to provide educational practitioners with new knowledge and understanding enabling them to improve educational practices or resolve significant problems in classrooms and schools.
- Action research derives from a research tradition emphasizing cyclical, dynamic, and collaborative approaches to investigation.

- A common process of inquiry includes:
  - Design of the study
  - Data gathering
  - Data analysis
  - Communicating outcomes
  - Taking action
- Action research may be engaged as a developmental process that systematically increases the scope of the investigation.

Understanding Action Research: Exploring Issues of Paradigm and Method

2

Introduction

One of the difficulties of engaging in research is the proliferation of methods employed to study educational issues. Thirty years ago, the term "research" was used in university or professional contexts to refer to "scientific research." This term, in turn, commonly referred to "experimental research," which was seen as the epitome of scientific method. The search for truth and certainty encompassed by this view of research has been replaced by an understanding that a variety of different methods provide strong and valid approaches to investigation. In such circumstances it is all too easy for novice researchers to become confused by this proliferation of viewpoints and approaches to research or to scramble them into a disconnected set of procedures that undermine the clarity and power of systematic investigation. This chapter explores the nature of action research to clarify the ways it differs from other commonly conceived approaches to research.

Although action research has much in common with traditional experimental research engaged by scholars and scientists, it has distinctive qualities that make it more specifically relevant to classroom practitioners. To assist our exploration, we will first review the concept "research," and then clarify distinctions made between the two major research paradigms, commonly called quantitative research and qualitative research. In all this the intent is to provide practitioners with effective approaches to research that have direct, practical applications to their schools and classrooms.

Distinguishing Between Different Approaches to Research: Objective Science and Naturalistic Inquiry

Research may be defined as a process of systematic investigation leading to increased understanding of a phenomenon or issue of interest. Though research is ultimately quite an ordinary activity, a process for looking again at an existing situation (re-searching it) and seeing it in a different way, systematic processes of investigation provide the means for ensuring strong and effective processes of inquiry.

As indicated, the term "research" in education was once commonly associated with "science," indicating a process of investigation or experimentation aimed at the discovery and interpretation of facts and the development of universal theories or laws. More recently "research" has been interpreted more broadly to include systematic inquiry by educational practitioners. There is now no approach commonly accepted as the best way to do research, but a variety of approaches using different methods in order to accomplish different types of purpose. To some extent, the juxtaposition of different methodological approaches has muddied the research waters, with researchers often inappropriately applying research methodologies. The intent of the following discussion, therefore, is to clarify major approaches to research to ensure that action researchers use research tools appropriate to the task at hand.

Two major paradigms compete for interest and attention, both providing powerful, but distinct, ways in which to investigate phenomena in the physical and human universe. Science, or scientific positivism—often referred to as quantitative research—and **naturalistic inquiry**—often referred to as *qualitative research*—provide powerful but different approaches to research, each based on a different set of assumptions about what is right and good as a way of acquiring knowledge.

Research holds the promise of assisting educational practitioners to investigate and find workable solutions to problematic events occurring on a day-to-day basis in classrooms and schools. There are times when they need to disengage themselves from subjective involvement in everyday events, to stand back and observe the situation objectively, and to see whether they can envisage the situation according to some underlying set of influences hidden in the day-to-day complexities of activity and interaction. At these times, they might engage the viewpoint of scientific positivism, seeking to establish the facts of the situation and to apply scientific formulated theories and explanations for events and behaviors.

At other times, however, these procedures will prove inadequate with the very concise nature of scientific method—the very procedures themselves—inhibiting the formulation of effective solutions to the problem investigated. In these circumstances, **qualitative** or **naturalistic** approaches to research provide a different set of tools to deal with the situation. These provide the means to investigate the complex ways people interact in their everyday lives and enable classroom and school practitioners to increase their understanding of the events they observe. In particular, they gain greater insight into the ways people interpret events from their own perspective, providing culturally and contextually appropriate information assisting them to more effectively manage problems they confront in classrooms and schools.

As Figure 2.1 indicates, objective and naturalistic approaches to inquiry have quite different purposes, processes, and outcomes. One acquires objective, factual information about a limited number of variables, and the other works to understand more clearly the multiple dimensions of socially constructed human behavior.

As will become evident in following sections, distinguishing between different research paradigms is not always straightforward. The problem partially relates to rather loose use of associated terminology. For example, the literature often refers to *quantitative* and *qualitative* methods as equivalent to the distinction between objective science and naturalistic inquiry and fails to differentiate between the research *paradigm* and the research *methods*. There is a difference, for instance, between qualitative *research* and qualitative *methods*. It is possible to use qualitative methods to acquire and partially analyze data in experimental science—to use qualitative data

SCIENTIFIC POSITIVISM	NATURALISTIC INQUIRY
Purposes	**Purposes**
Studies events and behaviors *objectively.*	Studies people's *subjective* experience.
Hypothesizes a relationship between variables of interest.	*Explores perspectives* on an issue or problem.
Processes	**Processes**
Precisely *measures* quantities of variables.	*Describes* people's experience and perspective of the issue/problem.
Carefully *controls* events and conditions within the study.	Allows events to unfold *naturally.*
Uses *statistical analysis* of data.	Uses *interpretive methods* to analyze the data.
Outcomes	**Outcomes**
Seeks *explanations* for events and behaviors.	Seeks to *understand* events and behaviors.
Describes *causes* of events and behaviors.	Constructs *detailed descriptions* of events and behaviors.
Generalizes findings to sites and people not included in the study.	Findings are *setting and person specific.*

Figure 2.1
Scientific Positivism and Naturalistic Inquiry

objectively. Conversely, it is possible to use numerical or quantitative data within a naturalistic study to clarify emerging perspectives.

The use of qualitative methods, however, does not necessarily constitute qualitative research, nor does the use of quantitative methods constitute a quantitative study. The way the data is manipulated and applied to research outcomes provides an indication of the appropriate use of the terminology. Objective studies seeking causal explanations and generalizable results are appropriately named quantitative or positivistic research. At the same time, interpretive studies resulting in detailed, descriptive accounts of people's subjective experience are appropriately identified as naturalistic or qualitative research.

While we can mix methods and data, it is difficult to mix research paradigms within the same study without damaging the utility and integrity of the research. Studies without a random sample, for instance, cannot generalize results. Similarly, qualitative studies that measure fixed variables limit the extent of holistic understanding emerging from a study. Neither paradigm is right or wrong, better or worse. Each seeks to attain different purposes, using different processes to attain different types of outcome. Each is evaluated by a different set of criteria to determine the strength, quality, or rigor of the research (see the section on validity in Chapter 3).

We need to be wary of setting up boundaries that make too fixed the distinctions between the two paradigms. Qualitative research does, for instance, sometimes make use of numerical data to extend or clarify information emerging in the research process. Conversely, quantitative researchers sometimes engage in preliminary qualitative studies to identify the variables to be included in their research. To ensure that their research does not become caught in the muddy waters between the paradigms, however, researchers need to frequently ask themselves, "What is the purpose or objective of this part of the research? How can I attain that purpose, and what type of methods should I use to achieve my purpose?" Answers to these questions help us assess the nature of the information we require and the appropriate research tools we must apply.

The following sections seek to clarify the nature of the difference between two essentially incompatible—or incommensurable—approaches to research to ensure that those engaging in research use appropriate tools for the differing types of problems they engage. The sections explore the essential differences between positivistic and naturalistic approaches to research—the one more intent on measuring in order to produce objective knowledge, and the other more focused on the subjective construction of meaning. The distinction has implications for different ways of viewing pedagogy—one perspective that seeks verifiable truths pointing to best teaching practices, and another more focused on ways of constructing teaching/learning processes that are meaningful to student life-worlds.[1]

Objective Science and Experimental Research

One of the enduring legacies of the modern world is that bestowed by science. So successful has science been at providing miraculous material benefits to human life that scientific knowledge has achieved a preeminent status that puts it above all others. In recent decades billions of dollars have been invested in scientific studies of education providing a huge body of knowledge that assists educators in enhancing teaching and learning at all levels of the education system. We now have high degrees of certainty about a range of issues, from the effects of gender, race, and class on educational achievement to the effects of different types of teaching practice on student learning and behavior. There are quite distinct limits, however, to the ways that experimental science can be applied to human affairs, and the results of research are often contradictory or limited in their ability to provide practical solutions to the huge problems still confronting many educational systems in culturally and socially diverse communities. It is worthwhile, therefore, to review the nature of scientific research in order to understand its strengths and its appropriate application.

---

[1]Again, we need to be wary of interpreting this simplistically, since a good teacher probably incorporates both elements into a pedagogy.

The scientific perspective is often associated with a set of assumptions and beliefs that is technically known as scientific positivism. Scientific positivism assumes a fixed universe that operates according to a stable set of laws defining the phenomena and the relationship between those phenomena. The universe is often envisioned as a huge machine with the various parts interacting in precise and ordered manner. It assumes that ultimately, in principal, everything in the universe can be measured with precision and the relationship between phenomena described accurately. The laws of the physical universe, such as the laws of thermodynamics, and so on, describe some of the unique and unchangeable properties of the physical universe. Continuing scientific efforts to refine and extend our understanding of the universe are carried out in the disciplinary spheres of physics, chemistry, biology, and so on. Each has a distinctive focus providing scientifically derived information that extends our understanding of the physical universe. Physiology and human biology focus on those aspects of the universe dealing with the human body but generally stop short of involvement of the "mind"—that aspect of the universe that is peculiar to human beings.

The purpose of scientific work is to describe with great precision the features of the universe and the stable relationships that hold between those features. Scientific work is often associated with accurate measurement of "variables" to determine the nature and extent of those relationships, with the ultimate goal being to establish causal connections between parts of the machine—the connection between heat and pressure of gas in an enclosed container, and the relationship between electrons and protons within an atom, are examples. The success of science in establishing those stable sets of relationships has enabled the production of the technological marvels of the modern world, from manufactured materials to fabrics, medications, food storage, flight, communications, and armaments.

Once science is able to measure and describe precisely the nature of a particular set of phenomena, it is able to predict how those phenomena behave with a great deal of certainty. If I heat a certain type of metal to a certain temperature, under certain atmospheric conditions, it will turn to a liquid. If I allow electrical charges to move through the machinery of my computer by depressing keys, it will behave in highly regulated ways, enabling me to successfully complete a large number of complex activities. My ability to do this is based on the outcome of the application of scientific principles to explanations of the behavior of electrons in certain environments. The high degrees of certainty engendered by these explanations provide the basis for the computer technology that continues to transform our world. Combined with explanations for the behavior of metals, plastics, and conductors, a highly sophisticated and rigorous stock of scientific knowledge enables the control of materials and processes for the production and use of this technology. The focus on prediction and control enables people to manufacture an enormous range of goods—clothing, vehicles, computers, structural steel, medicines, and computers that have the potential to dramatically enhance our lives.

This has obvious implications for education. If we can scientifically measure and describe the precise nature of the learning process, then we should, in theory, be able to control all of the factors likely to influence a student's learning and produce a highly effective education for each and every person. Armed with scientific knowledge, we should be able to predict with precision the conditions required for any child to acquire the knowledge necessary to achieve success in education, irrespective of his/her gender, class, ethnicity, or any other factor likely to impinge on learning.

Experimental and Quasi-Experimental Methods

The primary method for establishing scientific explanations is experimental method. The purpose of experiments is to provide the means for establishing cause-effect relationships between phenomena. Early experiments with gases in enclosed containers, for instance, were able to establish direct relationships between the heat of the gas and the pressure within the container. Rising pressures were seen to be caused by increases in heat. In the same way, experimental studies have attempted to establish the conditions under which learning takes place, such that a student's achievement can be attributed to the particular ways that learning occurred. Educational experimental studies, therefore, try to establish what causes successful learning to occur. That is, to enable people to explain the factors causing learning or the lack of it, to help them predict the conditions under which learning will occur, and then to establish those conditions in classrooms. Experiments are constructed by defining a set of variables (the factors causing or being acted upon), postulating a set of relationships between those variables, and testing to determine the nature of the relationship between the variables. Experiments must be carefully constructed to ensure that plausible rival explanations for relationships emerging from an experiment may not be attributable to other variables not included in the experiment.

Experiments are carefully designed so that random assignment of subjects to experimental groups and the controlled application of experimental treatments or interventions allows researchers to state with high degrees of certainty that the effects observed were related to the treatments or interventions. Many studies, for instance, have observed the effect of different teaching strategies on student learning. With researchers controlling the conditions under which these strategies were applied in classrooms to selected groups of students, the experiments operated in carefully controlled classroom conditions. The intent of such designs is to eliminate rival explanations for the results obtained. Controlling extraneous variables is an important aspect of experimental design, since the potential influences on learning are many and varied, including such variables as class size, student learning styles, ethnicity, race, gender, social class, type of school, parenting style experienced by students, motivation, personality, illness, drug use, intelligence, aptitude, school size, exposure to media, and so on. Researchers want to be sure that any result they obtain from experimentally manipulating teaching strategies may not, in fact, be attributable to one or more of these or any other factors.

Quasi-experiments, or non-experiments as they are sometimes called (Johnson 2001), are used where it is not possible to manipulate variables experimentally, either for ethical or pragmatic reasons. It would be difficult, though not impossible, to set up an experiment to test the effect of lengthening or shortening the school year. What is possible, in these situations, is studying school systems with different length school years. In these types of studies, variables are controlled or manipulated statistically rather than experimentally, establishing the nature of the relationship between variables by carefully contrived statistical manipulation. McEwan (2000) provides a clear description of quasi-experimental studies of school voucher programs, which show how, in conditions where it is not possible to control who enters private and public schools, researchers are able to employ statistical methods that control for the background of families and students. In this manner, a researcher can minimize the possibility of plausible rival explanations for the effects of school voucher programs and control for the effect of variables like parental education, family income, gender, race, and ethnicity.

Both experimental and non-experimental research is subject to quality control to ensure rigor in procedure and stability of results. Experimenters want to be able to say with a high degree of certainty that the results obtained could be obtained with other groups of people in other contexts and that replication of the experiment in similar contexts would yield similar results. For these reasons, experiments are evaluated according to their reliability, internal validity, and external validity—the extent to which similar results may be obtained from different settings, samples, and times (reliability), the extent to which results might be attributed to the experimental variables (internal validity), and the extent to which results apply to the broader population from which the sample was drawn (external validity or generalizability).

Experimental method, as a hallmark of scientific positivism, is based on the belief in a fixed and knowable universe. Experiments and quasi-experiments attempt to establish the nature of phenomena and the relationship between features of the physical and human world. Precise measurement of the degrees of relationship between variables enables scientific experiments, in theory, to establish the ability to predict and in many cases control important features of the world. In education, experimental and quasi-experimental research have provided a large array of information having the potential to dramatically improve classroom and school learning. As will become evident in the following discussion, however, there are limits on the utility of experimental studies on human subjects. Although experimental science has established scientific laws enabling powerful explanations for the nature of the physical universe, the laws of human behavior have proven much more elusive, and other approaches to research have emerged enabling different, but useful, ways of understanding people.

Understanding Human Social Life: Naturalistic Inquiry

The problem with applying science to human affairs lies in the nature of humanity. We are at once physical, biological, and sociocultural beings, and attempts to understand our behavior need to take into account each of those facets. While the methods of positivistic science are powerful ways of understanding our physical being and provide deep insights into our biologic nature, they come up short as a vehicle for providing explanations for the sociocultural aspects of human life. Although experimentation still assists us to understand certain features of human social and cultural life, ultimately positivistic explanations fail to encompass some of the fundamental features of human life—the creative construction of meaning that is at the center of every social activity. It is the need to investigate meaning that is at the heart of naturalistic inquiry.

While experimental science has provided much useful information, the reality of this knowledge is that any theory of human behavior can only be a tentative, partial explanation of any individual or group's acts or behaviors. Two things intervene in attempts to describe scientific laws of human behavior. One is the nature of human beings themselves. As cross-cultural studies have demonstrated convincingly, people perceive the world and respond to it in many different ways. Given the same sets of "facts," people will interpret both what they are seeing and what that means in many different ways. No amount of explanation or clarification can provide a set of foundational truths about the way people should behave since behavior is predicated on sets of beliefs that are not, in principle, verifiable. Any "truth" of human experience is true only within a given framework of meanings.

This becomes increasingly clear if we consider some of the fundamental conditions of human social life and the way it impacts the lives of individuals. The concept of the life-world comes to us from the work of sociologists like Peter Berger (Berger and Luckman, 1967; Berger, Berger, and Kellner, 1973) who engage research from the perspective that people construct reality as an ongoing social process in their everyday lives. The life-world refers to the consciousness of everyday life, carried by every individual, that provides coherence and order to their existence. The life-world is not a genetically inherited view of the world, but is learned by individuals as they experience everyday events and interactions within the compass of their families and communities. Therefore, the life-world is socially constructed so that individuals learn to live in a social world according to sets of meaning, deeply embedded in their everyday conduct, that are shared by others living in that particular place and time.

The life-world is not a random set of events, but is given order and coherence by a patterned, structured organization of meaning that is so "ordinary" that people literally do not see, or are usually not conscious of, the depth and complexity of the worlds they inhabit. A child learns to associate with parents and siblings in particular ways, and to communicate using a particular language, to act in particular ways, and to participate in events like meals, conversation, play, and work using appropriate behaviors and routine ways of accomplishing his/her everyday life. Like a fish in the sea, people cannot see the "water" of this patterned, structured everyday life but live in a taken-for-granted social world providing order and coherence for every aspect of their everyday lives—the interactions, acts, activities, events, purposes, feelings, and productions that comprise their lives.

We get some idea of what this means when we visit a new place for the first time, especially if it is in a foreign country. We feel uncomfortable to varying degrees until we learn the "rules" that enable us to operate in the new setting—the appropriate words to use, how to sit or stand, how to eat, how to dress appropriately, and so on. We become aware of a myriad of small behaviors that those living in the context take for granted because it is so much an ordinary part of their life-world.

I remember people's consternation when I visited an Aboriginal community for the first time and sat with my wife in church, not realizing that the sexes had been strictly segregated and that I was sitting with the women. I've also entered a school staff room and felt the embarrassed silence when I inadvertently sat in "Mr Jeffries' chair." Small and apparently inconsequential behaviors can sometimes have dramatic impact on our ability to interact comfortably with people.

The anthropologist Goodenough (1971) conceptualized this life-world in terms of the concept "culture", which he defines as the socially learned rules and boundaries that enable a person to know what *is* (how the world is *defined*, structured, made up), what *can be* (what is *possible* in the world, whether it be ancestral ghosts, the existence of God, or faster-than-light travel), what *should be* (the system of values enabling the individual to distinguish between good and bad, appropriate and inappropriate), *what to do* (what acts or behaviors are required to accomplish a purpose), and *how to do it* (the steps required to accomplish that purpose). Individuals, therefore, inhabit a life-world comprised of taken-for-granted rules and boundaries giving order and coherence to their lives. Without these patterns and structures of meaning, people would live in a bewildering, chaotic world of sensation and events that would make human life as we know it impossible. It is this cultural cradle that enables us to live together in harmony and to accomplish day to day tasks such as eating meals, dressing, communicating through talk and discussion, working, resolving disputes, and mowing the lawn.

The distinctive aspect of our cultural life-world is that we share it with people who have learned similar sets of meanings and who act according to the patterns and structures of meaning with those who have had similar life experiences. But beneath the apparent order and coherence of the social life-world is a deeply chaotic system of meanings that continually threaten the possibility of an ordered and productive daily life. For each person has had somewhat different experiences, and each has built a system of meanings that works superficially to accomplish ordinary tasks but has slightly different nuances and interpretations that at any one time can be magnified and distorted, causing confusion or conflict as people try to accomplish their everyday lives. This is readily apparent when people get married and discover that a person with whom they thought they shared deeply consonant views of the world evinces acts and behaviors not in accord with their own. Small acts, the dropping of a sock or tissue, the use of a word, can trigger discomfort, discordance, and even conflict. The art of marriage requires people to learn new sets of meaning, to negotiate acts and behaviors consonant with a partner's existing habits and values, in order to accomplish a life together. It is something that is sometimes astonishingly difficult, even for people closely committed to each other.

Social scientists have long studied the intricacies of interaction between people. Ethnomethodologists (e.g. Garfinkel, 1967) provide us with glimpses into the ways that people negotiate these worlds of meanings to accomplish everyday social life, constantly constructing activity and behavior together, negotiating meaning, trailing behavior, repairing disjunctures in perspective, and so on. The French writer Lyotard (1984) speaks of a social world atomized into flexible networks of "language games"—individual people selecting from a number of possible games depending on the context in which they are operating. Similarly, another French writer, Derrida (1976), views social life as being lived at the intersection of a large body of "discourses," or "texts." We get some idea of how this operates if we were to follow a teenager into a classroom, the school yard, home, or a sports team. Both behavior and language change from context to context—"What's happenin'" becomes "Hello," "Hi," or "How are you," with accompanying changes in body language and "attitude." The wonder of human life is that we are able to accomplish so much ordered activity in the context of the seemingly chaotic jumble of meanings likely to intrude on any interaction between people.

Though we live within a particular life-world made of sets of meaning deeply embedded in our life histories, we are usually not conscious of those rules and boundaries or patterns giving meaning and coherence to our lives. The taken-for-granted world is not seen, or apprehended, but *lived.* It is only when we come in conflict with another, or where disjuncture occurs in our interactions or our experience, that we start to become aware of that which we have come to take for granted. Since research revolves around a search for solutions to problematic issues and events, one of its major tasks is to uncover the meanings implicit in the acts and behaviors of interacting individuals. By exploring the world of others in a setting or by getting involved in events, we seek to understand the meaning behind their actions and behaviors—to enter their life-worlds, and through an increased understanding of those divergent life-worlds to seek ways of re-doing or re-enacting those actions and behaviors in ways that will make sense to all those engaged in the problematic events.

This is not just a technical task, but involves deeply held feelings associated with the meanings implicit in a person's life-world. Not only are people attached to their particular life-worlds emotionally, but they react unfavorably when they are threatened. A denial of the veracity or validity of any aspect of a person's life-world is likely to create negative feelings that inhibit the possibility of productive interaction. The world of human life is meaningful, interactional, emotional, and constructive, and accomplishing human productive and harmonious human activity requires all these aspects of experience to be taken into account. It is this understanding that is at the heart of action research—the need to clarify and understand the meaning implicit in the acts and behaviors of all people involved in events on which research is focused, and the need to use those extended understandings as the basis for resolving the problems investigated.

This lesson is deeply inscribed in my consciousness. As a young teacher, I worked with the children of Australian Aboriginal people who lived a very traditional hunter-gatherer lifestyle. It soon became evident to me that they literally lived in a different universe—that the way they viewed the world, the way they acted towards each other, their aspirations and responses, were so dramatically different from my own that my teaching made absolutely no sense to their everyday world. I became aware of the need to know something of that world in order to provide a bridge of understanding between their world and the curriculum that I was teaching.

Even the simplest aspects of the syllabus entailed elements that were deeply engaged with the different visions of the world and the lifestyles attached. As I watched the people gathering seeds and fruit from desert plants to provide for their immediate needs, I became aware of how deeply embedded I was in the world of technological production when I cut a slice of bread for my lunch. Behind that simple act lay the mining and production of metals needed for the knife, as well as that required for the production of the machinery needed to grow and process the wheat, and to fabricate the ovens and other machinery needed to make the bread. What I had seen as a simple loaf of bread became a complex technological production.

My eyes began to see a different world when I asked the question, "What do I need to know in order to understand where this bread came from?" A very different order of understanding came to mind when I asked, "What do Aboriginal people need to know when they ask a similar question about their own food?" Not only does the actual world of technological production intrude, but the web of work and economic relationships enabling me to acquire that loaf of bread are likewise complex and very different from the web of relationships surrounding Aboriginal meals.

This experience changed forever the way I see teaching. I now realize the need to find ways of making connections between what my students know—how they perceive and understand the world from the standpoint of their own experiences—what they need to learn, and how they can learn it. That fundamental perception has been recently reinforced as I've worked in schools in the United States where the experiences and perspectives of Hispanic and African American students and communities have enriched and challenged my educational endeavors. As I worked in the South Valley in Albuquerque, NM, and the poorer suburbs of Columbia and Richmond, VA, I had a lot to learn before I could frame my knowledge in ways that made sense to people in those places. As a teacher, I had to do some on-the-spot research to enable me to do my work effectively.

Differences in cultural perspective do not relate to ethnic differences alone. We have only to look at the differences in the way teenagers and their parents interpret events to realize the extent to which their age difference creates differences in cultural experience and perspective in everyday life. Parents listening to their children's music often shake their heads in wonder that *anyone* could find the experience pleasurable—a response shared by teenagers listening to their parent's music. They all are hearing the same music, in terms of the sounds emanating from the instrument or recording, but they have very different experiences of the sounds and associate very different meanings to them.

Phenomenology: Exploring Everyday Experience

Action research in education is clearly informed by **phenomenology,** a philosophical standpoint that explores the subjective dimensions of human experience. Van Manen's perspective on the study of pedagogy provides useful insights into ways that teachers might view their work, which are quite different in approach to that of the objective, clinical viewpoints that dominate much of the research literature. Through a continuing body of work, Van Manen (1977, 1982, 1984, 1988, 1990) focuses on phenomenological approaches to research and teaching that put us subjectively in touch with *knowledge of people's everyday experience.* Van Manen suggests that phenomenology does not offer us theory to explain and/or control our classrooms, but rather offers plausible insights that bring us in more direct contact with the world of our students (Van Manen, 1984). He emphasizes the need for contact rather than control, thus modifying the traditional, detached, and observational standpoint taken by experimental researchers and placing them in the posture of active participants in the contexts they study.

Phenomenological research attempts to reveal meaning and to understand how that meaning is connected to a person's life experience. Phenomenology does not *give* meaning to lived experience since meaning already exists in each person's everyday world. We discover the ways people give meaning to events in their lives by being *in* their world, not by observing it objectively. It is through interaction with their worlds that we discover a human world rather than an objectively scientific world. William Dilthey (quoted in Van Manen, 1990) sees human science as investigation concerned with those areas of human existence involving *consciousness, purposiveness,* and *meaning.* Dilthey suggests that people consciously enact their lives according to a set of purposes meaningful to them within the logic of their own life-world. Other writers extend this notion, focusing also on the willfulness of human activity—in its most extreme form, the "will to power" (Neitsche, 1979; Rosenau, 1992) that can be interpreted as the need to have control.[2]

The purpose of research and teaching, according to Van Manen, is not to put us in command of our students, but to put us in touch with them. The emphasis is on insight rather than explanation and to reveal meanings and the way they are connected to a person's life-world. To gain phenomenological insight, we do not ask How do these children learn this material?, but rather What is the nature of the children's experience of learning? with the intent of better understanding what this learning experience is like for these children (Van Manen, 1984).

Van Manen's perspective should not be taken as a prescription for the totality of all classroom interaction or all research, since it will sometimes be appropriate for teachers and researchers to stand back and observe the situation objectively, assessing and evaluating events in an unemotional and disengaged term. At other times, educators need to enter the life-world of students to understand how to construct educational activities that are truly meaningful and worthwhile within their everyday lives. Qualitative research provides the tools for these tasks.

---

[2]Phenomenology is the study of phenomena, or ordinary occurrences.

Meaning, Interpretation, and Qualitative Methods

The need to understand how people experience and make meaning of events and phenomena is at the heart of naturalistic qualitative research. One of the central features of qualitative research is that it provides the means for researchers to understand the ways in which people interpret any event. Thus, we find the term **interpretive research** increasingly applied to qualitative investigations. In his book *Interpretive Interactionism,* Norman Denzin (1989b) argues that interpretation and understanding are key features of everyday social life—people interpreting and making judgments about their own and others experience and constructing their life in an ongoing way according to meanings and taken-for-granted procedures that are embedded in the everyday practices of the world in which they have lived.

Denzin suggests that the problem with many human services is that programs, policies, and practices are based on interpretations and judgments of people responsible for their development and delivery. In schools, for instance, faulty or incorrect understandings arise when teachers mistake their own experiences and perspectives for their students' experiences and perspectives. A consequence of this dynamic, however, is that teaching doesn't work adequately because the teaching/learning strategies bear little relationship to the students' meanings, interpretations, and experiences.

The importance of the interpretive perspective to educational contexts is clear. If we are to solve many of the problems that continue to make our classrooms and schools problematic, then we must engage in research that provides understanding of the perspectives of all people who are involved. We need to take seriously the experiences and perspectives of students, parents, teachers, and administrators in formulating programs and practices providing effective solutions to problems experienced in schools and classrooms.

Research, therefore, should employ qualitative processes of interpretation as a central dynamic of investigation. Its purpose should be to describe and give meaning to events, showing how a set of events or phenomena are perceived and interpreted by actors in the setting. By studying events in this way, we are able to better understand or comprehend people's experience. This reflective, reflexive process also helps in untangling and clarifying the meanings embedded in a set of experiences, leading an audience or those who have experienced the events to greater or extended understanding. Interpretive research, therefore:

- Identifies different definitions of the problem
- Reveals the perspectives of the various interested parties
- Suggests alternative points of view from which the problem can be interpreted and assessed
- Identifies strategic points of intervention
- Exposes the limits of statistical information by furnishing materials that enable understanding of individual experiences

Denzin's take on interpretation suggests that far more is involved than "theorizing" another person's experience. It is an essentially phenomenological[3] process requiring one to enter into or take the point of view of another; in Mead's (1934)

---

[3]Anyone having doubts about this should consider the difficulties experienced by people whose tasks involve making young adolescents engage in desired behaviors against their will.

words, "taking the attitude of the other," or in Berger and Luckman's (1967) terms, entering their "consciousness of everyday life." Denzin (1989b) suggests that understanding is more than a cognitive event; it requires an audience to enter or take account of the emotional world of those studied. Cognitive understanding is rational, orderly, logical, and detached from emotional feeling. Emotional understanding encompasses emotionality, self-feelings, and shared experience.

Understanding, in an interpretive sense, enables us to project ourselves (enter) into the experience of the other, to understand what they think and feel about particular acts and events. As Denzin says (1989b), "the goal of interpretation is to build true, authentic understandings of the phenomena under investigation" (p. 123). More particularly, though, it seeks to reveal how significant experiences—epiphanies—are embedded in the taken-for-granted world of everyday life. They record the agonies, pains, tragedies, triumphs, and peaks of human experience. The actions, activities, behavior, and deeply felt emotion—love, pride, dignity, honor, hate, and envy—of people's lives experience enable educators.

This perspective has direct implications for teaching. If we consider teaching to be the transmission of objective knowledge, then knowing something of a student's life-world will be peripherally relevant to the task of teaching. Where it is engaged as a process of socially constructed knowledge, then it becomes a process of assisting learners to make sense of the material being learned from within their own frames of reference. If we cannot frame our teaching/learning processes in ways that enable diverse learners to understand what they are learning and that are meaningful within their own social and cultural life-world, then we run the risk of engaging in a series of mechanistic or ritualistic acts that we impose on our students by means of systems of rewards and punishments.

The need to understand the world of the classroom and the school in these ways has resulted in a proliferation of naturalistic investigation so that the literature on qualitative research is now both extensive and diverse. Some recent useful contributions, largely focusing on education, include Cresswell (2002), deMarrais (1998), Weis and Fine (2000), delaine (2000), Merchant and Willis (2001), Marshall and Rossman (1999), Silverman (2000), Connelly and Clandinin (1999), and Bogdan and Biklin (1992).

Qualitative, interpretive approaches to inquiry, therefore, provide the principle means for enabling teachers to engage action research to devise pedagogical strategies more attuned to the realities of students' lives. While it is useful in some contexts to think of students in objective terms, to plan strategies and interventions that enable good learning processes to occur, there will be times when the collaborative construction of pedagogical processes or the formulation of socially and culturally appropriate curricula will be enhanced by the processes explored in the coming chapters.

When I first entered teaching, I was the sole arbiter of the content and processes of teaching in my classroom. I formulated the syllabus from a preordained state curriculum, established teaching/learning processes that I had learned in my professional preparation to provide the greatest likelihood of successful learning, and maintained sound classroom management processes in order to ensure that students in my class worked systematically.

As a result of my experiences in many different cultural contexts my preparation for classes and my teaching is now much more flexible and participatory. I engage my students in the process of assisting me to formulate a syllabus and, in the process, try to accommodate the diverse backgrounds and learning styles they bring to my classes. That doesn't mean that I do not prepare thoroughly, or that classroom management is never an issue, but preparation and management have necessarily become a collaborative process. At first, as I learned how to do this, it seemed like extra work, but having become more skilled I can now accomplish it easily. Further, I've learned that by engaging students in these processes they not only become more interested and enthusiastic about their learning, but have some wonderful ideas about both the content and the processes of learning.

While I still appreciate and make use of the information acquired from my studies of educational psychology, sociology, and anthropology—much of it gained through experimental or quasi-experimental research—I am able to place that alongside the knowledge I acquire of my students' experience using naturalistic techniques of inquiry. Each has its place. Each provides tools for acquiring knowledge.

Research Relationships in Classrooms and Schools

Traditional approaches to experimental research place a strong emphasis on the need for researchers to remain objective, work at an emotional distance, and interact as little as possible with research subjects and the context. Action research works on the supposition that researchers will be both subjectively involved and will interact with the research participants and the research environment. In technical terms, action research participants are *positioned* quite differently, taking different roles and having different sets of responsibility within the research act. Researchers are no longer seen as having sole responsibility for enacting the technical processes of the investigation but act more like team leaders, coordinators, or facilitators. Their role is not to engage in research but to assist other participating stakeholders to carry out an investigation and search for a solution to problems they perceive as significant. In the most ideal version of action research, stakeholders do the work of clarifying the issue, acquiring information, analyzing the data, constructing reports, and formulating actions. Stronger versions of action research have stakeholders taking central responsibility for these activities, with the research facilitator/coordinator assisting participants by supporting and advising them on procedures.

The importance of this issue, broadly speaking, is that a set of **relationships** has been built into professional life that sometimes need to be modified in order to carry out an effective action research process. A common assumption built into the interactions between professionals and their client groups says, in effect, "I'm the expert.

I know what needs to be done." The assumption here is that training and experience have provided professionals with special knowledge enabling them to make definitive judgments about the nature of the problem experienced and to formulate appropriate solutions to the problem. While this works in some instances, or in instances where the clients are culturally and socially similar to the professional, there are many, many instances where the "expert" knowledge of the professional does not provide the basis for an effective solution to the problem. Some of the deep-seated and long-standing problems in education and other human services relate to the imposition of Eurocentric, middle-class systems of understanding onto people—students, clients, and sometimes fellow professionals—whose social and cultural orientations are quite different.

Interpretive action research, therefore, starts from quite a different position. It says, in effect, "Although I have professional knowledge that may be useful in exploring the issue or problem facing us, my knowledge is incomplete. We will need to investigate the issue further to reveal other relevant (cultural) knowledge that may extend our understanding of the issue." Expert knowledge, in this case, becomes another resource to be applied to the issue investigated and stands alongside the knowledge and understanding of other people whose deep and extended experience in the setting provides knowledge resources that might usefully be applied to the solution of the problem investigated.

This change in status of the researcher also signals a change in relationships, since the researcher is no longer the director of the investigation, but acts more like a consultant. In this latter case, research participants may be seen as employers or customers with the right to determine the nature of the research as well as the research processes. As a good business principle, "the customer is always right" signals the nature of the change in relationship between researcher and participants. As John Heron indicates in *Cooperative Inquiry* (Heron, 1996), "self-directing persons develop most fully through fully reciprocal relations with other self-directing persons. Autonomy and co-operation are necessary and mutually enhancing values of human life. Hence experiential research involves a co-equal relation between two people, reversing the roles of facilitator and agent, or combining them at the same time." As the anthropologist, George Marcus (1998), indicated "[social] affiliations and identities give [research participants] an immense advantage in shaping research. . . . There is control of language and a well of life experience that are great assets for achieving the sort of depth [of understanding] that anthropologists have always hoped for from one- to two-year fieldwork projects."

Classes accustomed to highly directive processes of instruction may not seem like a fertile field for this type of research, but most students respond quickly and easily. They may, however, need to be introduced systematically to this style of operating, and some students will take time to develop the capacity for self-direction. Over time, students will become increasingly attuned to these rich educative processes. Shelia Baldwin describes the change in relationships that occurred when she, as teacher, became facilitator of her high school students' ethnographic research. "Throughout our time together, I likened our project to a journey we were taking together to discover our community and school culture." One student commented, " I really like that word 'ethnographer.' It makes me feel special." As Shelia indicates, there is some uncertainty at the beginning of the project as students learn that there is not one correct answer to the research question. She was surprised, however, at the level of commitment of her students and realized that she could have established higher degrees of trust and lesser degrees of control from the earliest stages of the study. Her students demonstrated their commitment by attending meetings outside of class hours, turning up at 7:00 A.M., and staying with the project to the end. She ends by saying "They have given me the confidence I needed to be a facilitator [of research]. Now I can allow my students to take ownership."

Many teachers have had similar experiences. One group (Stringer, 1997) spoke of the ways that a participatory approach to research had enhanced their understanding of teaching. "We discovered that teaching is a complex art that requires teachers to facilitate learning, to enact or model what is to be learned, and to create appropriate organizational and social conditions that enable learning to occur. . . engaging students in learning processes that not only enable them to acquire discrete pieces of information, but also to engage in active inquiry and discovery that lead them to see and understand their real-life experiences in new ways." The end product is students who not only take on ownership and responsibility for their own learning, but teachers who are able to engender these feelings. One teacher wrote of her experience doing research with other teachers and some of her students:

> We're much more aware. We're not so definite or absolute anymore in who we are—in a productive way. We're able to absorb so much more when we don't deflect what comes our way. We went through a process of evolution . . . went in with preconceived notions of school, but became aware of different life perspectives and realities. We started from one point, became different people, and have continued to evolve as we tried to recreate the learning experience. We're different teachers for it. (Stringer, 1997, p. 202)

The orientation of this approach to research, therefore, is to enable people, including students, teachers, administrators, parents, and others, to construct different ways of accomplishing their teaching/learning tasks; to improve practices and behaviors in the classroom; and to accomplish effective teaching and learning for all. As I indicate in the following section, these research procedures are not just objective, technical routines for acquiring objective knowledge; they embody particular social and ethical principles that make them fit for a humane and democratic society and provide the means to dramatically transform the quality of the human environment in classrooms and schools.

The Social Principles of Action Research: Not Just a Technical Routine

Much of the material that follows describes technical routines for engaging in action research. The changes in methods signaled by the move from experimental to qualitative research, however, also reflect a change in the human dimensions of investigation. Where experimental research starts from the assumption that the researcher take a disinterested, objective view in order to acquire an unbiased, objective truth, action research assumes an engaged and subjective interaction with people in the research setting.

There are, however, deeper issues to be considered in engaging participatory action research as a mode of inquiry. Modern social life, with its tendency toward centralized, bureaucratic forms of organization, too easily slides into a form of autocratic operation at odds with the democratic intent of its institutions. Too often, powerful figures in school contexts take on the manner and style of a dictator, imposing their perspectives and agendas on others and disregarding the needs and views of others. Though this sometimes works—the father-figure principal who keeps an iron hand on the reins of the school; or the demanding, disciplinary teacher who will not countenance poor behavior or performance—it provides a poor socialization for life in a democratic society. Too often people accept the unacceptable and are passive contributors to processes that inhibit or sometimes damage their lives or the lives of their children.

Participatory action research, therefore, enacts systematic inquiry in ways that are:

- Democratic
- Participatory
- Empowering
- Life-enhancing

These changes highlight the nature and exciting potentials of action research, providing opportunities for teachers, principals, students, and parents to engage in exciting and sometimes exhilarating work together. Processes of investigation, therefore, not only provide information and understanding as key outcomes of a process of inquiry, they enable people to develop a sense of togetherness, and provide the basis for effective and productive relationships that spill over into all aspects of their life together. As they participate in action research, people develop high degrees of motivation and are often empowered to act in ways they never thought possible. Action research is not only empowering, therefore, but provides the basis for building democratic learning communities that enhance the life of schools and institutions.

Recently, I engaged in an action research process in a school in a poor part of town. Debriefing parent participants in the latter stages of the process, I was struck by the excitement evident in their lively talk, shining eyes, and the enthusiasm with which they reviewed their experience. "You know, Ernie," said one, "It was such an empowering experience for us." Asked how it had been empowering, she responded, "Because we were able to do it ourselves, instead of having experts come and do it and tell us. We learned so much in the process, and now we know how to do research." She and another woman who participated in the project indicated a desire to extend their understanding of research processes and to extend their skills. Enrolled as extension students, they sat in on my graduate research class, participated actively, and provided class participants with great insight into effective ways of practicing action research in community contexts.

This is not an isolated instance—I've shared the excitement and experienced the feelings of accomplishment of young children, teenagers, teachers, principals, parents, student teachers, graduate students, and professors in large cities, small country towns, and remote communities. My experience encompasses a wide range of social and cultural contexts on two continents, yet the power of participatory processes to engage enthusiasm and excitement still excites me. For me, action research is not a dreary, objective, mechanistic process, but a vital, energizing process that engages the mind, enhances the spirit, and creates a unity that enables people to accomplish highly significant goals. At its best, it is a transformational experience enabling people to see the world anew, and in some cases, to literally change their lives.

There is another side to action research, however, that continues to sustain me professionally; the ability to provide the means to accomplish exciting work in the most difficult of circumstances. In a world made increasingly problematic by the forces of economic rationalism and accountability, where every activity must be justified in terms of a pre-specified benchmark and justified in dollar terms, the spiritual and artistic side of education can easily be lost in a maze of technical, mechanistic, and clinical procedure that too easily dulls and nullifies the creative, life-enhancing outcomes of a truly educational experience. The energy and excitement generated by collaborative accomplishment not only provides the means to accomplish the technical, clinical goals of our work, but to do so in ways that are truly meaningful and enriching.

These things do not come automatically, however, since they are, to some extent, at odds with commonly accepted practices in classroom and school situations. Teachers as research facilitators take on quite a different role from that required as learning facilitator, though these roles have much in common. Accomplishing the skillful, socially principled application of research requires new understandings and the application of new practices that are somewhat different from those required in teaching. The following sections signal that researchers need to learn not only the technical skills of inquiry but also the human capacities of dialogue, affirmation, engagement, and responsiveness. These human qualities differentiate a participatory approach to action research from the technical-mechanical work of the objective scientist or the instructor-teacher and provide the basis for work that is not only technically effective but joyful and life-enhancing.

Participation: Building a Community of Learners

[R]ather than seeing ourselves as privileged owners of education, generously willing to bestow it upon others, we have to look at ourselves humbly as learners who can join in solidarity with those who are also learning, and thus bring about a shared process of liberation. By sharing the joy of learning and discovery with our students, we reaffirm the human capacity, inherent in all of us, to generate knowledge and transform the world. (Ada, 1993, p. 25)

The need for people to live and work together in harmony is inscribed in many religious texts—the Bible, the Koran, the Bhagavad Gita, and so on—and in political documents such as the Magna Carta or the U.S. Constitution. While the search for happiness is rarely recognized in literature focused on technical efficiency or social justice, it should be seen as an inherent part of both. Technical processes are most effective when they accommodate the needs of the people subject to those processes—a point now recognized in modern management practices. Highly successful participatory models of management are to be found in the writings of Block (1990), and Senge et al. (1994) in the processes of Total Quality Management and in the operation of successful modern corporations like the Taurus division of Ford, and the Saturn division of General Motors.

Participatory research provides a technical means for accomplishing both a sense of community and a living democracy. It provides the dialogic means to create and/or implement rules, plans, and procedures that make sense to all those involved. Their purpose is to bring people together in a dialogic and productive relationship that creates a sense of community through the sharing of perspectives, the negotiation of meaning, and the development of collaboratively produced activities, programs, and projects.

These principles should not be interpreted as an idealized, utopian fantasy, but as pick and shovel, bread and butter issues that are an ordinary part of school and community life. The factory, school, office, or store should embody elements of harmony that are more human-like than machine-like. The essential features of a participatory approach to inquiry has these outcomes incorporated as central elements of the research process—not just the technical working of a machine, but the working out of a negotiated social order to produce harmonious, effective, and humanized educational practices. The search for harmony, peace, love, and happiness needs to be inserted into the equation for technical efficiency to become an integral part of the daily processes of school life.

The clear message of a participatory approach to action research is that all stakeholders whose lives are affected by an issue need to be incorporated in the search for solutions to that issue. The process of collaboratively working toward that goal not only provides a wide range of expertise, both professional and cultural, but also generates positive working relationships. By including students and parents in the search for solutions to these type of problems, we open the possibility of making use of their wisdom and acknowledging the concrete realities effecting student behavior and performance. Moreover, by engaging them in processes of inquiry that recognize their competence and worth, we provide the basis for developing productive relationships engendering trust and understanding. Even the poorest communities have a store of experience and local knowledge that can be incorporated into exciting and meaningful activities having the power to transform the education of people and children.

Martin Buber, (Annett, 1986) a German scholar, was able to articulate some of the foundations of a sound social life as he witnessed the dangers emerging from overzealous social movements in Nazi Germany. Buber recognized the need to foster the formation of communities within the daily routines of everyday life, not only on a grandiose level, but in the day to day interactions of people—"there must exist cells, small community cells out of which alone the great human community can be built." Buber's "community" was not the natural community of the family, village, or town that was often ruled by powerful traditions and fraught with coercion, violence, and exploitation.

As Arnett reveals (1987, p. viii), "Buber's community was a community of choice around a common center, the voluntary coming together of persons in direct relationship."

Buber alluded to the need to change the nature of relationships between people in bringing rules into operation. Where rules of conduct or operation are imposed uncaringly or without possibility of real input by those subject to the rules, he suggests, the likelihood of a sense of community is dramatically diminished. As Buber noted, rules are but "empty shells when justice does not manifest itself between persons. The true revolution demands a powerful will toward community. The divine emerges in the possibility of genuine life between persons and wills to reveal itself only through its realization in true community." Buber suggests that no structure leaving unchanged the nature of the relationship between persons can bring about a true transformation. Further, time and processes are needed for people to work through differences in perspective and experience and to find common ground in their struggle to accomplish desired ends and purposes. Where compliance is forced on people by the demands of authority, then community disintegrates from within, mistrust becomes a basic feature of life, and a crisis of confidence in the institutions emerges.

For Buber, the basis for formation of a community lay in the principles of an ethical communication that had the following characteristics:

- A felt need to communicate
- An atmosphere of openness, freedom, and responsibility
- Dealing with the real issues and ideas relevant to the communicator
- Appreciation of individual differences and uniqueness
- Acceptance of disagreement and conflict with the desire to resolve them
- Effective feedback and use of feedback
- Mutual respect and trust
- Sincerity and honesty
- A positive attitude for understanding and learning
- A willingness to admit error and allow persuasion

Versions of these types of principles abound in the literature on good management and good teaching practice. They present an idea of the type of interactions and relationships that provide the basis of a productive working environment in any social setting. They are particularly relevant to an approach to action research seeking to provide practical and effective ways of engaging in inquiry in classroom, school, and community settings.

Conclusion

Research texts quite often work on an unspoken assumption that applications of the technical routines of scientific research provide the basis for enlightened and improved professional practice. This chapter has suggested the need to broaden ideas about the nature and function of research to ensure that they acknowledge and take into account the social and human dimensions of educational life. While scientifically validated knowledge truly has the potential to increase understanding of significant features of our social life and educational practice, to the extent that it fails to acknowledge or take into account the social, cultural, ethical, and political nature of social life, it fails to provide the means to improve people's educational endeavors.

The participatory and interpretive approach to action research found in this text seeks to provide a more balanced approach to inquiry and provide research procedures that are conducive to democratic and humane social processes within classrooms and schools. The intent is to provide a rigorous approach to inquiry that legitimizes the perspectives and experiences of all people involved, takes account of scientifically validated information in the processes, and encompasses the means for accomplishing sustainable and effective educational practices that really make a difference in people's lives.

In the chapters that follow, the technical routines of research are accomplished within a set of principles that values the human dimensions of educational life. These principles are expressed more clearly in the next chapter as a precursor to the detailed articulation of action research processes.

Summary

- The chapter distinguishes between two major research paradigms: Scientific positivism, sometimes called quantitative research, and *naturalistic inquiry,* often referred to as qualitative or interpretive research.
- Objective science assumes a fixed universe that can be observed and explained with precision. Through experimental method, it seeks generalizable information with high degrees of reliability that can be applied across diverse settings. It seeks high degrees of predictability and control of events.
- Naturalistic inquiry focuses on understanding the systems of meaning and interpretation inherent in people's everyday social lives. It makes use of qualitative methods to understand how people experience and make meaning of events.
- Action research requires a different set of relationships than those often engaged by professionals. It seeks to make use of the deep-seated and extended understandings people have of their own situations.
- Action research embodies a set of social principles that are both democratic and ethical. It seeks to engage processes of inquiry that are democratic, participatory, empowering, and life-enhancing.
- These are accomplished, in immediate terms, through the formation of learning communities within classrooms, schools, and their associated communities.

Initiating a Study: Research Design

3

RESEARCH DESIGN	DATA GATHERING	DATA ANALYSIS	COMMUNICATION	ACTION
INITIATING A STUDY	CAPTURING STAKEHOLDER EXPERIENCES AND PERSPECTIVES	IDENTIFYING KEY FEATURES OF EXPERIENCE	WRITING REPORTS	CREATING SOLUTIONS
Setting the stage			Reports Ethnographies Biographies	Solving problems
Focusing and framing	Interviewing	Analyzing epiphanies and illuminative experiences	PRESENTATIONS AND PERFORMANCES	Classroom practices
Literature review	Observing			Curriculum development
Sources of information	Artifact review	Categorizing and coding	Presentations Drama Poetry	Evaluation
Ethics	Literature review	Enhancing analysis	Song Dance Art	Family and community
Validity		Constructing category systems	Video Multimedia	School plans

This chapter presents ways of initiating a research study. It describes procedures for:

1. Creating a productive research environment
2. *Designing* the study (i.e., formulating an action plan for the research processes)
3. *Focusing* the study and stating it in researchable terms
4. *Framing* the scope of the inquiry
5. Engaging in a preliminary *review of the literature*
6. Identifying *sources of data*
7. Describing methods of *data analysis*
8. Taking account of *ethical* considerations
9. Establishing the validity of the study

Setting the Stage: Creating a Productive Research Environment

As the previous chapter indicates, action research is not just a technical routine providing information to improve a mechanical or ritualized learning process. Where scientific research is characterized by detached objectivity, action research is an *engaged* approach to research that enmeshes researchers in the life-worlds of the people with whom they work. In its best forms, research provides opportunities to develop good working relationships between participants, providing a "meaning-ful" basis for shared understandings and, in educational terms, the development of a learning community. In such circumstances, teaching and learning become infused with a creative energy that enables people not only to perform at the top of their capabilities, but to engage their full human potential. While action research can certainly enhance the routine day-to-day functioning of classrooms and schools, its greater potential lies in the extent to which it can transform the socio-emotional environment of classrooms and schools.

As we approach the technical routines of investigation, it is necessary to articulate the general working principles of action research to maximize the possibility of effective and productive outcomes. The holistic approaches to inquiry inherent in the need to find real solutions to practical problems in the classroom and school imply a need to focus on the broader dimensions of human conduct and interaction. As with school learning processes, action research necessarily involves solutions that have the potential to take into account the physical, emotional, aesthetic, spiritual, intellectual, moral, and social life of those involved. Since the process is as important as the product, these features must also be taken into account in developing positive working environments that form the basis for effective action.

With Head, Heart, and Hand: The Human Dimensions of Action Research

When we can work with head, heart and hand, we begin to shape a kind of community that is responsive to many different communities, in different places and in different times, and one that opens many ways forward. (Kelly and Sewell, 1988)

Too often, students move through routinized reading and writing tasks, engaging their hands, and to some extent their heads, but without having their heart in it. Teachers may likewise move mechanically through a teaching routine, maintaining order in their classes as they "keep the kids quiet" and "cover the content of the curriculum" with their heart disengaged. In such circumstances, classroom life threatens to become tedious, boring, and irrelevant—something to be endured by students to gain a class credit, certificate, or diploma. Good teaching provides learning experiences that excite students and provide knowledge and skills that enhance their lives. One of the very productive aspects of both teaching and research is the ability to fully engage all dimensions of experience, to employ the heads, hands, and hearts of the people who participate in classroom and school.

This is not always an easy task, as teachers often face groups of students who are disinterested, fractious, or rebellious. One of the enduring tasks of teaching is to develop and sustain student interest, and experienced teachers engage a broad repertoire of strategies with this end in mind. We speak of the need to motivate students as part of the language of instruction, often attributing student disinterest to personality factors like poor self-concept, poor concentration, or to their home or community background. Motivation is often seen as extrinsic to the content of learning, so that grades, assessments, or reward systems become primary means for encouraging students to maintain their focus and/or interest in their work. Motivation, however, may be more broadly conceived as engaging the *heart* or the *spirit* of the students and others with whom we work so they do not just "go through the motions" but take ownership for their work and engage it joyously, enthusiastically, and creatively. The same is true for teachers themselves, who must constantly find ways to develop and sustain the creative energy required for their demanding day-to-day work with children in schools.

Classroom teachers sometimes have difficulty imagining that research could make such a difference to their classroom life. As a teacher myself I discovered the energy emerging from participatory processes of inquiry. Over the past decades, however, I have been humbled by the sometimes impassioned comments of ordinary teachers who have embraced these tenets. Often working in the most difficult of situations, they have been able to transform their classroom and teaching lives, engaging creative energies of students, families, and community people. One pre-school teacher, engaging this form of research for the first time, commented, "It has been a long time since I have had a paradigmatic shift like this in such a profound way. [It] is like a small earthquake or miniature shock of lightning arousing me from my day-to-day automatic pilot semi-slumber." This type of response continues to sustain my excitement and enthusiasm. The technical routines I learn and teach are important, but the processes by which they become instilled in people's experience are a central ingredient of a truly educational experience. When I teach, I still aspire to a productive and enjoyable classroom experience for my students and myself. After decades in the classroom, I can still accomplish this, most times, in most places.

One of the problems of engaging the heart of our students, however, lies in the complexity teachers face in their daily class lives. My work alongside Australian Aboriginal people, whose needs are often quite different from the mainstream population, has sensitized me to this facet of school life. These experiences have been reinforced by my work in American schools and universities where African American, Hispanic, Native American, and other groups of students provide a rich tapestry of humanity that not only holds a fertile cultural resource but challenges teachers to accommodate the diversity that exists in their classrooms. Often the complexity of these situations encourages us to ignore the implicit differences in students, so we speak of them in technical or objectifying language—organisms, the learner, or the student—and characterize their failure to accomplish learning objectives in terms of deviance or other personal inadequacies. We often focus on interventions or strategies to repair their inappropriate or inadequate performances without acknowledging the possibility of engaging the resourcefulness of the students with whom we work.

The approach to action research presented in this book works on the assumption that people, even very young people, have deep and extended understandings of their lives that enable them to negotiate their way through an often bewildering and unpredictable life-world. It is our willingness to acknowledge the legitimacy of their world-views, and the wisdom that enables them to survive and sometimes thrive in difficult circumstances, that is at the heart of the participatory processes described in this book. The use of interviews as a central component of action research enables us to listen carefully to what people say, to record and represent events in their own terms, and to use their perceptions and interpretations in formulating plans and activities. The task is not to convince them of the inadequacies of their perspective but to find ways of enabling them, through sharing each other's perspectives, to formulate more productive understandings of their own situation.

This orientation to research seeks to enhance people's feelings of competence and worth by engaging them in processes that provide an affirmation of themselves, their friends, their families, and their communities. Our work with others—students, colleagues, parents, and administrators—enables them to maintain a constructive vision of themselves, anchoring them in a productive perspective of their worlds, and enabling them to work easily and comfortably with those around them. Engaging the heart means caring, in an ongoing way, about those facets of human experience that make a difference in the quality of their day-to-day lives. When we talk of the heart of the matter, or engaging the heart of the people, we are talking about their feelings of pride, dignity, identity, responsibility, and locatedness (see Figure 3.1).

The energy and joy emerging from research processes that hear the voices of the people, engage their knowledge and skills, and enable them to actively participate in the construction of activities, events, projects, programs, and services have been an integral part of my professional experience for many years. When I see people talk with shining eyes of their accomplishments, when I see them deeply engaged in work affecting their lives, when I see them moved to upgrade and extend their education, and continue to move in often-difficult terrain over extended periods, I know that their hearts have been engaged. They rarely do so in isolation, however, and the work they accomplish is enhanced by the common unity they share with those with whom they have worked.

Working Principles of Action Research

In a previous publication (Stringer, 1999), I presented a group of key concepts holding the principles of action research. The key principle is that of *relationship* because when relationships are wrong, it is hard to accomplish the desired outcomes of any project. *Communication* is also a central feature of action research, enabling all participants to remain informed and in harmony with the different activities in which people are engaged. The principle of *inclusion* speaks to the need to ensure that all people whose lives are affected or who have an effect on the issue investigated are included and that all significant factors having an effect are taken into account. Finally,

Pride
Feelings of personal worth

Dignity
Feelings of competence

Identity
Acknowledging the worth of social identities: female, mother, person-of-color, parent, etc.

Responsibility
Acknowledging their ability to be responsible for their actions

Space
Feelings of comfort that result from working in non-threatening physical environments

Place
Feelings of having a legitimate place in the social context

Figure 3.1
The Human Dimensions
of Action Research

the principle of *participation* signals the need to ensure that people are actively engaged in the work of the project, gaining energy from the resulting feelings of ownership and accomplishment. As we learn the technical aspects of research, we also need to encompass and integrate behaviors and interactional styles that facilitate the work we wish to accomplish. We need to take into account, therefore, the features of our work in all that we do.

Relationships
Good working relationships enable individuals and groups to trust each other, provide high levels of motivation, and provide the basis for continuing research activities. Good working relationships:

- Promote feelings of equality for all people involved
- Maintain harmony
- Avoid conflicts, where possible
- Resolve conflicts that arise, openly and dialogically

- Accept people as they are, not as some people think they ought to be
- Encourage personal, cooperative relationships, rather than impersonal, competitive, conflictual, or authoritarian relationships
- Are sensitive to people's feelings

Communication

Maintaining good relationships depends, to a significant extent, on the ability of people to communicate effectively. The quality, consistency, and honesty of communication have a vital effect on interactions between individuals and groups. Their work together is likely to be short lived or ineffectual if people talk to each other in disparaging or demeaning ways, if they fail to provide information about their activities, or if they distort or selectively communicate information.

Effective communication occurs when all participants:

- Listen attentively to each other
- Accept and act upon what is said
- Can understand what has been said
- Are truthful and sincere
- Act in socially and culturally appropriate ways
- Regularly advise others about what is happening

Participation

It is normal practice for professional practitioners to take responsibility for all that needs to be done in their sphere of operation. They either do things themselves or engage someone to do it for them. While this is quite necessary for many activities related to schooling and other professional spheres, one of the purposes of action research is to engage the natural expertise and experience of all participants. Where people are able to see that their worth is acknowledged by the activities in which they are able to engage, high levels of personal investment—both time and emotion—often result. Active participation is very empowering, especially for people who have a poor self-image. Another key feature of action research, therefore, is for facilitators to provide opportunities for people to demonstrate their competence by engaging in research-related activities themselves. Sometimes people may commence with quite simple tasks and take on increasingly complex activities as their confidence increases. Although this sometimes requires more time and considerable patience on the part of research facilitators, the long-term benefits easily outweigh the initial outlay of time and effort.

Participation is most effective when it:

- Enables significant levels of active involvement
- Enables people to perform significant tasks
- Provides support for people as they learn to act for themselves
- Encourages plans and activities that people are able to accomplish themselves
- Deals personally with people rather than with their representatives or agent

Inclusion

Often people are tempted to carve out a piece of "territory," or to take charge of an issue. In professional life, teachers and administrators almost automatically take responsibility for any actions required to deal with issues within their professional realm. Further, there is often pressure to find short-term solutions to complex problems with a long history, providing teachers and/or administrators with the temptation to take immediate action themselves. Usually, these actions fail to take into account many of the factors contributing to the problem or fail to include people integral to the context or whose lives are substantially affected by the problem.

Inclusion requires participants to:

- Involve all relevant groups and individuals whose lives are affected by the issue investigated
- Take account of all relevant issues affecting the research question
- Cooperate with related groups, agencies, and organizations where necessary
- Ensure all relevant groups benefit from activities

An Index of Engagement: Excitement, Interest, Apathy, and Resistance

A productive research environment is one in which people are actively engaged in the project at hand. Action research works best when research facilitators gauge the extent of participant involvement—always ensuring that major stakeholding groups continue to be part of the ongoing activity, or to maintain their interest in the project. The following index provides the means for facilitators to ask the question, "To what extent are the individuals and groups engaged?

In the best projects, people are highly engaged, and their **excitement** is evident. They talk animatedly, meet frequently to share ideas or explore issues, spend long hours working on required activities, are happy with their work, and resolve problems easily and cooperatively. At this level of engagement, highly productive and enjoyable work is a continuing and easily sustainable feature of the situation.

The work is also relatively easy when there are high degrees of **interest.** People work purposively and productively, talking easily and collegially as they share ideas and resources and work collaboratively. Interested participants produce good work that accomplishes the point of the project and gives them high degrees of satisfaction.

Apathy is a common response when people do not see the point of a process, when its purpose is merely ritualistic, or when participants can't see the relevance of research activities. Lethargic interactions are matched by token responses requiring a minimum of effort and producing minimum outcomes. You can see this in many classroom situations where students provide the teacher with poor quality work that they have engaged with the minimum amount of energy and time.

Resistance is a response of people engaged in activities they see as pointless, threatening, or coercive. Goffman (1961) suggests these are common responses in contexts where people have no freedom of choice or where they are forced to comply to rules over which they have no control. Critical theorists (e.g., Kincheloe and McClaren, 1994) suggest that resistance is a natural response to coercive systems of authority and people employ a variety of strategies to alleviate what they consider to be oppressive conditions. Productive work is rarely possible in these situations, and efforts to engage people in any sort of activity focuses mainly on systems of reward and punishment to attain required behaviors.

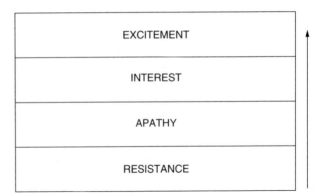

Figure 3.2
Index of Engagement

An Index of Engagement (Figure 3.2) provides a rule-of-thumb measure of the extent to which people are dedicated or committed to the work in hand. By enacting the principles of action research articulated previously, researchers provide the conditions that maximize the likelihood of interested or excited participants. Where it becomes apparent that some participants have begun to slide toward that line where interest fades into apathy, then the likelihood of an effective outcome for the project diminishes considerably. At this stage it would be expedient to engage in a brief review of the project using an evaluation cycle (see Chapter 7) to understand where and how interest has faded and to take steps to act on issues emerging. The intent of these processes is to engage people who may have become either apathetic or resistant in ways that enable them to become interested or excited. The best research outcomes occur where the interest of all stakeholders has been maintained and where people know that their voices are heard and their issues acted upon. Where even a small group remains apathetic or resistant, productive work is difficult to attain.

Research Design

As teacher researchers engage in action research they need to have a clear view of the details of the investigation in which they will be engaged. Initially, they will construct a preliminary picture of the project but will work with other stakeholders to refine this picture and incorporate more detail of research activities.

As they commence the work of inquiry, they will design the research and detail an action plan listing the steps to be taken. The design will include:

- **Building a preliminary picture:** Identifying the research problem and the people affected by or having an effect on the problem
- **Focusing:** Refining the statement of the research problem, the research question, and research objectives
- **Framing:** Establishing the scope of the inquiry
- **Preliminary literature review**
- **Sampling:** Procedures for identifying project participants

- **Sources of information/data:** Identifying stakeholding groups, sites and settings, statistical records, and other sources of documentary information providing input to the study
- **Form of the information/data:** The type of information that will inform the inquiry—interview transcripts, observational records, review summaries, televisual documentaries, formal research reports, school records, and so on
- **Data gathering procedures:** How information will be gathered—including interviews, focus groups, observations, review of materials and equipment, and so on
- **Data analysis procedures:** Ways of distilling information to identify key features, concepts, or meanings—e.g., event analysis, categorizing, and coding
- **Ethics:** Steps taken to ensure that no harm is done to people through their inclusion in the research
- **Validity:** Procedures used to enhance the strength of the research

Building the Researcher's Picture: The Reflective Practitioner

Reflective teacher-practitioners are curious about their work, wish to learn from it, and consciously engage in cycles of observation, reflection, and new action—conscious trial and error—to improve their practice. Their professional education and experience provide a toolkit of concepts and frameworks enabling them to systematically reflect upon the complex and inspirational art of teaching. The approach to research described in this text extends the possibilities for this informal look-think-act cycle. It outlines systematic methods of investigation and conceptual frameworks that will enable teachers to tackle the more difficult and long-term classroom and school problems. Such an approach can generate powerful understandings that inform strong educational practices.

While investigations by individual researchers can provide an effective means to solve classroom problems, the power of research is greatly enhanced when teachers engage in exploration with students, parents, other teachers, and others affected by the issue. By engaging in dialogue and discussion with others, collaborative researchers not only engage a larger pool of knowledge, but also form the basis for learning communities that have truly transformative potential.

One of the first difficulties confronting researchers is to acquire clarity about the nature and purpose of the research. Classrooms and schools are highly complex social contexts, containing myriads of interactions between teachers, students, administrators, parents, and others. In their day-to-day work, teachers deal with a vast array of inter-related issues and problems that have a continuing impact on their work. The initial processes of focusing, framing, and designing an action research study constitute the first of a number of cycles of observation, reflection, and action—depicted here as a Look-Think-Act sequence of activity. In the first research cycle, teacher-researchers carefully observe relevant classroom or school settings and then reflect on their observations to clarify the nature of the research problem. They identify the people who will be involved and with them further clarify the issue, formulating the research question upon which the study will initially focus, and delineating the scope of inquiry. Continuing cycles of the Look-Think-Act process enable the teacher-

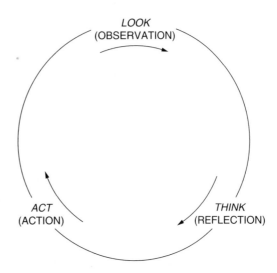

Figure 3.3
The Look-Think-Act Research Cycle

researcher and other participants to further refine these details as they engage in their investigation (see Figure 3.3).

LOOK entails building a preliminary picture of the situation and enabling the researcher to describe *who* is involved, *what* is happening, and *how, where, and when* events and activities occur. Information is acquired by observing, interacting, and talking informally with people.

THINK requires researchers to reflect on the emerging picture. It is the essential preliminary analysis of the situation enabling researchers to develop a clearer understanding of what is happening, how it is happening, and the stakeholding groups affected by or affecting the issue.

ACT defines the actions emerging from reflection. It requires people to *plan* their next steps and *implement* appropriate activity. *Evaluation* of these steps requires another cycle of the Look-Think-Act process.

Focusing the Study

In the everyday world of the classroom, teachers are confronted with an ongoing series of small crises and problems that they solve using a repertoire of skills and knowledge acquired through their professional training and school experience. More systematic research becomes necessary when they find themselves unable to find an effective solution to a persistent or serious problem. Identifying the point of entry is sometimes not easy since any problems tend to occur as an interrelated or intertwined series of events. Behavioral problems are often associated with poor academic performance, negative attitudes, lack of engagement, and so on. Trying to define what is *the* problem can easily become a "chicken-and-egg" process having no particular beginning or end or no clearly defined cause-and-effect relationships.

Sometimes our first analysis of a situation focuses on related events that prove to be peripheral to the problem about which we are concerned. A recent meeting of a school board I attended focused on the problem of low parent participation, with members discussing ways of increasing parent participation. Eventually, I asked board members whether, in fact, parent participation was the real problem, and asked them to consider the problem behind the problem. They spoke of a number of issues about which they were concerned, including the failure of parents to engage in required actions to remediate their children's poor academic performance or inappropriate behavior. In this case, the problem upon which the school board initially focused turned out to be multidimensional with parent participation being one facet of more deep-seated educational problems. Once the underlying problems were identified, the board was able to reflect more broadly on the issues about which they were concerned. The *problem* of parent participation turned out to be a suggested *solution*. In the first stages of research, therefore, research participants need to carefully reflect on the nature of the problem about which they are concerned.

One of the major strengths of qualitative research is its ability to allow researchers to tentatively state the problem, then refine and reframe the study by continuing iterations of the Look-Think-Act research cycle. In one study, for instance, researchers focused initially on after-school vandalism in the local district and attributed it to poor parental supervision. Preliminary investigations revealed, however, that youth from their school suffered from boredom and frustration because of the apparent lack of activities or facilities in their small town. The investigation took a markedly different turn at this point, focusing more clearly on exactly what facilities were available and what might be developed. In another investigation, preliminary inquiries indicated to a classroom teacher that an apparent lack of interest in reading in her class could be attributed more clearly to her teaching methods and the reading material she used. She refocused her research at this point from her students to her own syllabus.

At this stage, the research is essentially a reflective process requiring research participants to think carefully through all dimensions of the issue causing concern. The first step is to reflect on what is happening that is problematic and what issues and events are related to that problem. To focus the research more clearly, the issue or problem is stated in the form of a researchable question and the objective of studying that issue identified. These should be clearly stated as follows[1]:

---

[1]Since this is a qualitative research study, a research hypothesis—a suggested answer to the research question—is not part of the design. Qualitative or interpretive inquiry is hypothesis generating, rather than hypothesis testing. "Testing" of the "answers" generated by an action research process is accomplished through continual cycling through the Look-Think-Act routine, so that actions put into place as a result of the first cycle of investigation are subject to evaluative processes through further observation and analysis—Looking and Thinking.

- **The *issue or topic* to be studied:** Defining which issues or events are causing concern
- **The *research problem:*** Stating the issue as a problem
- **The *research question:*** Reframing that problem as a question—asking, in effect, "What is happening here?"
- **The *research objective:*** Describing what we would hope to achieve by studying this question[2]

Shelley Jones' study of reading in her class was defined in the following terms:

Issue: Students are consistently failing to complete their reading homework, are listless in reading lessons, and score poorly on reading proficiency tests.

Problem: The students are uninterested in reading.

Question: How do students experience reading?

Objective: To understand what the experience of reading means to students.

The preliminary reflective process for developing the focus of the study is assisted by dialogue with both potential participants and colleagues. While it is possible that the research focus may later change as other participants pose their own particular questions, initiators of the project should be clear about their own research questions and its significance to them.

The initial development of the research question should focus on *how* participants and other stakeholders experience the problematic issue and *how* they interpret events and other information. How is it that these problems occur? How do students perceive that they manage to complete their assignments? How do students describe learning processes that are stimulating? In action research the focus is largely on events and their interpretation, rather than factual information or strongly developed causal connections explaining why events occur.

By developing a clear, precise, and focused research question, researchers take an essential reference point into their inquiry. Once investigations have commenced, they are able to evaluate the emerging data according to its reference to the research questions. The initial research question should be shared by all participants and reiterated consistently throughout the research cycles as a constant guide to investigation.

---

[2]Qualitative studies usually focus on understanding people's experience and perspectives as a common outcome of the research process. Quantitative or experimental studies, however, more often focus on causal explanations that explain how one group of variables is "caused" by the effect of preceding variables.

Framing the Study: Delimiting the Scope of the Inquiry

As research participants identify and clarify the research issues and questions, they will also need to define the broad parameters of the study, determining whether it will be limited in scope involving a small number of people over a small time period, or whether more extended study is required. Sometimes it is a relatively simple matter to work with students within a classroom to formulate successful strategies to solve the problem studied. At other times, it may be necessary to work in conjunction with teachers from other classes, with the school administration, and/or with families. Before commencing research, therefore, participants will make decisions about the sample of people to be included in the study, the sites or settings in which the research will take place, and the times research activities will take place. Decisions will also be made about the extent of participation by those involved in the study, which will define who will be involved in the various research activities and who will monitor and support people in their research work.

These considerations run hand-in-hand with the need to consider the breadth of issues to be incorporated into the study. By including too many issues, the study is likely to become complex and unwieldy, but delimiting the study too closely may neglect issues that have an important bearing on the problem. In the Barrios Juntos study, for instance (see pp. 197–201), participants concerned with ways of improving parent participation in the school decided to focus their study on parent-teacher conferences rather than investigating the other possible forums and vehicles of parent participation. In this instance, the research revealed ways in which parent-teacher conferences could be improved, but also identified a range of related issues that would need to be addressed. Researchers, therefore, will initially broadly identify:

- **Problem:** *What* is the problem requiring investigation? What is my central research question?
- **Participants:** *Who* are the stakeholders? Which people are affected by or have an effect on the issue being studied? Students? Teachers? Administrators? Parents or other family members? Others?
- **Place:** *Where* will the research take place? Which sites or settings will be included in the study? Classrooms? School yard? Offices? Homes? Other locations?
- **Time:** *When* will the research begin? How long might it take?
- **Scope:** What is the likely scope of the issues to be investigated? Student academic experience? Student reading experience? Reading comprehension experience? Student experiences of the curriculum, classroom, learning? Student and teacher experiences of school organization? Student, teacher, and parent perspectives on student experiences?

Once the research participants have clarified the focus, frame, and scope of the research, they will undertake a preliminary review of the literature to identify other perspectives on the issue embedded in the literature. This may assist them to further clarify the nature and extent of their investigations.

Preliminary Literature Review

As Cresswell (2002) points out, literature reviews for qualitative research have different purposes than those in quantitative research. While substantial use of the literature provides the basis for formulating a quantitative study, qualitative studies use the literature review quite minimally in the earlier phases of a study. Since the latter focuses on stakeholder experiences and perspectives, pre-formulation of the issue according to concepts and analyses in the literature are deemed inappropriate at this point. Because of the nature of qualitative research, initial conceptions of the research are always assumed to be provisional, thus limiting the possibility of an exhaustive review of the literature.

Understandings and information emerging from the literature, however, may augment, complement, or challenge stakeholder perspectives as the study progresses. Since classroom and school life have been the subject of study for many decades, research participants may increase the power of their investigation by reviewing literature that speaks to emerging concepts and issues. In some cases, they may identify potential solutions to the problem that have been successfully enacted in other contexts, or acquire information that clarifies issues emerging in the study. Frequently, salient issues emerging in the data collection phase influence the direction of the investigation, causing participants to pursue different, but related, questions. Hence the literature search will evolve as an ongoing feature of the research process, emerging in accordance with the directions and agendas indicated by participant-constructed descriptions of the situation.

Literature Search

The first phase of a search requires researchers to identify relevant literature. This task is greatly enhanced by the capabilities of computer-assisted search engines available in most libraries. It will be necessary to identify three to four key concepts related to the issue to feed into the search routine. Where large numbers of items are identified, it may be necessary to delineate further key concepts to narrow the search to the most relevant sources of information. Perusing annotated collections, such as ERIC, which provide a brief description of the content of the reading, may enhance this process.

An increasing body of material is available on the web providing researchers with useful resources for their study. Sole reliance on the web, however, is not recommended, as the information available from this source tends to be incomplete and patchy. As in library searches, researchers will need to identify key concepts to feed into the search process.

Researchers often distinguish between:

- **Primary sources** providing direct reports of original research
- **Secondary sources** that report on or summarize primary source material
- **Professional literature** based on the perspectives of experienced professionals
- **Institutional reports** from government or institutional authorities
- **Practice literature** presenting or advocating particular approaches to professional practice

University and professional libraries provide a wide variety of relevant literature, including theses and dissertations, journals, books, handbooks, abstracts, and encyclopedias. Library staff can often assist in identifying initial reading pertinent to the problem being investigated, but review of any material will identify other sources of information, so that a review of the literature becomes an ever-expanding search. Researchers should note sources cited in journal articles, research reports, and texts, then review those for further information.

Identifying Different Perspectives in the Literature

The preliminary literature review extends the think/reflect part of the research cycle and provides new possibilities for conceptualizing or interpreting the issue. The preliminary search, therefore, should be sufficiently broad to provide researchers with an understanding of the different perspectives and types of information presented within the literature. These will not only differ according to the disciplines of the authors—psychology, sociology, cultural studies, and so on—but according to different theoretical positions from within each discipline. The literature may also vary according to the formal and informal reports from a variety of educational sources, including school, district, state, and national documents. It may include video/television documentaries, as well as information on projects and activities available on the web.

As the project progresses, participants will select, review, and evaluate relevant literature as part of the process of data collection thereby, identifying pertinent information to enhance the understandings emerging from other sources (see Chapter 4). Studies by other people within the literature become other perspectives (or stakeholders) to be incorporated into the process of data collection and analysis. The preliminary review of the literature within the first iteration of the action research cycle is conducted through the lens of the initial research question, alerting participants to other findings about similar problems, assisting with the refinement of the research question, and/or providing insight into research methods.

Sampling: Selecting Participants

In most studies, limits on time and resources make it impossible to include all people who might potentially inform the research process, therefore it is necessary to select a smaller group to provide the information (data) on which the research is grounded. A technique called *purposive, or purposeful, sampling* seeks to ensure that the diverse perspectives of people likely to affect the issue are included in the study. Cresswell (2002) suggests that purposive sampling seeks to select participants for a variety of purposes. These include:

- People who represent the diverse perspectives found in any social context (maximal variation sampling)
- Particularly troublesome or enlightening cases (extreme case sampling)
- Participants who are "typical" of people in the setting (typical sampling)
- Participants who have particular knowledge related to the issue studied (theory or concept sampling)

In all cases, researchers need to purposively select a sample of participants that represents the variation of perspectives and experiences across all groups and sub-groups who affect or are affected by the issue under investigation—the stakeholders in the study.[3]

The first task is to identify the primary stakeholding groups[4]—that is, the group most centrally involved or affected by the issue studied. If a study is concerned about poorly performing boys in a classroom, the poorly performing boys would be the primary stakeholding group, while a study of parent participation in school would have parents as the primary stakeholders. Sometimes the primary stakeholding groups are complementary groups. A study of a classroom issue might include teachers and students as primary stakeholders, while a study of parent participation might include parents, teachers, and students.

The next task is to identify, within those stakeholding groups, the different types or groups of people likely to have an effect on the issue studied. Issues of gender, class, race, and ethnicity are paramount, since these factors are likely to be related to significant variation in experience and perspective. Researchers might need to ensure that girls and boys are included in their sample, that poorer students are represented as well as those from more middle-class backgrounds, and that each racial and ethnic group is included. Depending on the context, it may be necessary for researchers to include members of different social cliques, religious affiliations, sporting groups, or other types of groups represented in the social setting.

While it is not always possible to include people from *all* groups in any setting, those selected should include participants from groups likely to have a significant impact on the issue studied or to be impacted by that issue. To fail to include participants because it is not convenient, because they show little interest, or because they are non-communicative is to put the effectiveness of the study at risk. The previous chapter talked of the need to establish research relationships to maximize the possibility of including everyone likely to affect the issue studied.

It is not always possible for researchers to nominate in advance those who need to be included in a study. A technique called *snowballing* enables researchers to ask participants who they think needs to be included, or someone they might nominate who has quite a different perspective or set of experiences related to the issue studied. In this way, researchers commence by defining likely participants, but extend their sample to be more inclusive of the diverse and significant perspectives included in the study.

Any group, however, is likely to include people who are natural leaders or who, in some way, are able to sway the opinions or perspectives of others in their group—sometimes referred to as opinion leaders. Researchers should try to ensure that the sample selected includes both natural leaders and opinion leaders. A general rule of

---

[3]Purposive sampling differs in nature and purpose from random sampling used for experimental studies. A random sample drawn from a larger population enables experimental researchers to use statistical procedures to generalize from that sample to a larger population. Rather than seeking to generalize, action research seeks solutions to problems and questions that are quite context specific.

[4]In some literature, the *primary stakeholding group* is referred to as the *critical reference group*. The intent, however, is similar—to focus on those primarily affected by the issue studied.

thumb in this process is to ask "Who can speak for this group? Whose word will group members acknowledge as representing their perspective?"

The research design may not specify a particular sample, but will describe the procedures for identifying those who will be active participants in the study.

Sources and Form of Information (Data Gathering)

The major source of information in action research is that provided by interviewing stakeholding research participants—the sample described previously. Researchers will also observe or review a variety of other sources with the intent of acquiring a body of relevant information to assist in developing a clearer understanding of events and phenomena studied. Common sources of information include cultural settings (places), events, activities, materials and equipment, work samples, documents, records, reports, relevant literature, and so on (to be discussed in Chapter 4). Data is collected from these sources by observation of settings and events or by reviewing documentary and other recorded information.

The research design should stipulate the methods employed to access these types of information, including interviews, focus groups, observations, reviews, photographs, video recording, and audio recording. Structured interviews, questionnaires, and observation schedules may also be used in the latter stages of a project.

Because of the nature of qualitative research, it is not possible to signal precisely all sources of information, but the design should provide participants with guidance about where, when, how, and from whom initial information will be acquired.

Distilling the Information (Analyzing the Data)

The research design should inform participants and those reading research proposals of the type of data analysis to be used in the study. The research design should clearly signal the type of data analysis employed and the use to which analyzed data might be applied to actions emerging in the latter stages of the study (see Chapter 5).

RESEARCH DESIGN

A qualitative action research design provides a description of:

1. *Focus:* A statement of the issue, the research problem, the research question, and research objectives
2. *Framing the scope of inquiry:* The place, the time, the stakeholding groups, and the scope of the issues included in the study
3. *Preliminary literature review:* Processes for reviewing the literature
4. *Sources of information/data:* The stakeholders, sites and settings, and literature from which information will be acquired
5. *Data gathering processes:* Ways information will be gathered— interviews, observation, review of materials and equipment, and so on
6. *Data analysis processes:* Procedures used for distilling information

---

Research Ethics

The research design also includes ethical considerations that protect the well-being and interests of research participants. Punch (1994) suggests that "the view that science is intrinsically neutral and essentially beneficial disappeared with the revelations at the Nuremberg trials." Some well-known studies have shown that researchers are not always aware of potential harm that may come to those who participate in research studies (e.g., Horowitz, 1970; Milgram, 1963). Most public institutions and professional organizations have formal procedures to ensure that researchers do not knowingly or unknowingly put research participants at risk. The research design includes procedures for ensuring the safety of their participants. As Sieber (1992) indicates, sound ethics and sound methodology go hand in hand.

Confidentiality, Care, and Sensitivity

When people talk for extended periods, they often speak of very private matters and reveal highly problematic events or even potentially harmful information. A prime directive of social research is to protect the anonymity of participants. In practice, it is best to assume that *all* information acquired is highly confidential. Where we require information to be shared with other participants or audiences, we must first ask relevant participants for permission to do so. When I read back my field notes, or share analyzed information with participants, I ask "Is there anything here you would not like to reveal to other people in this project?" If they appear unsure, I inform them that it may be possible to present the information but to disguise its source. We can do this by using fictitious names or by reporting it generally—"Some people suggest that . . ." and "Other participants provide a different perspective. . . ."

Aligned with confidentiality is the duty of care we have to participants. We need to ensure that information is stored securely so that others do not inadvertently see it. We certainly should not share recorded information with others without permission of the persons concerned, even if that information points to apparently harmful events in the person's life—drug abuse, physical abuse, and so on. This points to another possibility occasionally arising in the processes of extended interview where the recall of distressing events creates a deep emotional response. Duty of care requires researchers to provide sufficient time for the person to debrief by talking through issues or events to a point of comfort, or by putting them in contact with a family member or counselor who can assist them to resolve the situation.

Permissions

Permission is not usually required when teachers engage in action research directly related to their ongoing work in the classroom. Where they engage in more extended studies involving other school staff, children from other classes, or parents, then they may need to obtain formal permission prior to commencing the project. To the extent that the research becomes a public process, therefore, where people's privacy or personal well-being is at risk, written permission from a person in a position of authority is warranted—a principal, school district superintendent, or other relevant authority. In these circumstances, it is necessary to provide information about the nature of the research, the significance of the study, and the ways in which ethical considerations will be taken into account. It is useful to attach a copy of the research design to the request for permission to pursue the study.

Where research is associated with a university course or program, the institution itself will usually have processes for reviewing research through an ethics committee. A similar system operates in school districts. Though the procedures are sometimes unwieldy and time-consuming, they provide a means of ensuring that people's privacy is not violated and that the research processes do not interfere with their well-being.

Informed Consent

In many contexts, protocols require those facilitating research to engage in processes of informed consent. This requires the research facilitator and others engaged in data gathering to:

- Inform each participant of the purpose and nature of the study
- Ask whether they wish to participate
- Ask permission to record information they provide
- Assure them of the confidentiality of that information
- Advise them that they may withdraw at any stage and have their recorded information returned
- Ask them to sign a short document affirming their permission

Figure 3.4 provides an example of how these processes are presented to participants and then documented. A consent form not only provides information but is a record of consent so that copies should be provided to each signatory.

RESEARCH ETHICS

Ethical procedures are established by:

1. *Confidentiality:* Privacy is protected by ensuring confidentiality of information.
2. *Permissions:* Permission is obtained to carry out the research by people in positions of responsibility.
3. *Informed consent:* Participants are informed of the nature of the study and provide formal consent to be included.

YOUTH RECREATIONAL FACILITIES IN LEDDINGHALL

Mrs. Miles' ninth-grade class at Leddinghall High School is concerned that no recreational facilities for young people are available in the district. They are now engaged in reviewing the services, facilities, and resources available to young people in the community and will invite young people who live there to tell of their experiences. On the basis of this study, the class will write a report on recreation for young people in the Leddinghall community to be presented to the town council.

Consent Form

I, _____ have read the above information and been informed of the nature of the study. I consent to being interviewed by a class member for this study. I understand that:

- All information will be kept confidential
- I may withdraw from the study at any time and have information I have given returned to me at that time
- I will not be identified in any way in reports arising from this study without my written permission

Signed: _____

Date: _____

Figure 3.4
Consent Form

Validity in Action Research: Evaluating Quality

When teachers engage in research in their own classrooms, they are usually able to ascertain the worth of research according to its usefulness in helping them accomplish their teaching objectives. Studies wider in scope, however, involving official approval or requests for funding, often need to satisfy more stringent requirements. People want assurance that sloppy, poorly devised, or unbalanced research is not likely to result in inadequate or potentially damaging outcomes. In these circumstances, they often require an examination of the rigor or strength of the procedures to be included in the methodology section of a research proposal.

Action research, being essentially qualitative or naturalistic, seeks to construct holistic understandings of the dynamic and complex social world of classroom and school. It reveals people's subjective experience and the ways they meaningfully construct and interpret events, activities, behaviors, responses, and problems. Although these types of studies provide powerful understandings enabling the development of effective practices and activities, they are mostly specific to particular contexts and lack stability over time—what is true at one time may vary as policies and procedures shift and the actors in the setting change. When a new principal arrives at a school or staff changes occur, for instance, then the life of the school is likely to change in significant ways. The truths emerging from naturalistic inquiry, therefore, are always contingent (i.e., they are true only for the people, time, and setting of that particular study). We are not looking for *the* truth or *the* causes, but truths-in-context.

Procedures for evaluating the rigor of experimental or survey research evolve around well-formulated processes for testing reliability[5] and establishing the validity[6] of a study (see pp. 19–20). Traditional experimental criteria for establishing validity, however, are inappropriate for qualitative action research, and debate continues about a broadly acceptable set of criteria to use for this purpose. Some researchers have approached this task by seeking to identify the foundational assumptions underlying the term "validity." "What does it mean," they ask, "when we seek to establish the validity of a study?" Two highly respected scholars, Denzin and Lincoln (1998b, p. 414), interpret validity in the following terms:

> . . . a text's call to authority and truth . . . is established through recourse to a set of rules concerning knowledge, its production, and representation. The rules, as Scheurich (1992, p. 1) notes, if properly followed, establish validity. Without validity there is no truth, and without truth there can be no trust in a text's claims to validity. . . . "Validity becomes a boundary line that "divides good research from bad, separates acceptable (to a particular research community) research from unacceptable research. . . " (Scheurich, 1992, p. 5)

Because qualitative methods are essentially subjective in nature and local in scope, procedures for assessing the validity of research are quite different than those used for experimental study. As Scheurich's quote suggests, a new set of criteria are required to provide people with trust that the research is acceptable. A common set of criteria for establishing the validity of research has been provided by Lincoln and Guba (1985). They suggest that because there can be no objective measures of validity, the underlying issue becomes to identify ways of establishing *trustworthiness*, or the extent to which we can trust the truthfulness or adequacy of a research project. They propose that the means for establishing trustworthiness involve procedures for attaining:

- **Credibility:** The plausibility and integrity of a study
- **Transferability:** Whether results might be applied to other contexts than the research setting

---

[5]Reliability is estimated by measures of the extent to which similar results may be expected from similar samples within the population studied, across different contexts and at different times. Reliability focuses on the stability of results across time, settings, and samples.

[6]Experimental validity is defined in two ways—external validity and internal validity. Measures of external validity estimate the probability that results obtained from the sample differ significantly from results we would expect. Internal validity focuses on the extent to which results obtained might be attributed to the dependent variables included in the study, and not some other cause. Researchers ask "Do our instruments actually measure what we wish them to measure," and "Are the results attributal to the dependant variables we have stipulated, or to some other related variable?" Internal validity focuses on careful research design and instrumentation. Both reliability and validity are verified by statistical and other techniques.

- **Dependability:** Where research processes are clearly defined and open to scrutiny
- **Confirmability:** Where the outcomes of the study are demonstrably drawn from the data

Trustworthiness, therefore, is established by recording and reviewing the research procedures themselves to establish the extent to which they ensure the phenomena studied is accurately and adequately represented. The following procedures are adapted from those suggested by Guba and Lincoln.

Credibility

Qualitative research is easily open to sloppy, biased processes that merely reinscribe the biases and perspectives of those in control of the research process. Careful adherence to the following processes assists researchers in minimizing the extent to which their own viewpoints intrude. They may also review and record the following features of the research process to provide evidence of rigorous procedure and enhancing the plausibility of their findings (Lincoln and Guba, 1985).

Prolonged Engagement

Brief visits to a research site provide only superficial understandings of events. A rigorous study requires researchers to invest sufficient time to achieve a relatively sophisticated understanding of a context: to learn the intricacies of cultural knowledge and meaning that sustain people's actions and activities in a setting. Prolonged engagement in a setting also enables researchers to establish relationships of trust with participants, and therefore gain greater access to insider knowledge rather than the often superficial or purposeful information given by strangers. Researchers therefore add to the credibility of a study by recording the time spent in the research context.

Persistent Observation

Being present in the research context for an extended time period is not a sufficient condition to establish credibility, however. Sometimes researchers mistake their presence in the field for engagement in research. In a recent study, one investigator indicated he had worked with a group of teachers for months. He had, however, not engaged in systematic research at that time and his "observations" were undirected, unfocused, and unrecorded. Participants need to consciously engage in data collection activities to provide depth to their inquiries. This is essential to interviewing processes, as a single interview lasting 15–20 minutes provides very superficial understandings that lack both detail and adequacy. Prolonged engagement signals the need for repeated, extended interviews to establish the adequacy, accuracy, and appropriateness of research materials. Researchers therefore need to record the number and duration of observations and interviews.

Triangulation

Triangulation involves the use of multiple and different sources, methods, and perspectives to corroborate, elaborate, or illuminate the research problem and its outcomes. It enables the inquirer to clarify meaning by identifying different ways the phenomenon is being perceived (Stake, 1994). In action research, we include all stakeholders relevant to the issue investigated, observe multiple sites and events relevant to the stakeholders and issue investigated, and review all relevant materials, including resources, reports, records, research literature, and so on. These multiple sources and methods provide a rich resource for building adequate and appropriate accounts and understandings that form the base for working toward the resolution of research problems.

Participant Debriefing

This process is similar to *peer debriefing* proposed by Lincoln and Guba (1985), but differs because of the change in status of the researcher in an action research process. It is not solely the research facilitator who is in need of debriefing, but other participants in the process as well. Debriefing is a process of exposing oneself to a disinterested person for the purpose of exploring and challenging aspects of the inquiry that might otherwise remain only implicit within the participant's mind (Lincoln and Guba, 1985). The purposes of debriefing are to review the appropriateness of research procedures and to clarify the participant ways of describing and interpreting events. Debriefing also provides participants with an opportunity for catharsis, enabling them to deal with emotions and feelings that might cloud their vision or prevent relevant information from emerging. Researcher facilitators often provide debriefing sessions with research participants, but may also require an interested colleague to engage in debriefing them on the processes of research they are guiding. The credibility of a study is enhanced where researchers record that participants were given the opportunity to debrief.

Diverse Case Analysis

In all research, it is necessary to ensure that other interpretations of the data are fully explored. Sometimes there is a temptation to include in a research process only those people who are positively inclined toward the issue under study, or to interpret the information in particular ways. Diverse case analysis seeks to ensure all possible perspectives are taken into account, and that interpretations of important, significant, or powerful people do not overwhelm others. Diverse case analysis enables participants to constantly refine interpretations so that all participant perspectives are included in the final report, and all issues are dealt with. The credibility of a study is enhanced if researchers can demonstrate that all perspectives affecting the study have been included. A clear statement of sampling procedures assists in this process.

Referential Adequacy

Referential adequacy refers to the need for concepts and structures of meaning within the study to clearly reflect the perspectives, perceptions, and language of participants. When participants' experiences and perspectives are reinterpreted through the lenses of other existing reports or theories, or in terms derived from existing practices, procedures, or policies, research outcomes are likely to be distorted. One of the key features of qualitative research is the need to ensure that interpretations are experience-near, grounded in the language and terminology used by participants to frame and describe their experience. Where it is necessary to use more general terms to refer to a number of phenomena, those terms should adequately refer to the specific details to which they refer. The credibility of a study is enhanced to the extent that researchers can demonstrate that outcomes of the study have a direct relationship to the terminology and language used by participants.

Member Checks

In experimental inquiry, research subjects rarely have the opportunity to question or review the information gathered and the outcomes of the study. The practical nature of action research, however, requires that participants be given frequent opportunity to review the raw data, the analyzed data, and reports that are produced. This process of review is called member checking and provides the means for ensuring the research adequately and accurately represents the perspectives and experiences of participants. Member checking is one of the key procedures required to establish the credibility of a study.

Transferability

Unlike quantitative research that assumes the need to generalize the results of the study, qualitative research by its very nature can only apply results directly to the context of the study. Nevertheless, researchers seek to provide the possibility that results might be transferred to other settings to enable people to take advantage of the knowledge acquired in the course of the study. Whether such application is possible, it is assumed, can be assessed according to the likelihood that another context is sufficiently similar to allow results to be applicable. A study from rural Australia, for instance, may or may not have import for suburban Holland. Qualitative research reports seek to provide sufficiently detailed reports of the context and the participants to enable others to assess the likely applicability of the research to their own situation. Thickly detailed descriptions, therefore, contribute to the trustworthiness of a study by enabling other audiences to clearly understand the nature of the context and the people participating in the study.

Dependability

Trustworthiness also depends on the extent to which observers are able to ascertain whether research procedures are adequate for the purposes of the study. Where insufficient information is available, or available information indicates the likelihood of superficial and/or limited inquiry, they will not feel the study is dependable. The dependability of research is achieved through an *inquiry audit* whereby details of the research process, including processes for defining the research problem, collecting and analyzing data, and constructing reports are made available to participants and other audiences.

Confirmability

Confirmability is achieved through an audit trail, with the inquirer having retained recorded information that can be made available for review. These include raw data such as field notes, photographs, diary entries, original and annotated documents, copies of letters, and materials generated at meetings. They also include data reduction and analysis products and plans and reports derived from the study. They enable participants or other observers to be able to confirm that research accurately and adequately represents the perspectives presented in the study. By this means, they enhance the trustworthiness of the study.

Validity and Participation

The strength of qualitative research derives from the methodological intent to build accounts that more clearly represent the experience, perspective, and voice of those studied. The credibility of accounts, to some extent, is derived from the extent to which researchers are able to enact the procedures delineated in the previous section. Throughout the process, however, researchers constantly run the risk of observing and interpreting events through the lens of their own history of experience, thus putting the validity of the study at risk (Stringer and Genat, 1998).

A much greater degree of credibility, however, is gained through the use of participatory processes. When research participants engage in the processes of collecting and analyzing data, they are in a position to constantly check and extend the veracity of the material with which they are working. As they read the data of their interviews, they not only "see themselves" more clearly (the looking-glass-self), but are drawn to extend and clarify the events they describe. As they engage in data analysis, they are able to identify more clearly and correctly the significant experiences, features, and elements of which they are comprised. As they assist in the construction of reports, they help formulate accounts that more clearly use familiar language to represent their experience and perspective.

Participatory processes respond to recent developments in qualitative research (Altheide and Johnson, 1998) that point to the multiple means now used to establish validity, according to the nature and purposes of the study, and the theoretical frames of reference upon which the research rests. In a very direct way, engaging people as direct participants in the research also enables a study to take into account such issues as emotionality, caring, subjective understanding, and relationships in research (Lather, 1993; Oleson, 1994, 1999) that are important features of feminist research. They are incorporated as a means of ensuring the validity/trustworthiness of a study, but also to enhance the possibility of effective change.

Validity and Utility

One of the greatest sources of validity in action research is the utility of the outcomes of research. Where participants are able to construct ways of describing and interpreting events that enable them to take effective action on the issue they have investigated, they demonstrate the validity of the research. The power of the processes is nowhere more evident than in effective actions emerging from the research, clearly demonstrating the success in identifying appropriate perspectives and meanings. High degrees of credibility are evident, since the understandings that emerge from the processes of inquiry are successfully applied to actions within the research setting. It becomes immediately evident that the features on which the research has focused are adequate to account for the phenomena investigated.

Summary

The validity of action research is verified through procedures establishing credibility, transferability, dependability, confirmability, degrees of participation, and utility. These are attained through:

1. **Prolonged engagement:** The duration of the research processes
2. **Persistent observation:** The number and duration of observations and interviews
3. **Triangulation:** All sources of data, including the settings observed, the stakeholders interviewed, and materials reviewed
4. **Participant debriefing:** Processes for reviewing research procedures
5. **Negative case analysis:** Processes for ensuring a diversity of interpretations are explored

6. **Referential adequacy:** How terminology within the study is drawn from participant language and concepts
7. **Member checks:** Procedures for checking the accuracy of data and the appropriateness of data analysis and reporting
8. **Transferability:** The inclusion of detailed descriptions of the participants and the research context
9. **Dependability:** Detailed description of the research process
10. **Confirmability:** The data available for review
11. **Participation:** The extent of stakeholder participation in the research process
12. **Utility:** Practical outcomes of the research process

Gathering Data: Sources of Information

4

RESEARCH DESIGN	DATA GATHERING	DATA ANALYSIS	COMMUNICATION	ACTION
INITIATING A STUDY	CAPTURING STAKEHOLDER EXPERIENCES AND PERSPECTIVES	IDENTIFYING KEY FEATURES OF EXPERIENCE	WRITING REPORTS	CREATING SOLUTIONS
Setting the stage			Reports Ethnographies Biographies	Solving problems
Focusing and framing	Interviewing	Analyzing epiphanies and illuminative experiences	PRESENTATIONS AND PERFORMANCES	Classroom practices
Literature review	Observing			Curriculum development
Sources of information	Artifacts review	Coding and categorizing	Presentations Drama Poetry	Evaluation
Ethics	Literature review	Enhancing analysis	Song Dance Art	Family and community
Validity		Constructing category systems	Video Multimedia	School plans

Contents of This Chapter

Chapter 3 described the first phase of inquiry in which participants focus their investigation and design a valid and ethical research process. This chapter presents the first steps of that investigation, describing procedures for systematically accumulating information that will contribute to extended understanding of the issue investigated. It provides details of:

• The *purposes* for gathering information
• Procedures for *interviewing* participants
• Procedures for *observing* setting and events
• Procedures for reviewing *artifacts*—records, documents, and materials
• Procedures for incorporating *statistical and numerical data*, including those obtained from *surveys*
• Procedures for reviewing the *literature*

Later chapters reveal how participants distill this body of information to crystallize and clarify their understandings of the issue investigated.

Building a Picture: Gathering Information

The first movement through the Look-Think-Act research cycle provided preliminary information from which participants defined the research problem and question
and provided a plan for enacting the investigation. During the next iteration of the
cycle, participants begin to build a picture of the problem they are investigating—
first focusing on the Look step to gather information from a variety of sources (see
Figure 4.1). Ultimately, this information will be used to develop detailed accounts
that clarify and extend their understanding of the acts, activities, events, purposes,
and emotions comprising people's everyday lives.

The major purpose of this phase of inquiry is to understand the experience of interacting individuals. When we work with children who are disengaged, disinterested, or misbehaving, for instance, we ask "What is happening for these children?
What is in their experience that is creating these responses to the situation?" This
approach differs from the detached, clinical perspective of the psychologist, another
useful viewpoint, that may explain those behaviors in terms of behavioral or personality disorders—depression, anxiety, attention deficit disorder, and so on. In action
research, however, we seek to understand the natural world of the child, searching
for ways to understand his or her experience. The information we acquire in this
process enables us to enter children's worlds, to understand and interpret events in
ways that mesh with their experience. Other types of information complement, enhance, or challenge the information we acquire and provide depth and clarity to the
understandings emerging from the investigation.

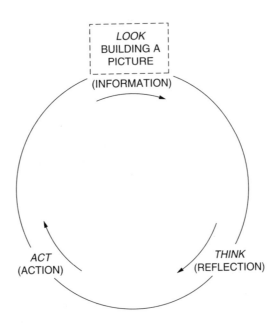

Figure 4.1
Information for Action Research

I've heard many stories of children refusing to go to school or misbehaving badly and the investigations revealing reasons for their behavior—a child who feared the departure of her mother after a parental argument; another scared to go to school because he didn't have the right pens; one who was scared of a bully; another whose brother had been sent to prison. In many cases, the reasons became apparent only when the children were asked to talk at length about their experience and provided the basis for effective actions to deal with the issue. Children are like adults in many ways. We can't assume that we understand ourselves perfectly, but what knowledge and understanding we have needs to be taken seriously when actions are affecting our lives.

In action research, **interviews** are the principle means of understanding people's experiences and perspectives. We also systematically **observe** settings and events, **review documents** and **records** pertaining to the issue investigated, and examine related **materials and equipment.** In doing so, we often acquire useful **numerical and statistical information** that complements other information we have acquired. As issues emerge, we also focus our attention on related literature, including academic research reports, professional publications, or official reports, that shed further light on the issue investigated. Each of these types of information—records of interviews, observations, and reviews of documents, artifacts, and the literature—has the potential to increase the power and scope of the research process. If we listen to people describe and interpret their experience, as well as observe and participate in events and read reports of those or similar events, then we enrich the research process. Multiple sources diminish the possibility that one perspective alone will shape the course or determine the outcome of an investigation. Multiple sources also provide a diversity of materials from which to fashion effective solutions to the problem. This **triangulation** of data adds depth and rigor to the research process.

Interviewing: Guided Conversations

Interviews enable participants to describe their situation and interpret the issue investigated in their own terms. They enable other participants to enter the world of the persons interviewed and to understand events from their perspective (Denzin, 1997; Spradley, 1979a; Spradley and McCurdy, 1972). Interviews not only provide a record of their views and perspectives, but also symbolically recognize the legitimacy of their points of view. They are the principal means by which we are able to hear the voice of the other and to incorporate their perspective in the inquiry process. The interview process, however, also provides opportunities for participants to revisit and reflect on events in their lives, and in the process, to extend their understanding of their own experience. This double hermeneutic—meaning-making process—serves as the principal powerhouse of the research process, enabling all participants to extend their understanding of their own, and others', experience.

Interviewing is best accomplished as a sociable series of events, not unlike a conversation between friends, where the easy exchange of information takes place in a comfortable, friendly environment. Although some people envisage interviewing as a form of authentic dialogue, we need to be wary of the way this dialogue emerges. When interviewers engage in exchanges of information or experience, as in a normal conversation, they unwittingly inscribe their own sets of meanings into the research process, constructing descriptions and interpretations that easily distort the experience or perspective of the participant interviewed. Authentic dialogue can only occur where a research facilitator is a natural participant in the setting, and where other participants have had opportunities to explore their own experience prior to engaging in dialogue. The following protocols provide ways to engage the interview process comfortably, ethically, and productively.

A wide range of literature provides information about interviewing (e.g., Chirban, 1996; Holstein and Gubrium, 1995; Kvale, 1996; Rubin and Rubin, 1995; McCracken, 1988). Researchers should use these materials selectively, however, since some interview techniques are used for clinical or hypothesis testing processes not suited to the purposes of action research. The key issue guiding selection of technique is whether it is used to reveal the perspective of the participant or it focuses on revealing specified types of information.

Initiating Interviews: Establishing Relationships of Trust

Initial stages of the interview process can be a little uncomfortable for both interviewer and interviewee, and the interviewer must establish a relationship of trust in order for the person interviewed to reveal his/her experience, either to a stranger or a colleague. Chapter 3 suggests using initial contacts with people to inform them of the issue being studied and exploring the possibility that they might participate. The researcher:

- Identifies himself/herself
- Identifies the issue of interest
- Asks permission to talk about that issue
- Negotiates a convenient time and place to meet

The actual conversation would sound something like:

Hi! I'm Ernie Stringer. The principal says he's informed the staff I'd be working here. I've been asked to assist staff to explore ways of improving parent-teacher conferences. I'd like to hear your views about that. Could we set up a time to talk? I'd need about half an hour of your time.

The prime directive in interviewing is for the interviewee to feel comfortable and safe talking with the interviewer. The preceding information should be presented in ways appropriate to the people and the setting and that enable people to feel in control of the situation—to make them feel they're not being put upon. Provide interviewees with the opportunity to determine the time and place of interviews, and ask them to suggest places to meet where they are comfortable. A classroom or school office may not be the best place to interview children or parents because the site itself may put them into a particular role or frame of mind. Behavior and talk are greatly influenced by the environment in which they occur. Research is a sociable process and should be treated as such. According to the circumstances, people may be comfortable in their own homes, in cafes or fast food outlets, or in a park or other public place. A meeting over coffee enables the interviewer and interviewee to chat about general events and establish a conversational tone in their interactions. This provides a context to move easily to the issue of interest.

Initiating interviews is sometimes a sensitive issue. You might manage, initially, short chats in hallways and lounges, which open possibilities for more extended conversations (interviews). It's important to keep these initial occasions low key and informal so people feel they aren't being imposed upon. After an initial interaction, you might indicate your desire to have them speak at greater length about issues arising in your conversation. Let them know of the focus of your interests and that you're interested in their perspective. "This has been interesting, Jack. I'd like to be able to explore this issue further. Could we meet somewhere and continue this conversation?" This provides a context for commencing more in-depth conversations that provide the basis for a continuing research relationship.

Questioning Techniques

Spradley (1979a) provides a useful framework of questions derived from his attempts to elicit natural structures of meaning used by people to describe and organize their social worlds. His essentially ethnographic methodology seeks neutral, non-leading questions that minimize the extent to which participant responses will be governed by frameworks of meaning inadvertently imposed by the researcher. A modified form of this framework provides the means to engage research participants in extended interviews revealing detailed descriptions of events and interactions in their lives and providing opportunities to explore significant issues in depth in their own terms.

A major problem with the interview process is that researcher perceptions, perspectives, interests, and agendas easily flavor questions when the major purpose of the process is to obtain interviewee perspectives. Common approaches to interviewing based on extended lists of pre-defined questions are therefore inappropriate for the purpose of this type of research. Ethnographic interviews are quite different from questionnaires that frame the issue in terms making sense to the researcher, often focusing on technical/professional concepts, agendas, procedures, or practices. This detracts from the ability of participants to define, describe, and interpret experience in their own terms and can sometimes alienate audiences central to the study. Questionnaires, therefore, are usually inappropriate in the early stages of action research. At later stages of the process, they may be used to gather data from a broader audience, but care must be taken to frame them in terms derived from participants' concepts and terminology (see pp. 87–89).

First Phase: Grand Tour Questions

Interviews will occur at a place and time convenient and comfortable for the interviewee. Participants should be relaxed, comfortable, and in as natural a setting as possible. Formal settings—participants behind desks, or in noisy, crowded places where privacy cannot be guaranteed—should be avoided.

An action research interview begins with one general grand tour question taking the form:

"Tell me about. . . . "—"Tell me about your work" or "Tell me about your school."

Though there are many extensions from this fundamental query, the simple framing enables respondents to describe, frame, and interpret events, issues, and other phenomena in their own terms. The question is not asked in bald isolation, but emerges contextually when sufficient rapport between participants has been established. It is also necessary to *frame* or contextualize the question:

There are a number of people in this school concerned about [students dropping out of school]. Last time we talked, you spoke briefly about this issue. Could you **tell me about** [students dropping out of your school]?

Often, it is best to contextualize the issue by starting with a more general question:

Last time we spoke of students dropping out of your school. I'm not very familiar with your school. Could you **tell me about** your school?

In most cases, people are able to talk at length on an issue about which they are concerned. It merely requires a listener with an attentive attitude to enable them to engage in an extended discourse. In some instances, however, participants may be unable to answer such a general question, which tempts the researcher to insert more specific questions that destroy the intent of the research process. Spradley (1979a) suggests alternative ways of asking grand tour questions when respondents are able only to give limited responses to the more general question:

- **Typical** grand tour questions, which enable respondents to talk about ways events usually occur (e.g., How does your group usually work? Describe a typical day in your school.)
- **Specific** grand tour questions, which focus on particular events or times (e.g., Can you tell me about yesterday's meeting? Describe what happened the last time.)
- **A guided tour** question is a request for an actual tour that allows participants to show researchers (and, where possible, other stakeholders) around their offices, schools, classrooms, centers, or agencies (e.g., Could you show me around your classroom/school?). As they walk around the school or classroom, participants may explain details about the people and activities involved in each part of the setting. Researchers may use **mini-tour** questions (see Figure 4.2) to extend the descriptions provided (e.g., Tell me more about what happens in this part of the room/office/class. Can you tell me more about the students/young people you've mentioned?).
- **A task-related** grand tour question aids in description (e.g., Could you draw me a map of the school/classroom?). Maps are often very instructive and provide opportunities for extensive description and questioning. You can also ask participants to demonstrate how things are done (e.g., Can you show me how you write up your syllabus? Can you show me how the children do this work?).

Grand tour questions comprise ways of initiating participant descriptions of their experience. Information acquired in this way provides the basis for more extended descriptions, elicited by similar types of questions, but emerging from ideas and agendas within the respondents' own descriptions.

Novice researchers sometimes find interviewing an uncomfortable experience because the process of working through structured questioning processes can be awkward and unnatural. It seems impossible that such a discomfiting process would enable people to speak freely, and they tend to fall back on conversation as a means of engaging participants. Practice and experience, however, show how it is possible for interview questions to freely and easily construct a conversation. In its best formulation, questions should emerge in a fashion similar to the streetwise informality inherent in media presentations of urban youth: "What's happenin', man? What's goin' down? What's up?"

Novice researchers should prepare for interviewing processes by memorizing the forms of questioning described in the following paragraphs and practicing mock interviews with friends and colleagues until they are able to translate the rather formal interview structures suggested in this book into the common language of the contexts they engage. Like any set of skills, practice may not make perfect but it certainly increases effectiveness.

An interesting outcome of the acquisition of these questioning skills is their application to educational contexts. Teachers will find them wonderful tools for classroom questioning procedures, and administrators will find them useful in defining their managerial work—consultation, planning, leadership, and organization. A teacher wrote of this work in a message to a colleague:

> Spradley's format is very helpful when I apply it for interviewing my kids. I use the visual cues, have them write stuff out on paper, make drawings and maps of the school. The work is shared. We physically walk the area—a guided tour. I first thought the idea was dumb, but it's a great success. It's engaged, it's shared, we are walking together. The movement stops the tape in the head. The experience is shared. It's generative.

Second Phase: Extending the Interview—Mini-Tour Questions

Interviews emerge and expand from responses to the initial grand tour questions. As people respond to the initial grand tour questions, a number of details begin to emerge, revealing events, activities, issues, and so on, that comprise their experience and perspective. Sometimes the information is limited and interviewers need to probe further to enable the respondents to dig deeper into their experience. At this stage, the source of further questions emerges from concepts, issues, and ideas embedded in respondent answers to the first questions. The interviewer asks **Mini-tour** questions enabling interviewees to extend their responses (see Figure 4.2).

Mini-tour questions are similar in form to the general, typical, specific, guided, and task-related grand tour questions, but the focus of the questions is derived from information revealed in initial responses. They take the form:

> You talked of the way students start their work in the morning. **Tell me more about** students starting their work."

Or "Tell me how your students **usually** start their work."

Or "Tell me how your students started their work **this morning.**"

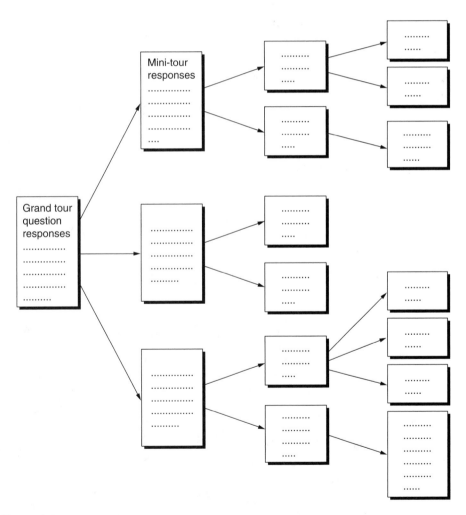

Figure 4.2
Mini-Tour Questioning Processes

Or "Can we **sit in your room** and have you tell me what's happening as students start their work?"

Or "Can you **show me** how students start their work?"

Responses to these questions may lead to other Mini-tour questions eventually providing extended detailed descriptions of the issues and contexts investigated (see Figure 4.2).

Extending Participant Responses: Prompt Questions

Further information may be acquired through the skillful use of prompts, which encourage participants to reveal more details of the phenomena they are discussing:

- **Extension** questions (e.g., Tell me more about. . . . Is there anything else you can tell me about. . . . What else?)
- **Encouragement** comments/questions (e.g., Go on. Yes? Uh huh?)
- **Example** questions (e.g., Can you give me an example of how children start their work?)

Prompt questions are not designed to elicit particular types of information the interviewer might see as desirable, but merely to enable the interviewee to think more closely about events or perspectives described.

As interviews progress, research facilitators may be presented with viewpoints that appear limited, biased, wrong, or potentially harmful. They should, however, not attempt to extend the participants' responses by suggesting appropriate responses—"Don't you think that . . . "—and definitely must avoid discussion or debate about information presented. They should certainly avoid criticizing the perspective presented or suggesting alternative acceptable viewpoints. Acceptance of diverse viewpoints is a prime directive in action research, even where those perspectives conflict dramatically with those of other research participants. Challenges to particular viewpoints will occur naturally as differing perspectives are presented in more public arenas. The task at this stage, to employ the words of a well-known anthropologist, is "to grasp the natives' point of view, to realize their vision of their world" (Malinowski, 1922/1961, p. 5).

In the course of work with senior government department managers, my Aboriginal colleagues and I sometimes faced people whose perspectives were fundamentally racist. I would converse with them with barely controlled rage, fuming at the insensitive nature of their remarks. On one occasion, an Aboriginal colleague later said "Take it easy, Stringer. He doesn't understand," to which I responded, "How do you stand it?" He looked at me quizzically and said, "You just get used to it." In many of these situations, we were able to engage in productive work with these departments that, in the longer term, sensitized the people with whom we had been speaking to their inappropriate behavior and/or perspectives. I learned at that time that immediate confrontation is not always an appropriate response to inappropriate speech or behavior.

Prolonged Engagement

The intent of action research is to help people develop new understandings of issues or problems. Asking them to explain, superficially, why and how the issue affects them often elicits merely taken-for-granted responses or perspectives that reproduce existing understandings and provide little basis for revealing underlying features of their experience. Interview processes should give people the opportunity to carefully explore their experience and examine how events and issues are embedded in the complex features of their everyday life.

The questioning techniques described help facilitate this descriptive process, but can usually only be effective if sufficient time is allocated to enable participants to explore the issue in depth. While simple problems or issues may require relatively small investments of time, larger or long-standing issues require prolonged periods of reflection and analysis. While a single 15–20-minute interview may suffice for a simple issue, significant issues require more than a superficial exploration. Multiple interviews of 30–60 minutes in duration enable participants to explore issues in depth, engaging the multiple dimensions of their experience and, in the process, extending their understanding of the complexity of the issues they face.

Except for simple research processes, repeat interviews become an essential feature of good qualitative research. Repeat interviews not only enable participants to reflect on issues more extensively, but provide opportunities to review and extend information previously acquired. Prolonged engagement, therefore, suggests the need for a significant time commitment and repeated interaction with or between research participants. Merely being in the context is not sufficient—one must be engaged in systematic inquiry required to research an issue in a context.

> When I queried the extent of the engagement of one researcher, she replied, "Oh, I was working with these teachers for months." Unfortunately, the intensive nature of the project work in which teachers and researchers were engaged provided little opportunity for them to discuss the nature of their experience, most of their attention being focused on the technical issues related to the project. The single 15-minute interview with each teacher was an inadequate vehicle for revealing the complex nature of their experience and provided only superficial comments that were uninformative and uninspiring.

Recording Information

Although action research processes often are informal, especially in small-scale or localized projects, it is important to keep a record of information acquired. This is especially important when different groups are involved, where personality differences are likely to create discord, or where sensitive issues are investigated.

Participants acquire a degree of safety knowing their perspectives are not forgotten or distorted over time. For reasons of accuracy and harmony, an ongoing record of information is a central feature of research. Field notes and tape recordings provide the two major forms of recording information, though increasing use is being made of video-recording.

> On numerous occasions, I have been engaged in action research projects that threatened to be disrupted by disputes about things people had said or decisions that had been made. Referring back to the recorded data and reading the actual words people had used usually restores order when disputes threaten to erupt. In numerous instances, a mollified participant has acknowledged his or her error by saying "Did I say that?" or "I forgot we'd decided that."

Field Notes

Verbatim record: Wherever possible, interviewers should make an immediate record of responses. You should ask permission for this before the interview, or in some cases, after the first few minutes, when the person has commenced talking. "This is very interesting. Do you mind if I take notes as you talk?" Handwritten field notes are a common form of recording with researchers writing a verbatim record of people's actual words. This requires researchers to be constantly aware of the need to record what is actually *said* by the person being interviewed, rather than a condensed or "tidied up" version. It is a "warts and all" procedure, where colloquialisms, incorrect grammar, or even blatantly incorrect information are precisely recorded. This all goes into the mix to ensure an accurate and authentic account of the person's perspective. At later stages of the interview (see member checking in following paragraphs), the interviewee will have opportunities to correct or add to the information given.

The following example is a record of an interview with a middle-school teacher:

Interviewer: Some teachers say they'd like greater parent participation in this school. Can you tell me what you think of the idea of greater parent participation?
Teacher: Well, parents should feel they are part of the school. . . . We could provide, like, inservices for parents on things like handling children, using computers. . . you know, Inspiration, web-searches . . . .

It would help parents to have skills to assist their kids, especially those who're struggling. Parents could be offered stuff at low cost, no cost. Like study skills, how to develop study habits with children. It'd be low pressure, low key. You could have staff volunteers with special skills, special expertise.

It helps establish good relationships with parents. Give them greater ability to communicate results. They'd be able to talk more easily about their children.
Interviewer: Are there other ways to increase parent participation?
Teacher: I like having parents in class who can guide and help a child, but not do the work for the kids. Some parents help, but they end up doing the work for

the kids. That's not on. But if they help the kids with their work, it's a great help to me.

One school had a parent scheduled to help a child. They'd have that child each time they came to the classroom, helping with, like, reading, if the child was having difficulty with reading. . . .

This type of handwritten record requires practice in writing at speed and the concomitant development of personal shorthand writing protocols—"&" for "and," "w/" for "with," "t" for "the," "g" for "..ing," missing consonants (e.g., writg, or wrtg for writing), and so on. It takes practice, but is essential if researchers are to record the respondent's actual words. Those responsible for recording information need to be wary of paraphrasing or abstracting, since this defeats the purpose of interviewing (i.e., capturing the voice of participants and describing things as they would describe them). Sometimes it may be necessary to ask the person interviewed to repeat information, or to pause momentarily so the interviewer can catch up on notes.

Member checking: Once an interview has finished, the interviewer should read back the notes, giving the respondent an opportunity to confirm the accuracy of the notes, or to extend or clarify information given. In some cases, it may also be possible to identify the key features of the interview to use in data analysis (see Chapter 5: Giving Voice: Interpretive and Qualitative Data Analysis). Some people type their notes and have the respondent read them to check for accuracy. It may also be appropriate, in some instances, to provide a copy of the field notes to the respondent for their own information.

Tape Recorders

Using a tape recorder has the advantage of allowing the researcher to acquire a detailed and accurate account of an interview. Researchers acquire large quantities of information from multiple sources, so they should keep a careful record of their tapes, noting on each tape the person, place, time, and date of the interview. Tapes should be transcribed as soon as possible after the interview, and the accuracy of the resulting text verified by the person interviewed.

Tape recordings have a number of disadvantages, however, and researchers should carefully weigh the merits of this technology. Technical difficulties with equipment may damage rapport with respondents, and people sometimes find it difficult to talk freely in the presence of a recording device, especially when sensitive issues are discussed. A researcher may need to wait until a reasonable degree of rapport has been established before introducing the possibility of using a tape recorder. When using a recorder, the researcher should be prepared to stop the tape to allow respondents to speak off the record if they show signs of discomfort.

The sheer volume of material obtained through tape-recording also may inhibit the steady progress of a research process. If tape recordings are used, they should be transcribed immediately so the relevant information becomes available to participants. This is particularly useful when contentious or sensitive issues are explored, since a person's own words may help resolve potentially inflammatory situations. Researchers should be wary of accumulating tapes for later transcribing—a lengthy and tedious process that may detract from the power of the research.

Working with Children

Action research works on the premise that children are active constructors of their own knowledge. By talking, listening, and reflecting on events within a system of mutually supportive relations, children are able to extend their understanding of events and experiences. An extensive amount of literature has revealed the possibilities of engaging children in research processes related to their own learning environments.

Some researchers, however, find working with children somewhat frustrating initially. For a variety of reasons, children sometimes have difficulty engaging in the forms of discourse common to adults and responding or reacting to events in immediate rather than abstract terms. Asking children a grand tour question such as "Tell me about . . . " sometimes elicits an abbreviated or non-committal response—"What do you want to know?" "I just like it!"—or a quizzical look.

In these circumstances, alternate forms of grand tour questions, especially those involving activity, may enhance opportunities to elicit responses from children and enable them to explore and express their experience. These include:

> **Typical** grand tour questions—"What usually happens . . . ?"
> **Specific** grand tour questions—"What happened last time the class . . . ?
> **Guided tour** questions—"Can you show me around your classroom and tell me. . .?
> **Task-related** questions—"Can you show me how . . . ?" "Draw me a picture of. . . ."

This latter form provides multiple ways for children to express their thoughts and feelings, or to reveal details of their experience. Activity questions are particularly fruitful in work with children. Art enables children to draw and talk about aspects of their experience. Care needs to be taken to ensure the child is engaging actual events, rather than extrapolating to an imaginary world as creative children sometimes do. You might ask the child to draw some aspects of his/her experience by requesting, "Can you draw me a picture of . . . ?" Then, "Tell me about the picture."

In some cases, especially where sensitive issues are explored, some people use scenarios, asking children to recount a story using imaginary or fictional characters representing types of actors in the context. Drawings or doll figures may be used for these purposes. It also may be useful to use reversal questions like, "If you were a teacher, what would you do if . . . ?", or future-oriented questions like, "What would happen if . . . ?" The problem with these types of questions, however, is the risk that children will engage in fantasies having little bearing on the reality at hand.

It is often difficult for children to talk openly and honestly with an adult, especially an authority figure like a teacher. For this reason, it is necessary to spend time and effort developing an easy and friendly relationship that allows a child to respond more empathetically to researchers. Teachers engaging in research in their class or school may need to develop a different type of relationship to enable children to speak freely. They may also provide training and practice in interviewing techniques so the children can interview each other. This is especially useful with older children, as it provides a safe environment for them to explore their experience. In these circumstances, group techniques (see Using Focus Groups to Gather Data following) masking the identity of the participants can also be fruitful.

The time, place, and style of interviews with children are particularly important. Children are likely to feel uncomfortable if interviewed individually by a teacher in a classroom. They may feel as if they are in trouble, or may feel wary of being asked to divulge information about classmates. This is especially true of "problem" students who may be central to a research process. Where they are included as participants in the research process, however, the rewards are often enormous, providing children with increased ownership and understanding of events and activities occurring in their school or classroom.

> Rhonda Petty (1997) describes her methods of working with a small group of boys from her class. She met with them in their homes, at McDonald's, in parks, and on small excursions. She was amazed at the difference in their demeanor and communicativeness in these contexts. They talked animatedly and easily, a far cry from the rather silent and uneasy conversations possible in the school context. She was able to elicit a broad range of information and gain a much clearer understanding of the boys with whom she worked. Petty was also able to provide a richly evocative account of the way those interactions dramatically changed the images she had formed of them.

As qualitative and naturalistic studies increasingly engage children, a variety of resources in the literature help researchers to include children in the processes of investigation (e.g., Edwards, Gandini, and Forman, 1993; Fine and Sandstrom, 1988; Graue and Walsh, 1998; Greig and Taylor, 1998; Helm, 1999; Malaguzzi, 1995; Meerdink, 1999; Selekman, 1997). It is essential that children are able to describe and interpret experience in their own terms, rather than being asked to respond to questions derived from a teacher or adult's perceptions of what *should be* important for a child. Often, there is a tendency for educational researchers to mentally list issues derived from their professional repertoire of experience—materials, lessons, learning processes, timetables, homework, reading, behavior, and so on. These issues may be of peripheral relevance to children as they focus on a more existential response to their situation. Ultimately, we wish to understand children's experience and perceptions of the issue we are investigating. The process enables the children to clarify and extend their understanding of events and to participate in plans to remedy the situation.

> I have many times had my faith in the integrity and good sense of children confirmed in research activities. I have seen high school drop-outs engaged in extended research processes culminating in the development of a new alternative high school in my city. I have seen how seriously even young elementary children engage processes of inquiry and focus on issues about which they are

concerned. Children, even those labelled "at risk" or "problem," generally respond intelligently and with passion when they are engaged as competent, in-
telligent persons, actively engaged as members of a team, rather than being
treated as miscreants or students subject to the directive dictates of authority
figures. The principles of participatory action research are especially rich and
rewarding when applied to young people.

Using Focus Groups to Gather Data

Traditional research practices focus largely on gathering data from individuals and
using that information for an abstracting process of analysis. Data gathering in action
research, however, becomes more effective when individuals are able to explore their
experiences interactively. Although it is important for people to have opportunities
to explore issues individually in the early stages of inquiry, joint processes of collaborative inquiry considerably enhance the power of a research process. Individual interviews followed by focus group exploration provide a context for participants to
share information and extend their understanding of issues.

In recent years, focus groups have emerged as a useful way to engage people in
processes of investigation, to enable people to share information and to "trigger" new
ideas or insights. A focus group may be envisioned as a group interview with questions providing a stimulus for capturing people's experiences and perspectives. It
provides the means for including relatively large numbers of people in a research
process, an important consideration in larger projects.

When we bring diverse groups of people or children together, however, we need
to carefully manage the dynamics of interaction and discussion to ensure the productive operation of focus groups. Too easily, they sometimes degenerate into "gab-
fests" or "slinging matches" where unfocused discussions or argumentative
interchanges damage the harmonious qualities characteristic of good action research.
Literature providing guidance for focus group facilitation includes publications by
Barbour and Kitzinger (1998), Morgan (1997a, 1997b), Morgan and Krueger (1997),
Krueger (1994, 1997a, 1997b), Krueger and Casey (2000), and Greenbaum (2000).

Bringing People Together

To initiate focus group explorations, the research facilitator should seek out opportunities to bring people together to discuss issues of common interest. "I've spoken
with a number of people about this issue, and some of them have similar views to
yourself. Would you be willing to meet with them to talk about the issues you've
raised?" Or "As you know, I've been speaking with other teachers, and many are concerned about. . . . Would you attend a meeting with people like Janet Jones, Bill Ro-
chon, and Maria Garcia to discuss this issue?"

As with interviews, the time and the place must be conducive to the process.
People should have adequate time to explore the issue and should be in a place where
they are comfortable and feel they can express their views and experiences freely. A
rushed meeting during recess time, or in a common room where others can overhear,

is likely to limit the information shared or to generate the types of interaction lead-ing to positive working relationships between people. These issues are especially im-portant when working with families or children. As with interviews, meetings away from school or other formal settings may be more conducive to an easy and commu-nicative atmosphere and may provide the basis for the ongoing development of pro-ductive action research processes.

Initially, research facilitators may arrange focus group meetings for small groups of stakeholders, but as the process of inquiry develops it may be fruitful to bring larger groups of participants together. Larger meetings become more productive when all individuals have opportunities to express their thoughts and experiences. In that way, focus groups may be used to enable greater active participation of all people present. Since information gathering is often concomitant with information processing (analysis or interpretation), processes for facilitating focus groups will be discussed in greater depth in Chapter 5.

The size of groups is important, with four to six being the optimal number of peo-ple in each group to enable everyone to participate effectively. When dealing with large groups, it is usually best to form sub-groups and have each sub-group record its exploration and report back to the whole group.

Focus groups can be used in contexts large and small. When I worked with the staff of the Brazos School to facilitate an internal evaluation, I interviewed each person individually, then wrote a short joint report revealing issues emerg-ing from these interactions. After staff had read the report, I facilitated a focus group meeting, which enabled them to clarify issues emerging in the report and to identify and prioritize issues on which they wished to take action. Because it was a small school, we were able to complete this process in only a few days.

On another occasion I worked with a small team of researchers to facilitate the review of a large regional organization. We spoke with staff and clients at local centers, helping them to talk of their perceptions of the purpose of the or-ganization, the services it was providing, and the problems they perceived. We then facilitated focus group meetings of staff and clients in each locality, which enabled them to clarify the issues that had emerged. Finally, representatives from each of these localities met to explore issues emerging from these meet-ings and to formulate an action plan. As a result of these activities, the organi-zation was restructured, resulting in more effective services and greatly increased activity. The process took six months, but was highly effective in re-vitalizing an organization that was in danger of closing.

Focus Group Processes

Research facilitators should ensure that focus group sessions are carefully planned and facilitated to guarantee the productive use of time. It is all too easy for poorly prepared groups to degenerate into gossip sessions, to be dominated by a forceful person, or to create antagonisms derived from intemperate debates. As with data gathering, researchers may engage a single focus group, though multiple groups may be used productively when meeting with diverse groups of stakeholders. The following steps provide a basic procedure for running focus groups:

1. Set ground rules
   - All persons should have opportunities to express their perspective.
   - All perspectives should be accepted nonjudgmentally.

2. Provide clear guidance
   - Provide and display focus questions.
   - Designate a time frame for each section/question.

3. Designate a facilitator for each group to
   - Ensure each person has an equal chance to talk.
   - Keep discussions on track.
   - Monitor times.

4. Record group talk in each group
   - Designate a person to record proceedings.
   - Record the details of each person's contribution, using their own words.
   - Where appropriate, each group should summarize their discussions, identifying and recording key features of experience, and significant issues or problems.

5. Feedback and clarification
   - Bring groups together and ensure adequate time is available for feedback and discussion.
   - Have each group present the summary of their discussions.
   - Provide opportunities for individuals within each group to extend or clarify points presented.
   - The facilitator should ask questions of each group designed to have them clarify and extend their contribution.
   - Ensure that new information emerging from this process is recorded.

6. Analyze combined information
   - Identify common features across groups.
   - Identify divergent issues or perspectives.
   - Rank issues in order of priority.

7. What Next: A plan for action
   - Define what is to happen next: What actions are to be taken, who will be responsible for them, where and when they will be done, what resources are required, and who will organize these.
   - Designate a person to monitor these actions.
   - Designate a time and place to meet again to review progress.

The rather bland description of these procedures masks the exciting and rewarding possibilities emerging from dialogue, discussion, and personal interactions common in these types of processes. There are many benefits gained through these processes. By providing participants with the space and time to engage in open dialogue on issues about which they are deeply concerned, they gain increased clarity and understanding of those issues and develop the productive personal relationships so important to the effective enactment of action research.

Focus Questions

Focus groups require careful facilitation to ensure people are able to accomplish productive purposes in the time they spend together. The purpose for meeting should be clearly described by the facilitator and discussion focused on specific issues related to that purpose. As with individual interviews, the major purpose of these types of sessions is to provide people with opportunities to describe and reflect on their own experiences and perspectives. A general statement by the facilitator contextualizing and framing the issue should be followed by a series of *focus questions* similar in format to those provided for individual interviews.

Grand tour questions. These enable people to express their experience and perspectives in their own terms: "We're meeting today to think about ways we might more effectively link with families in our community. I'd like to give you time, initially, to talk about ways you currently link with families, then extend our discussions from there. Please focus initially on the first question 'How do I currently link with families?'"

Mini-tour questions. As people explore these issues, further questions may emerge from issues arising in their discussion. "There's not enough time," "There are some parents who never contact me," and so on. These statements are reframed in question form and become subject for further sharing of information: "What are the different ways we currently make time to link with parents?" "What are the ways we currently link with parents who are difficult to contact?" The sharing of information in this way not only enables people to benefit from each other's experience, but also provides possibilities for directly formulating solutions to issues as they emerge.

Guided tour questions. Focus groups may engage in a *guided tour*, in which people tour a classroom, school, or other sites and share their experiences or perspectives of events related to those environments.

Task-related questions. Groups may also benefit from *task-related* questions, so that members are able to demonstrate how they go about achieving some purpose: "Could you show us how you organize the lessons you've been talking about?" "Could you show the group how you present this type of material in your class?" Having people express their perspective artistically can sometimes provide very evocative understandings of their experience, and maps and diagrams provide highly productive ways for people to explore and express their ideas or issues. Facilitators may ask people, either individually or as a group, to draw a picture, a map, or a diagram illustrating their experience of the issue on which they are focused. These productions then become the focus for further discussions extending people's understanding of participant experiences and perspectives.

Facilitators should ensure that each group keeps an ongoing record of their discussion. This may take the form of notes, recorded by a volunteer in the group, but sometimes may be recorded in summary form on charts. Where multiple groups are engaged in discussions, a plenary session should provide opportunities for participants to share the results of their exploration.

Participant Observation

The principal purpose of observation is to familiarize researchers with the context in which issues and events are played out, or to provide participants with opportunities to stand back from their everyday involvement and watch purposefully as events unfold. This extends both their perceptions and understanding of the everyday features of their life-world, and provides information for the construction of reports. Careful observation enables participants to build a picture of the context and the activities and events within it, revealing details of the setting as well as the mundane, routine activities comprising the life-world of teachers, students, and administrators. Sometimes, however, the opportunity to observe is revelatory, providing keen insights or illuminating important but taken-for-granted features of school and classroom life.

Observation in action research is very different from the highly structured types of observation required in experimental research. Here the researcher notes the frequency of specific types of behavior, acts, or events using a highly structured observation schedule. Participant observation in action research is much more open-ended—its purpose being to provide more detailed descriptions of the people's actions and the context in which they occur and to come to a deeper level of understanding through extended immersion in that context and interaction with people and events within it.

As I facilitated the internal evaluation of BSIC (see Chapter 8), I recorded observations of the school as field notes. This information provided the basis for a description of the school and the community context in which it was located. Readers of the report were able readily to locate themselves and their context as a precursor to reflecting on the events and activities on which the remainder of the report focused. A number of people commented favorably on this process, noting the way the description enabled them to focus on the events described as part of their own experience.

At another time, I engaged in an extended study of classrooms in a school in my state. As I watched children and teachers interact in classrooms over an extended period, a different picture of classroom life emerged for me. As a teacher, I had experienced classrooms as intensively busy places, with activities and events unfolding in rapid and complex interaction. As I observed each child for an extended period, however, I saw a completely different picture emerge, one composed of long periods of silence and inactivity. The boredom and patience of the children was almost palpable. I now see classrooms in quite a different way.

Although research facilitators may engage in observations of their own, they may also engage in collaborative observation processes using questions to elicit participant descriptions of events and the context. As with interviews, observation needs to be focused so that relevant details of the setting, activities, and events are recorded. Spradley (1979) suggests observations should always be accompanied or preceded by relevant questions for this purpose. A research facilitator may ask participants for a "guided tour" with the underlying question in mind: "What do I need to know about this school/classroom to understand the issue investigated? Tell me about this school (or classroom, community, etc.)." General observations will be extended and become more focused as the observer responds to questions about:

- **People:** students, teachers, administrators, specialist staff, and so on
- **Places:** classrooms, play areas, offices, homes, community contexts, locations of activities and events, and physical layouts
- **Acts:** single actions that people take (e.g., a child erasing some words)
- **Activities:** a set of related acts (e.g., a child writing a story)
- **Events:** a set of related activities (e.g., a language arts class)
- **Objects:** buildings, furniture, equipment, books, and learning materials
- **Purposes:** what people are trying to accomplish
- **Time:** times, frequency, duration, and sequencing of events and activities
- **Feelings:** emotional orientations and responses to people, events, activities, and so on

Working with participants in this way enables researcher facilitators to check the veracity of their own observations. This is an important issue, since it is all too easy for an outside researcher to focus on irrelevant issues or to misinterpret events.

> In one study, I summarized a meeting in this way: "The principal met staff to present the new school policy. The faculty appeared rather disgruntled with the new policy but made no comment about it." Here I noted information related to (a) the purpose of the meeting and (b) the feelings of the staff. When I checked with the staff to verify the authenticity of my interpretation, I discovered that I had misinterpreted the situation. They were not particularly concerned about the new policy, but they were unhappy with other (hidden) agendas they felt to be implicit in the principal's presentation.

Recording Observations

Field Notes

Field notes enable researchers to record detailed descriptions of actual places and events as they occur naturally. As researchers meet members of stakeholding groups, they will have opportunities to gain a clearer picture of the research context by observing the settings and events in which participants carry out their daily educational activities. They should record their observations in field notes that provide ongoing records of important elements of each part of the setting. In some contexts, it is not possible to record field notes immediately. In these cases, observers should record events as soon as possible after they occur.

The task may appear quite daunting as any context contains huge amounts of information that could be recorded. As indicated, researchers should record that information needed by an audience to understand the *context* and *social processes* related to the issue investigated, using the framework provided previously as a guide (people, places, events, etc.). The recorded information provides material that will later be used for descriptions of the context of the research or of events and activities.

Written descriptions may be supplemented by hand-drawn maps or pictures that provide increased clarity. A map of a school or classroom, for instance, provides a pictoral representation that may later be used to provide increased understanding and clarity. Observers may "set up" their observations by describing and drawing the setting, recording pertinent events and activities as they occur over a period of time, and then checking to ensure appropriate renditions of both setting and events.

Photographs

Photographs provide a useful record that enables later audiences to more clearly visualize settings and events. Photographs may be used to stimulate discussion during focus groups or provide the basis for focusing and/or extending interviews. A grand tour question, such as "Tell me what's happening in this photograph," can provide richly detailed descriptions—an especially useful process when working with children. Photographs may also be used to enhance reports presented to participants or to other research audiences.

Video Recording

The increasing availability of video equipment provides an important research resource. Written descriptions are necessarily limited, focusing on specific features of the situation and providing what is really a rudimentary understanding of the events and the context. Video recording has the advantage of making the scene immediately available to viewers, providing a far greater depth of understanding of the acts, activities, events, interactions, behaviors, and the nature of the context. Extended video recordings can reveal highly informative pictures easily viewed by large audiences.

Careful consideration needs to be given to the specific settings and events to be recorded. Schouten and Watling (1997) suggest a process by which participants "beacon out" fields of concern by exploring the extent of their investigation through dialogue, then focusing on salient features to be recorded. They suggest the following basic procedures:

- Leave a 10-second gap at the beginning of each tape.
- Make a trial recording to ensure equipment is working.
- Enable people time to warm-up before recording.
- Check the material immediately after recording.
- Stick to a designated time limit.
- Allow time for people to comment after recording.

Videos, however, do not reveal "the facts" or "the truth." They still provide only partial information, since only small segments of time may be recorded, and the lens focuses only on particular features of the context or events according to the particular interest or interpreting eye of the photographer. A useful way of using this particular tool is to record events identified by preliminary analyses of interview data. The camera then focuses on features of the scene identified as significant by participants in the process.

Artifacts: Documents, Records, Materials, and Equipment

In traditional anthropological investigations, understanding a cultural context sometimes required an intensive study of artifacts related to the daily social life of the setting. To some extent, this is true in action research, though the focus on artifacts is somewhat different in nature. Information related to educational issues investigated in schools can be found in documents and records, and useful insight may be gained by perusing books, materials, and equipment used for teaching, learning, or administration. A survey of the physical facilities—furniture, buildings, classrooms, offices, and so on—may also be instructive.

Researchers, however, need to be parsimonious and focused, since huge and unwieldy piles of information, most of which have little apparent pertinence to the issue investigated, may overwhelm an investigation. In participatory action research, participant accounts provide a frame of reference to focus further observation. Preliminary analysis of interview data reveals the features and elements of experience or context that might benefit from the gathering of additional information. Comments such as "I hate the text were using. It's so boring," or "I'm learning so much more this semester" may lead to a review of texts used in the class or an examination of achievement records.

Researchers should be wary of gathering information just for the sake of doing it, or gathering information indicated by common practice or traditional formulations. One of the strengths of action research is its ability to work by or through common, everyday practices and taken-for-granted knowledge to reveal underlying dynamics or features that are central to the problem investigated. People's perspectives as revealed in interviews, therefore, provide the central point of reference for reviewing artifacts. Ultimately, however, material is collected according to whether or not it appears pertinent to the issue investigated. Researchers do not determine which artifacts are to be reviewed prior to commencement of the study, however, since their pertinence or relevance to the research question is revealed as participant perspectives emerge. Whether school grades, classroom texts, furniture, school facilities, or other items are included becomes evident when they are included in participant interview responses. Reviewing interview field notes or transcripts, therefore, enables researchers to identify the artifacts to be included in the study.

Documents

Researchers can obtain a great deal of significant information by reviewing documents in the research context. In classrooms, a syllabus, curriculum, or timetable may provide crucial information about the teaching/learning features of the setting. At the school or district level, policy documents may include rules and regulations providing insight into institutionally approved behaviors, activities, or procedures. Policy documents also provide information about a school, school district, or state department. These may be complemented by annual reports containing details of the structure, purposes, operations, and resources of the school, district, or state department. Memos, meeting minutes, procedure statements, school or district plans, evaluation reports, press accounts, public relations materials, information statements, and newsletters likewise extend our understanding about a school's organization and operation.

In some environments, documentation is prolific. Researchers need to be selective, briefly scanning a range of documents to ascertain the information contained and its relevance to the project's focus. They should keep records of documents reviewed, noting any significant information and its source. In some cases, researchers may be able to obtain photocopies of relevant documents.

In reviewing documents and records, research participants should always keep in mind that they are not finding "the facts" or "the truth." Information is always influenced by the authors or written in accordance with particular people's motives, agendas, and perspectives. This is as true at the organizational level as it is at the level of the individual, since people or groups in positions of influence and power are able to inscribe their perspectives, values, and biases into official documents and records. Documents and records, therefore, should always be viewed only as information from another source or stakeholder that has no more legitimacy or truth value than any other stakeholder.

Records

Confidential records often are not available for public scrutiny, and researchers may need special circumstances and appropriate formal approval to gain access to them. Where research is conducted in-house, however, review of records can often provide invaluable information. Individual records of student behavior and achievement, school records of student numbers and attendance, and district or state records may provide information central to the investigation. Comparisons with other students, classes, or schools often reveal interesting information providing much needed perspective to an investigation. Perceptions that a school is poorly funded or achievement levels are low may not be borne out by a review of the records of other schools in a district or state. As with all information, however, such information needs to be carefully evaluated, since much of it is recorded in statistical form requiring careful interpretation. In circumstances where statistical information is used, the research team needs to include someone with the relevant expertise to interpret the information acquired. Figure 4.3 lists examples of documents and records that can be used.

Student-Work Samples

Student-work samples are a wonderful resource for providing highly informative, concrete visual information. They enable research participants to gain rich understandings of the activities in which children have engaged in classrooms or of lesson

Lesson plans	Research reports
Syllabi	Demographics
Curricula	Statistics
Project	Databases
Assignments	
Timetables	Legislation
	Rules and regulations
Grades	Policies and procedures
Achievement records	Annual reports
Work portfolios	Budgets
Attendance records	Archives
Report cards	
Case records	Constitutions
	Meeting minutes and
Books	agendas
Texts	Rosters
Book lists	Correspondence
Reading lists	E-mail
Bibliographies	Memos
	Reports
Diaries	
Calendars	Circulars
Phone logs	Notice boards
Schedules	Pamphlets and brochures
Appointment books	Lecture notes
Mileage records	

Figure 4.3
Documents and Records

plans and syllabi used by teachers in formulating teaching/learning processes. Work samples provide useful material when constructing reports. This enables audiences direct access to the outcomes of people's activities. As with documents, however, they should be collected parsimoniously since they tend to accumulate with astonishing speed. Work samples should be gathered once preliminary analysis of interview data provides a focus for selection.

As with participant sampling, work samples may be selected to demonstrate:

- Variation in student work
- Extreme examples of student work
- Typical student work
- Student work that exhibits particular characteristics
- Exceptional cases of student work

As with other artifacts, student-work samples should be selected according to their relevance to the research issue as becomes evident in the course of interviews with participants.

Materials, Equipment, and Facilities

A review of material and equipment provides useful input to the investigation because education is affected by a vast array of artifacts that influence events in classrooms and schools. Books, stationery, storage space, furniture, laboratory equipment, computers, art equipment, music materials and instruments, physical education equipment, play space and equipment, buildings, rooms, offices, and so on may all have a significant effect on schooling. Students and schools may, for instance, be hampered by a lack of equipment or by facilities in a poor state of repair. Research participants should carefully review these types of item, in conjunction with other data-gathering processes.

As with other observations, the focus and direction of reviews will depend, to a large extent, on information acquired in interviews. Researchers should be wary of focusing on details that participants interpret as having little significance to the issue investigated. This should not be seen as a fixed rule, however, since an outside observer may focus on features that are so commonplace other participants don't think it worthy of comment. It is possible, for instance, for people to take for granted dilapidated equipment in poor repair that significantly affects their activities. Research facilitators may record this information but then judge its significance only in conjunction with other stakeholders. See Figure 4.4 for a list of materials, equipment, and facilities that may prove useful in an investigation.

> One of the best schools for Aboriginal children I have observed was also the poorest in material terms. Despite the dilapidated furniture, obsolete texts, and the paucity of materials, the school rang with the life and vitality of the children and parents who participated in its programs in an ongoing way. It made me rethink my cherished notions about what was necessary for an adequate education for chil-

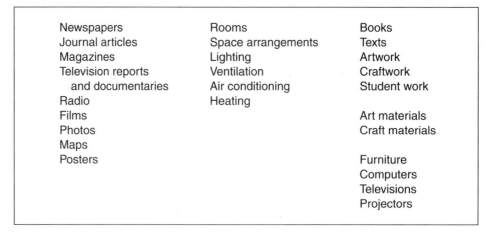

Newspapers	Rooms	Books
Journal articles	Space arrangements	Texts
Magazines	Lighting	Artwork
Television reports	Ventilation	Craftwork
and documentaries	Air conditioning	Student work
Radio	Heating	
Films		Art materials
Photos		Craft materials
Maps		
Posters		Furniture
		Computers
		Televisions
		Projectors

Figure 4.4
Materials, Equipment, and Facilities

dren. Sometimes in focusing on the material artifacts of schooling we miss important truths about the emotional, intellectual, and spiritual features of people's experience. Observations need to be treated warily as a source of understanding.

However, teacher perceptions of deficiencies in teaching and learning materials in a recent school evaluation were confirmed by a review of the school inventory. Triangulation, the comparing of different sources of data, can greatly enhance participant perspectives.

Recording Information

As researchers review artifacts, they should take careful note of information they consider relevant to the investigation. They should list information they have reviewed together with a summary description of the nature of the material. In the process, they should record which information may be made public and which must be kept confidential. The intent of the summaries is to provide stakeholders with information about materials that might enhance their investigation. If, for instance, stakeholders have a perception that student achievement levels are declining, then access to appropriate records will enable them to check whether or not this is so. This information will enable participants to extend, clarify, or enhance existing issues and perspectives as they emerge.

Surveys

A survey is another means of providing input into an action research process. Unlike quasi-experiments that use statistical analysis to test a hypothesis, surveys are sometimes used in action research to acquire information from larger groups of participants. A survey may be used, for instance, to acquire information from parents whose children attend a school. The major advantage of surveys is that they provide a comparatively inexpensive means to acquire information from a large number of people within a limited time frame. Their disadvantages are that it is frequently difficult to obtain responses from those surveyed and the fixed nature of the information that can be obtained by this means.

Creswell (2002) describes the different ways surveys can be administered—self-administered questionnaires, telephone interviews, face-to-face interviews, computer-assisted interviews, and Website and Internet surveys. He suggests there are two basic survey designs: a cross-sectional design that collects information from people at one point in time, and a longitudinal design studying changes in a group or population over time. Surveys always obtain information about people's perspectives on an issue rather than their actual behaviors. A study of student perspectives on homework, for instance, may focus on student attitudes, beliefs, and opinions, or be designed to elicit information about their perceptions, feelings, priorities, concerns, and experiences of homework. The latter is more appropriate for action research, which focuses largely on revealing the perspective and experience of participants.

Researchers may increase the validity of a survey by ensuring it is grounded in concepts and ideas that more closely fit the experience and perspective of those surveyed, and by doing face-to-face interviews with a small sample of participants (see Interviews). They may then use that information to formulate questions for the survey instrument. Surveys can be conducted through face-to-face interviews or through paper and pen questionnaires, and each may be administered to individuals or groups. Paper and pen questionnaires are useful when researchers require specific information about a limited number of items or where sensitive issues are explored.

Questions in action research surveys may be comparatively unstructured and open-ended to maximize opportunities for respondents to answer questions in their own terms or highly structured to acquire specific information related to issues of concern.

Conducting a Survey

- **Determine the purpose, focus, and participants.** Prior to constructing the survey instrument (questionnaire), carefully define:
  - Issues to be included
  - The type of information to be obtained
  - The people from whom it will be acquired

- **Formulate questions.** Ensure that questions:
  - Cover all issues and all types of information identified
  - Are clear and unambiguous
  - Do not include two issues in the one question (e.g., Should students be able to be in classrooms at lunch time and after school?)
  - Are framed in positive terms, rather than negative
  - Do not contain jargon likely to be unfamiliar to respondents
  - Are short and to the point

- **Responses:** Provide appropriate response formats. Formats should provide sufficient space for responses to open-ended or semi-structured questions. Closed response questions may take the following forms:
  - *Open response:* How many minutes should be allocated for lunch break? _____ minutes
  - *Fixed response:* When should children leave school after classes finish—within 5 minutes, within 15 minutes, or within 30 minutes?
  - *Dual response:* Responses choosing between two alternatives (e.g., yes/no, agree/disagree, male/female)
  - *Rating response:* Using the following scale, circle the most correct response: 1 (strongly disagree), 2 (disagree), 3 (neutral), 4 (agree), 5 (strongly agree)

- **Provide framing information:** Inform potential respondents of the purpose and nature of the survey. Include information about the likely duration of the interview/session and the types of response required (e.g., extended responses or precise responses).
- **Trial:** Test the adequacy of the questions by having preliminary interviews or questionnaire-completing sessions with a small number of people. Modify questions that prove to be inappropriate or ambiguous.

- **Administer** the questionnaire or conduct the survey.
- **Thank** people for their participation.
- **Analyze** the data.

Where more complex, extended, and/or analytic surveys are contemplated, researchers should use an appropriate source to ensure effective valid designs (e.g., Bell, 1993; Creswell, 2002; Cook and Campbell, 1979; Fink, 1995; Oppenheim, 1966; Youngman, 1966).

The Barrios Juntas Neighborhood Collective worked with parents and teachers to improve communication between families and the schools. They interviewed parents and teachers to explore ways of improving parent-teacher conferences. Parents were asked the following questions following their conference with teachers:

1. How do you feel about your parent-teacher conference?
2. How does it compare with other conferences?
3. What did you and the teacher talk about?
4. What would you have liked to talk more about?
5. How could teachers make your next conference better?
6. How could parents make the next conference better?

Similar questions were put to teachers. Results of both sets of information were analyzed separately using categorizing and coding techniques. They suggested a number of ways in which parent-teacher conferences could be improved. The school was able to put several recommendations emerging from this survey into practice in following parent-teacher conference days.

Statistical and Numerical Data

Surveys need to be analyzed statistically to obtain accurate information related to the large number of responses generated. Statistical and numerical data, however, may be used in action research to clarify issues related to issues studied. Schools generate large amounts of numerical data related to student achievement scores in classroom tests and standardized tests; administrative data related to student numbers; attendance records; student and staff composition data in terms of age, gender, race, and so on and information related to school materials, equipment, and resources. Other sources of quantitative data in action research include information in official reports and records as well as that available in studies of special issues (e.g., studies of student drop-out rates in a school district or state and in the research literature).

Unlike experimental research, where statistical data is used to test hypotheses, action research uses numerical and statistical data as another way to extend or clarify participant understandings of an issue or problem. Surveys also provide numerical information that can be used to test the applicability of specific concepts and ideas to broader populations. Numerical and statistical data are particularly useful where there is a lack of clarity about the occurrence of particular phenomena. Depending on the nature of the study, statistical information may provide descriptive information related to:

- *Occurrences* of a phenomenon (e.g., the number of girls in a school, the number of students in a class)
- *Comparisons* of different occurrences (e.g., the number of girls compared to the number of boys, or girls' scores compared with boys' scores on reading tests)
- *Trends, or history* of occurrences over time (e.g., reading scores are declining over time)
- *Central tendencies* (e.g., the mean score of students on an achievement test)
- *Distribution of scores* (e.g., whether there is a wide spread of scores in a classroom achievement test, or whether most students have similar scores)
- *Correlations* that measure the degree of relationship between any two phenomena (e.g., whether success in reading is related to gender, social class, or ethnicity)

Inferential statistics, sometimes found in formal research reports, use a variety of techniques—analysis of variance, multiple regression analysis, factor analysis, and so on—to tease out the effect of different factors on a phenomenon of interest (e.g., the extent to which scores on an achievement test may be attributed to or affected by age, gender, social class, race, or ethnicity). A wide range of studies and reports related to schooling and student learning has been amassed in the research literature, providing a rich body of information with the potential to inform research participants about particular aspects of issues they investigate.

Rarely, however, does statistical data provide the answer to an issue or problem since the information must first be interpreted to understand precisely what it is saying and to judge its relevance to the people and the setting of any study. Part of the job of qualitative interpretation, therefore, is to find out what the numbers are saying, to ensure that people understand the significance of the information, to clarify what it means in terms of the issue investigated, and to assess its relevance to the current context. Statistical information, however, can provide useful information that assists people in their deliberations. Where people are adamant about the efficacy of particular approaches to instruction, the incidence of drop-outs, the levels of funding available for particular purposes, and so on, numerical data often clarifies the situation and enables research participants to move forward in their investigations. It is important, however, that people ensure that "all the evidence is in" because it is easy to extract the results of a single study or to focus on one part of a table of statistics and interpret them out of context. As with all other information, quantitative data needs to be carefully interpreted to ensure it helps in clarifying and extending understanding emerging in the study.

Numbers must always be interpreted. Numerical results do not always lead to a self-evident truth—whether something worked or not. I became sensitized to that issue at a conference presentation given by a teacher who had won many local, state, and national awards for the quality of his teaching. He was in the process of a Masters degree seeking new instructional techniques. When asked why he should change what were obviously highly effective methods of instruction, he replied that although his students always scored highly in achievement tests he suspected they didn't really understand the material they learned; that they were responding to tests and exams according to formulae they had learned in class. In this case, the teacher's deeply intuitive knowledge of his students' understanding belied what the results indicated they had achieved.

Reviewing the Literature

As indicated in Chapter 3, reviewing the literature is an ongoing facet of stakeholder processes of inquiry. As issues and perspectives emerge, the literature review becomes more focused and enriches the information base of the investigation. In action research, the literature is positioned quite differently from that in traditional academic research. The literature is viewed as the source of other views or perspectives rather than as the source of "truths" or "facts." Facts, according to Smith ([Denzin] quoted in Frus, 1994), are social constructions and as much in need of investigation and exploration as other features of the context. Literature reviews also should be quite thorough to ensure that limited studies are not used as ammunition to force particular types of action. The voices of proponents of both phonics and whole language, for instance, should be included in any review of literature related to methods of teaching reading.

In an action research process, therefore, the literature might best be seen as another set of perspectives that provides useful information to be incorporated into the accounts emerging in the research process. In Figure 4.5, teacher and student perspectives are obtained through interviews. An analysis of the interviews provides understanding of stakeholder experiences and perspectives on an issue. A review of literature may reveal perspectives, interpretations, or analyses emerging from other studies of that issue—providing research participants with information that can enhance, complement, or challenge the constructions emerging within their study.

Processes for Reviewing and/or Deconstructing the Literature

A variety of sources may contain useful literature that speaks to the issue investigated, including academic texts and journals, professional journals and publications, and institutional or departmental publications and reports. These may include

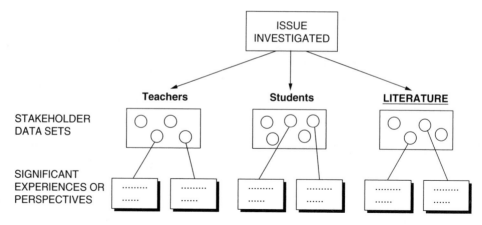

Figure 4.5
Including Perspectives Within the Literature

accounts of successful practices, projects, or learning processes; demographic information pertinent to the location or group studied; or indications of factors likely to have an impact on the study. They also may provide information about previous research on the issue, existing programs and services, or accounts of similar projects. Care needs to be taken in applying generalized information to the specific site of the study, however, because it is possible that the conditions in the setting, or the nature of particular groups, differ significantly from those in other studies. Although they may provide generalized analyses of an issue, the results of other studies may not provide the basis for action in any particular local setting.

The literature is not a body of truth, however, since studies may be comprised of a range of different theories; diverse ways of conceptualizing an issue; and different assumptions, values, and ideologies embedded in the research texts. These often unrecognized assumptions and sets of ideas sometimes are either inappropriate to the research in which participants are engaged or unconsciously impose a way of conceptualizing a situation or an issue that fails to take into account the concrete realities facing people in their specific situations. Part of the researcher's task, therefore, is to deconstruct the literature to reveal the inherent concepts, ideas, theories, values, and ideological assumptions embedded in the texts of their writing.[1]

Reviewing and deconstructing the literature requires participants to:

- Identify sources containing information relevant to their investigation.
- Distill the main features of lengthy articles or reports.

---

[1] The emphasis on deconstruction is another facet of qualitative research. Quantitative research assumes value-free or value-neutral research generalizable to all contexts. Qualitative research highlights the cultural and context-specific nature of knowledge and the importance of understanding an author's perspective, since they often infer truths about an issue on the basis of their own experience and perspective and fail to take into account the often different experiences and perspectives of those about whom they write.

- Identify information, concepts, or ideas that illuminate or resolve emerging issues.
- Deconstruct concepts and ideas that reveal unintended preconceptions, assumptions, or biases.
- Include distilled information in ongoing processes of reflection and analysis.

A review of the literature may incorporate materials in libraries, community organizations, government agencies, or on Websites. Often, material may be accessed through computerized search processes and databases such as ERIC. Research participants may use a Web search engine to locate resources or gain assistance from the help desk at their local or university library. They should be wary of using abstracts, however, since they often contain distorted or poorly formulated information. If a piece of literature seems pertinent, then it should be read in full text form.

Using the Literature Review

As information from the literature enters the research cycle, participants can make decisions about its worth or relevance. It may provide information enhancing or confirming the perspectives already reported or challenging the views and experience of stakeholder participants. The literature may also contain information suggesting actions to be taken or providing examples of actions taken in similar contexts. For formal reporting procedures, an extended review of the literature also provides evidence that participants have thoroughly investigated a variety of sources and taken this into account in their investigations.

Information emerging from the literature review, therefore, may be used:

- As part of the ongoing processes of reflection and analysis
- As information to be included in emergent understandings
- As material to be included in reports

Emergent Understandings

As participants accumulate information from a variety of sources, they acquire the materials from which new understandings emerge and enable them to take action to remediate the issue or problem that provided the focus of the study. The information may be encapsulated in reports detailing the outcomes of the research (Chapter 6) or in practice frameworks providing the basis for changed practices (Chapter 7).

As indicated in Figure 4.6, participant accounts derived from interviews provide the primary material for constructing emerging understandings—incorporating, as they do, information that resonates with the experience and perceptions of research participants. These preliminary accounts, however, are modified, clarified, enriched, or enhanced by information from other sources. Information from observation, together with material derived from reviewing documents, records, and other artifacts, may extend and enrich accounts derived from participant perceptions. Insightful or useful information may also be obtained from the literature reviewed during the processes of inquiry.

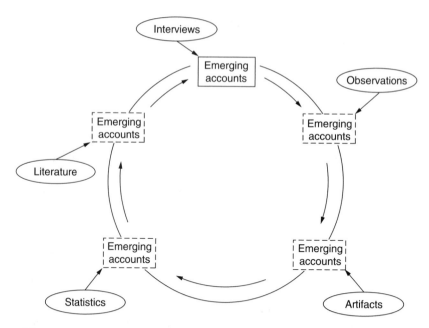

Figure 4.6
Building the Picture: Emerging Accounts

The accounts and understandings emerging from these processes of data gathering and analysis are not static, however, and continue to be enriched, enhanced, and clarified as researchers enter continuing cycles of the process that add further information from the same or other sources. The continuing Look-Think-Act cycle may incorporate information from the diverse sources identified in previous sections of this chapter.

Figure 4.6 typifies the process of data collection, though the reality is messier since information and analysis converge in the research arena from a variety of sources, sometimes serendipitously, and at odd moments in the research process. The art and craft of research is in the skillful management of this diverse body of information and the distilling and organizing of data into a coherent and clear framework of concepts and ideas that people can use for practical purposes.

Summary

The major purpose of this part of the research process is to gather information from a variety of sources. *Stakeholder experiences and perspectives* are complemented by *observations* and reviews of *artifacts* and *literature*.

This process requires research facilitators and other participants to develop *trusting rela-* *tionships* that enable the easy interchange of information.

The *interview* is the primary tool of data gathering—providing extended opportunities for stakeholders to reflect on their experience. Key features of the interview process include:

- *Initiating* interviews

- *Grand tour* questions to elicit participant responses
- *Mini-tour* and *Prompt* questions to extend participant responses
- Special techniques for *working with children*
- Using *focus groups* to work collaboratively

Information is also acquired through *observing* settings and events.

A review of *artifacts* provides a rich additional source of information. These may include:

- *Records*
- *Documents*
- *Student-work samples*
- *Materials, equipment, and facilities*

Numerical and statistical information from these sources, or from a project survey, can provide other useful resources.

Academic, professional, and institutional *literature* also provides useful information to extend participant understanding.

Giving Voice: Interpretive and Qualitative Data Analysis

5

RESEARCH DESIGN	DATA GATHERING	DATA ANALYSIS	COMMUNICATION	ACTION
INITIATING A STUDY	CAPTURING STAKEHOLDER EXPERIENCES AND PERSPECTIVES	IDENTIFYING KEY FEATURES OF EXPERIENCE	WRITING REPORTS	CREATING SOLUTIONS
Setting the stage			Reports Ethnographies Biographies	Solving problems
Focusing and framing	Interviewing	Analyzing epiphanies and illuminative experiences	PRESENTATIONS AND PERFORMANCES	Classroom practices
Literature review	Observing			Curriculum development
Sources of information	Artifacts Review	Coding and categorizing	Presentations Drama Poetry	Evaluation
Ethics	Literature review	Enhancing analysis	Song Dance Art	Family and community
Validity		Constructing category systems	Video Multimedia	School plans

Contents of This Chapter

This chapter presents detailed procedures for two approaches to data analysis.

It commences by explaining the *purpose* of data analysis in naturalistic inquiry/qualitative research.

The first data analysis section presents procedures for analyzing *epiphanies or illuminative experiences*. The main thrust of this method is to identify and *deconstruct*, or "unpack," epiphanies (significant experiences) to reveal the key features of participant experiences.

The next section describes *categorizing and coding* procedures for analyzing data. Researchers *"unitize" the data*, and identify discrete pieces of information people reveal in interviews, then select and sort data into a *system of categories*.

Introduction

The diagram shown in Figure 5.1 signals the move from data gathering to data analysis. In terms of the simple Look-Think-Act of action research, the Think component indicates the need for participants to *reflect* on the information they have gathered, and transform the sometimes large and unwieldy body of information into a relatively compact system of ideas and concepts that can be applied to solutions to the problem at hand.

The process of data analysis requires participants to sift through the accumulated data to identify that information most pertinent to the problem they are investigating. This process of distillation provides the material for an organized set of concepts and ideas that enable them to achieve greater insight, understanding, or clarity about events of interest. The intent is to accomplish common-sense solutions to problems by finding concepts and ideas that make sense to the stakeholders involved. One of the essential features of action research is the move to directly engage the experience and perspective of all participants to ensure that the sense made of the data is common to all.

This differs from common research practice in which researchers analyze data in isolation from the research context and subjects and formulate categories and schema that appear to make sense when applied to a particular theory. In much research, therefore, theoretical formulations often dominate proceedings by inscribing academic perspectives into the process and silencing the voices and perspectives of other participants. Though there is still a need for objective research that engages these types of practice, action research tends to focus on a more phenomenological approach to analysis.

This chapter, therefore, first presents an approach to data analysis that seeks to preserve participant perspectives by using epiphanic moments (Denzin, 1989b)—illuminative or significant experiences—as primary units of analysis. The ultimate

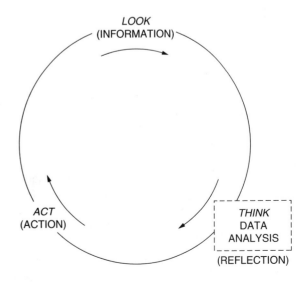

Figure 5.1
Reflection in Action Research

intent is to give voice to those participants and provide a body of ideas and concepts that clearly mesh with important elements of their experience and provide the basis for action. The second process presented is a more traditional form of qualitative analysis categorizing and coding data that distills large amounts of data into a more manageable body of ideas. The purpose of this process is to reveal patterns and themes within the data that expose the key features of events and settings.

Teachers rarely have time during the busy and demanding routines of everyday life in their classrooms to stand back and reflect on their work. Having the luxury to sit back, talk about, and reflect on their classroom practices often provides them with opportunities to gain significant insights into their professional life. I've frequently seen teachers' eyes light up in the course of interviews or focus group dialogues as they see themselves or aspects of their work in new ways. Merely having time to focus their attention in a systematic way is illuminative.

This does not always happen immediately, however. The students in the sexual harassment study (see Chapter 9), for instance, required an extended period of reflection and analysis to identify the nature and key features of their experience of harassment. The Barrios Juntos group (see Chapter 9) also needed to work through a systematic process of data analysis to reveal the key features of parent experiences in parent-teacher conferences. In each case, however, the process of data analysis enabled participants to extend their understanding of the issue investigated—providing concepts and ideas that enabled them to devise effective actions related to the problems they investigated. Data analysis, for them, was not just a technical research routine, but the means to inform their actions.

Data Analysis (1): Analyzing Epiphanies

The processes of inquiry described in this book largely emerge from the history of research in the academic disciplines. While action research has much in common with the general methodologies of naturalistic inquiry/qualitative research, its purposes are distinctly different. Traditionally, research has sought to provide scientific, objective theories of human conduct and conceptual schemes to explain how and why people act as they do. Action research, however, uses these types of theory as background information—choosing to focus instead on the ways people purposefully construct their own social worlds. The intent is to understand the ongoing, experienced reality of people's lives rather than seeking an objective truth that explains observed events. We, therefore, employ modes of inquiry that make the world of lived experience directly accessible to an audience, capturing the voices, emotions, and actions of those studied and focusing on those life experiences that shape the meanings persons give to themselves and their own experiences.

The intent of action research is to provide an approach to data analysis more clearly focused on processes and outcomes resonating with people's own meaningfulness and supplying the basis for effecting positive change in their lives. Action research, therefore, employs processes that engage the concepts and ideas people naturally use to observe, describe, and interpret their own experiences (Spradley, 1979a; Spradley and McCurdy, 1972). This represents an approach to research having the clear intention to learn from and with people, rather than studying them. Denzin (1989b) has suggested that the focus of interpretive research on meanings persons give to themselves and their life experiences requires researchers to capture the voices, emotions, and actions of those studied. The following analytic procedures enable participants to enter each other's worlds and to understand the events, actions, activities, behavior, and deeply felt emotions that represent the ongoing reality of human experience (Denzin, 1996).

The intent of these procedures is to enable researchers to accurately and authentically represent people's lives in non-authoritative, non-colonizing, and non-exploitive ways. They employ processes that not only maintain people's voices, but also capture the concepts, meanings, emotions, and agendas that can be applied to problems affecting their personal, institutional, and professional lives. Recent research experience (Genat, 2002; Young, 1999) suggests the need for voices of the participants, their structures of meaning, their interpretive processes, and their conceptual frameworks to dominate the process of data analysis. The procedures are based on a process of interpretive analysis suggested by Denzin (1989b) and focus on *epiphanies*—illuminative moments that mark people's lives. By exploring and unpacking these epiphanies, we seek to reveal features and elements of experience, often not apprehended in the normal course of events, that provide significant insight into people's lives.

Epiphanies and Illuminative Experiences

As noted previously, epiphanies are illuminative moments of crisis, or transformational, turning point experiences, which result in significant changes to people's perceptions of their lives (Denzin, 1989b). Epiphanies take a variety of forms—from the devastating experience that enters a person's life but once, through cumulative epiphanies that emerge over time, to minor epiphanies that are significant but not highly momentous. Epiphanies can be either positive or negative. They may include the experience of exhilaration at passing (or failing) a particularly significant examination, the sense of wonderment (or frustration) emerging from a difficult learning process, or a sense of injustice emerging from an unfair or distressing comment from a teacher, colleague, or administrator.

Epiphanies may vary in intensity, from the life-changing experience of complete failure or triumphant success, to less calamitous events that have significant, but not dire, effects on people's lives. They emerge as moments of human warmth or hurt, or they can be moments of clarity that add new dimensions to a person's life experience and invest them with new ways of interpreting or understanding their lives. An epiphany may emerge instantaneously—the "ah-ha" experience, or the "light bulb" that enables a person to say "so that's what is going on"—or it may emerge gradually through a cumulative sense of awareness after an ongoing process of experience and reflection.

Rhonda Petty reveals how she came to understand the concept "epiphany". She writes (Petty, 1997) "When I first read Denzin's (1989b) definition and description of epiphanies, I associated them with psychotic behavior or life-threatening diseases. My interpretation was too narrow. As Denzin wrote, epiphanies are turning-point experiences, interactional moments that mark people's lives and can be transformational. My own experience demonstrates, however, that epiphanies can stem from the unlikeliest of sources—a book, a conversation, or the click of a telephone." Epiphanies can emerge from seemingly minor events and may be best thought of as significant experiences that are set aside from the hum-drum, routine events that have little impact. They are experiences that are in some way distinct and are cause for particular comment or response from those involved.

Interpreting Epiphanies and Illuminative Experiences

Interpretive data analysis first identifies epiphanic or illuminative experiences in the lives of research participants, then deconstructs or unpacks those events to reveal the elements of experience of which they are built. We deconstruct those events using terminology, concepts, and structures of meaning derived from participant accounts. By starting with events significant from the participants' perspectives, and building understanding of events in their terms, we seek not only to give voice to the participants, but to create understandings that emerge from, resonate with, and are consistent with the world as they know and understand it. We seek emic (insider) constructions that are true to their worlds and their purposes.

We seek not only accounts of individual experience, but to understand the experience of different **groups** since individuals will interpret events according to their membership in a particular group. Teachers, parents, and students, for instance, are likely to see an issue from quite different viewpoints. We seek to formulate joint accounts providing insight into the perspective and experience of each stakeholding group.

Figure 5.2 shows how data related to the perspectives of teachers, students, and parents is analyzed and used as the basis of a report on a school issue. Researchers:

- *Review information* acquired from stakeholders in the data-gathering phase.
- Identify *epiphanies, or illuminative moments,* within individual participants' experience.
- Deconstruct or "unpack" those events to reveal the detailed *features and elements* of which epiphanies are constructed.
- Use those features and elements to construct *individual accounts* describing how selected individuals experience and interpret the issue investigated.
- Use the features and elements within individual accounts to construct *joint accounts* revealing the perspectives and experiences of each stakeholding group.

Finally, joint accounts provide the material for a *collective* account—an overall version chronicling events by comparing and contrasting the perspectives of the different stakeholding groups within the setting. Analysis identifies points of commonality of perspective and experience and points of discrepancy, diversity, or conflict. Points of commonality provide the basis for concerted action, while discrepant perspectives, viewpoints, or experiences signal the need to negotiate agendas and actions around unresolved issues.

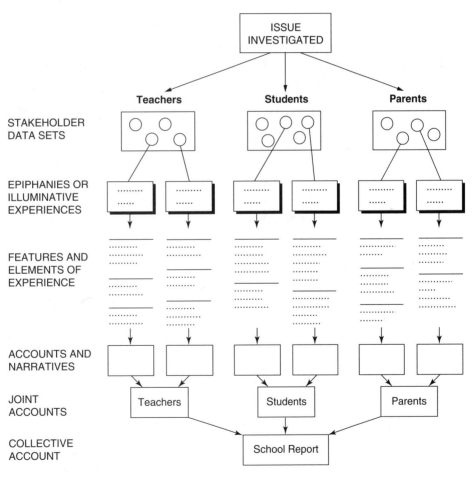

Figure 5.2
Analyzing Epiphanies

Selecting Key People

In many studies, it is not possible to focus on every person's perspective because of constraints of time or resources. As in other forms of research, it is necessary to select a sample of people who will become the focus of research activity (see Chapter 3). When we come to the process of data analysis, it is sometimes beneficial to focus attention on a smaller number of people to explore their experience in depth and to reveal with clarity the elements and features of their experience driving events in the setting. Our purpose in selecting people, therefore, is to isolate those individuals whose experiences or perspectives seem either typical of other people within the setting, or whose experiences or perspectives appear particularly illuminating or significant (Creswell, 2002).

Sometimes persons may be chosen because other people in their group hold them in high esteem, or because their contribution to the life and work of the group is seen as particularly significant. Significance is a flexible term since it may connote negative as well as positive events and behaviors. A child in a classroom whose behavior is disruptive, or a teacher who constantly complains about school organization, may have a significant effect on ongoing events in the classroom or school. Their perspective may be as important to a research process as the school principal or a highly popular student or teacher in illuminating events.

Key people may be thought of as those likely to provide important information or to have a significant impact on events within the school. In commencing interpretive analysis of data, research participants will select a number of persons from each stakeholding group who:

- Represent diverse perspectives from within the group
- Are likely to have a significant impact on the group
- Have seemingly typical experiences and perspectives
- Have particularly unusual or significant experiences or perspectives

Participatory processes help researchers to select people whose experiences and perspectives are likely to illuminate the complex and diverse nature of people, events, and other relevant phenomena. Even in non-participatory processes, however, participants may assist in identifying key people as researchers ask questions such as "Who do you think might provide useful perspectives on this issue?" or "Who in your group would give me a quite different perspective?"

The first step in interpretive data analysis, therefore, is to identify those people from within each stakeholding group whose combined experiences and perspectives will provide the material from which an understanding of that group will be drawn. The following steps of analysis provide the procedures through which these accounts are drawn.

Identifying Epiphanic or Illuminative Experiences

There is no magical recipe for revealing the true or real epiphanic or illuminative experiences. Rather, data analysis commences with a process of selecting those events or features of a person's experience that are especially *significant* in relation to the issue investigated. Sometimes they are most evident when strikingly significant events emerge within the research process itself or are revealed in accounts presented in interviews. At other times, however, judgments are made on the basis of an intimate knowledge of the person, events, and context that comes from extended engagement. Significant or epiphanic events are identified according to the expression of the participant.

The first reading of the data by a researcher, therefore, requires an empathetic, interpretive analysis responding to the internal question "What are the most significant experiences for this person (in relation to the issue investigated)?" The participant's descriptions of events provide clues, but the complex nuances of emotion and nonverbal cues displayed in interviews also provide information, suggesting those events that might usefully be singled out for further analysis. Sometimes significant events or features of experience are self-evident with the participant providing animated, agitated, or emotional descriptions of events and experiences that touch their lives in dramatic and consequential ways. At other times, a more focused and subtle reading is required to identify those features of experience that have a significant impact on the lives of the persons involved. In still other instances, it is evident in the extent to which the person focuses on a particular event or experience, in the person's tone of voice, their language and terminology, their countenance, or their body language.

My colleagues and I often use analysis of epiphanic or illuminative moments in the course of our teaching and research work. These provide a basis for understanding those aspects of people's experience that are particularly significant and help us to understand more clearly the issues and events that most concern the people with whom we work.

During a recent class evaluation, I asked participants to identify the most significant features of their experience. They interviewed each other in pairs, then each person identified those aspects of the class that were particularly significant from their perspective. As each person shared his or her experience, others were able to comment on those features that were similar to their own. Participants were able to construct an emerging picture of the class using this information (Stringer et al., 2001).

In a study of health workers, Bill Genat (2002) focused on an epiphanic event within the work life of one of the participants. Though other health workers were not involved in that particular event, they were able to identify similar experiences that were characteristic of their own situation. The information acquired by exploring one person's experience provided the basis for a richly textured description relevant to others.

Epiphanies and significant events, therefore, take on a range of complexions in terms of their intensity and their meaningfulness to participants. Sometimes a relatively trivial event can create great emotion, while at other times what appear as momentous events create little response. Examples of epiphanies and significant events include:

"If he does that one more time I'll scream!"
"Is she just dumb? I've explained it to her six different ways, and she just doesn't get it."

"I passed! I passed! I passed! I passed!"

"Oh, Jane. That is just wonderful. That is the best work I've seen from you in a long
    time. I knew you had it in you."

"It was so important that we did this work ourselves. If others had done it for us we
    wouldn't have learned anything!"

Sometimes the meanings of the words are self-evident, but more often it is necessary to provide information about the ways in which the words were delivered and
associated information. It is not unusual for people to be led to tears as they speak of
events. In the previous examples, the meanings are reasonably clear, but it would be
necessary to take into account the levels of excitement, frustration, and anger as well
as the voice tone and facial expression of the research participant in order to understand the significance of the words spoken. The **expression** of the words is at least
as important as the words themselves.

> Sometimes epiphanies are revealed unexpectedly. Many times, as I've inter-
> viewed people, I've been struck by the emotive force of their description of par-
> ticular events. I was recently surprised, however, to find my eyes "leaking" as I
> was being interviewed about a cross-cultural training program in which I had
> been involved. Though I thought I was recounting events in a fairly objective
> way, I had not realized the extent to which they had moved me. The interviewer
> informed me that it was not unusual for people to be moved to tears as they de-
> scribed events within this program. I coined the phrase "ethnographic tears" as
> a way of indicating the possibility of engaging people's deeply felt experience
> within an interview.
>
> Recently, I interviewed a student who revealed, in the course of a very or-
> dinary discussion, that she had recently failed a test. As she spoke of her dis-
> appointment, the tears welled up in her eyes. She described events that seemed
> related to her failure and the effect it had on her schoolwork. In the process,
> she revealed much about her classroom life, her approach to school, and her re-
> lationship with her teachers and classmates. In this case, the "real" life that ex-
> isted beneath the surface of her apparently benign experience provided
> significant insight into her experience of school.

Ultimately, however, the choice of epiphanies or significant events requires direct use of member checking since it is easy to misinterpret or wrongly choose events
in other people's lives. Ideally, when the data is member checked, that is, when the
research facilitator allows the participant to read or read back the information they
have provided, they should be asked which events were most significant—a grand
tour question (Spradley, 1979a) framed something like, "What, in all this, is most significant for you?" This provides an opportunity for the person interviewed to identify
those events that have had the biggest impact on their lives. One step back from this
is a procedure in which the researcher identifies significant events and checks their
importance with the participant.

Although I focus on events, sometimes significance is found in people's actions and responses or in the impact of features of the environment—physical space, dress, and so on. Significance is revealed in the body language and the nonverbal communication that gives us clues about the impact of events. A frown, a smile, a look of pain or anger, or forceful language suggests the need to focus on what is said. For example:

"She's such a *bitch*—dressing like that and talking like that. I can't stand being around her."

"I won't work there much longer. The office is so small I can't even *think* let alone do my work."

"When I saw the work that kid had produced I almost cried. It was fabulous."

As we explore people's description of events, therefore, we may identify a set of related elements impacting on their lives. The feature of experience—"The office is so small I can't even think"—may lead us to explore related components of a participant's experience. Comments on the size of an office, in this instance, were related to the number and complexity of the person's work activities and the space she felt she needed to store materials and do the work required of her. As became evident in reviewing the data, the work itself was the significant feature of the experience, even though the size of the office was the last straw and became the immediate focus of the agitated comment. Identifying epiphanies and significant experiences, therefore, requires a researcher to search for significant events in people's lives, but also to make connections between related phenomena.

Epiphanies do not need to be associated with momentous events. Minor epiphanies occur quite regularly as people reflect on their experience; sometimes calling on the "little light bulb that went on in my head" as they realize the significance of something they have described. These might be more appropriately called illuminative moments since they reflect processes of understanding and clarity that sometimes emerge as people reflect on their own experience or hear other people's stories.

Deconstructing Epiphanies: Features and Elements of Experience

Ultimately our purpose is to evoke an understanding of the way people experience events and phenomena in their lives. We need, therefore, to identify the information that will enable us to construct accounts for that purpose. The next step in this process is to deconstruct the epiphanies, thereby ascertaining those elements and/or features that enable an audience to understand the nature of the experience. We need to ask, "How is this event significant for the person? What are the features of this event they would see as significant?" By doing this, we are, in effect, unpacking or interrogating the epiphany to reveal the web and warp of the tapestry of people's lives. Information drawn from the data uses the concepts, terms, and language of the people interviewed as they described events, behaviors, responses, and so on—applying the verbatim principal described previously (see Chapter 4).

Figure 5.3 provides an example of this process. The participant, reflecting on her experience, described how doing research had been, for her and other parents, "an empowering experience." The major features of this empowering experience, revealed in interview field notes and member-checked with the participant, were that "we did it

In reflecting on the community-school research process enacted by Barrios Juntos, one parent-researcher exclaimed excitedly, "It was such an empowering experience!" Her framing of events as "empowering" was obviously significant, taking into account the excitement of her voice, her shining eyes, and the intensity signaled by her body language (i.e., body leaning forward and hands gesturing). From her talk, it was possible to ascertain that the empowering features of the research process related to the fact that "We did it ourselves," "We were listened to," and "We learned so much."

Exploration of what was involved in "We did it ourselves" revealed the processes of making up the questions, doing interviews with parents, analyzing the data, and writing reports as key elements of this feature of her experience. Structurally, we could map this out in the following way:

Epiphany   [Doing research] was an empowering experience.

Major Features   We did it ourselves.
                          We were listened to.
                          We learned so much.

Key Elements (of "We did it ourselves.")
                          Making up the questions
                          Doing interviews with parents
                          Analyzing the data
                          Writing reports

Deconstruction of other features—"We were listened to," and "We learned so much"—revealed the elements of those aspects of her experience. The final structure of the analyzed information—epiphany, features, and elements—provided materials from which an account of this person's experience could be formulated.

Figure 5.3
Deconstructing an Epiphany

ourselves," "we were listened to," and "we learned so much." Further analysis of field notes indicates the elements of experience associated with each of these. "We did it ourselves," for instance, was associated with making up the questions, doing interviews with parents, analyzing the data, and writing reports. Elements of "we were listened to" and "we learned so much" would, likewise, emerge from further exploration of the data.

Having identified an epiphany, therefore, researchers should ask: "What are the major features of this epiphany? What comprises the key features of the experience? And what detail (elements) would need to be included in a description so that an audience could understand its significance?"

Researchers should deconstruct each epiphany to reveal the different features of experience inherent in the event. Sometimes a single epiphany is sufficiently powerful to provide the basis for a detailed analysis of a person's experience, while other accounts may require ongoing analysis of several minor epiphanies, illuminative moments, or significant events.

As research participants work through this process of deconstruction, they may use other analytic frameworks that alert them to the types of information that might usefully be extracted from the data. A framework of concepts drawn from ethnographic observation (Spradley, 1979b) indicates the types of phenomena that might be used as epiphanies, features, or elements of experience. These include **acts, activities, events, times, places, purposes,** and **emotions.**

Another useful framework—asking **what, who, how, where, when,** and **why**—also may be used to assist in identifying useful or relevant detail. In all this, we are not attempting to include **every** possible detail since the possibilities are infinite. We do not need an extended description of the more mundane, taken-for-granted properties and features of everyday life, but we do need to identify the essential features of people's experiences or perspectives. It's important that we do not let the framework drive the data analysis process—i.e., starting with acts and working down through the concepts. The trigger for selecting features and elements are those aspects that are seen or felt by participants to be a central part of their experience. Framework concepts merely serve as reminders of the type of phenomena that might be included.

In all this, researchers need to focus their analysis by ensuring that the information revealed is associated with the issue or question that provides the focus for the study. They should ask, "How does this event illuminate or extend our understanding about the issue we are investigating? Does it provide answers to the questions that helped us to frame our study?" In some cases, the analysis will reveal information indicating the need to extend the boundaries of the study or to focus on issues that were not part of the original plan. The iterative or cyclical nature of the research process enables us to build understanding and extend our study accordingly.

Epiphanies in Observations and Representations

Sometimes epiphanic moments occur in the course of observing events and activities within a research setting. Any classroom or school is likely, over a period of time, to experience disruptive events that disturb the orderly routines of school life. A student outburst, conflict between a teacher and student, or an altercation between staff members signals an epiphanic event that may provide worthwhile focus for further exploration. The event itself tells part of the story, but description and analysis by participants reveals the meanings and experiences associated with the event that have the potential to greatly increase understanding about the issue investigated. Significant events, therefore, provide the focus for follow-up interviews to enable participants to explore and deconstruct events and explore the meanings embedded in singular events. A single event can provide a great deal of insight into the underlying structures of behavior or the ways everyday events are experienced or interpreted by the people involved.

Epiphanies may also appear as representations. They may be depicted in artwork that enables students to explore or represent their experience of a particular issue or in naturally occurring representations like graffiti that often appear on school buildings or furniture in the form of pictures, or slogans—"Mr Jones is a . . . ." and "School sucks"—and so on. While not all graffiti is significant, it may be associated with particular events or people that signal unresolved issues in the life of a school. They may provide a focus or a context for further exploration revealing key features of school life.

Constructing Conceptual Frameworks

Once epiphanies have been deconstructed to reveal the key features and elements inherent in participant experiences, the analyzed information is organized into a carefully structured system of concepts that assists people to clearly understand the import of what has been revealed. This structured system of concepts not only provides a summary of important information, but also supplies the basis for writing reports and planning actions.

The following outlines provide examples of how deconstructed epiphanies—the analysis of significant events within two action research projects—provided the framework for written accounts of each.

EXAMPLE ONE:
"EVERYTHING IS DIFFERENT NOW:
SURVIVING ETHNOGRAPHIC RESEARCH." (PETTY, 1997)

This account emerged from the study of a small group of African American boys from a school in an undesirable neighborhood. An elementary school teacher describes how she came to understand herself and her place in society differently, and how, in consequence, she was able to explore larger issues related to minority students on the basis of what she learned in a very small arena. She uses four *major features* as the basis for constructing her account, representing particularly illuminating aspects of her experience—"Doing Ethnographic Study: A Wake-Up Call," "Contextualizing Experience," "Surviving Qualitative Research," and What Can Be Learned from My Experience." The *key elements* of each are used as subheadings—"Setting Myself Up," and so on. Her account emerges from an analysis of one key epiphanic incident she describes in the section labeled "Doing Ethnographic Study: A Wake-Up Call." The structure of concepts derived from the study include:

Lived Experience: In which she presents the methodology of the study.
Doing Ethnographic Study: A Wake-Up Call: This section presents the difficulties she experienced initiating a "minority study." Key elements of her experience are described under three headings:

Setting Myself Up reflects on her perspective in the early stages of this study.
"Is This a Minority Study?"—Suspicion and Resistance describes the negative responses of some parents when approached for permission to study their sons and the feelings of devastation she felt as a result.
Aftermath provides an account of how she came to terms with the situation and the sense of hope she developed for these boys as she continued her work with them.

Contextualizing Experience: "As I reflected on these events, emergent themes helped me understand the nature of my experience, organize my thoughts, and think constructively about a situation that had once seemed hopeless." These themes (key elements) included:

> **Contradictions: Expectations and Experience** describes the discrepancy between the expectations with which she entered the boys' social worlds and the reality of the events that occurred.

> **Assumptions and Stereotypes** reveals how the boys failed to live up to her assumptions or to manifest behaviors her stereotypes had predicted.

> **Ignorance and Indifference** describes how she became aware that "my unconsciously purposeful ignorance showed my indifference" to the issues of race surrounding her study.

Surviving Qualitative Research: Articulates the lessons she learned from the *processes* of the study. Broken into its subcategories:

> **Naïve realism** reveals how she originally viewed the project through her own cultural lenses and acted accordingly.

> **Support for Survival** presents an account of how others supported her as she worked through these experiences and explored her responses so that the events became a learning experience.

What Can Be Learned From My Experience?: Reveals the broader lessons emerging from the research; that policies and programs fail because they fail to consider the perspectives and attitudes of those who formulate and implement them. "In the end, I realize that developing a genuine connection with someone of another culture or race requires an approach that acknowledges the person as authentic rather than as someone with quaint customs or unexplainable beliefs or desires."

EXAMPLE TWO:
"HIGH SCHOOL STUDENTS' PARTICIPATION IN ACTION RESEARCH: AN ONGOING LEARNING PROCESS." (BALDWIN, 1997)

This project presents an interpretive account of how Shelia Baldwin taught a group of high-school students to use ethnographic methods to explore cultural diversity in their school and community. The following framework emerged from deconstruction of a major epiphany—that students could be researchers. Exploration of the data revealed the *major features* (called themes by the author) of participant experiences—"Getting Started," "Relationships," and so on. *Key elements* of each of these features provide sub-headings and descriptive details within each section—"Teacher as Facilitator" and "Students as Ethnographers." These were formulated in a framework that became the basis for the project report.

> **Introduction:** Describes how the project was initiated.
>
> **Ethnographic Methods:** Describes the research methods.
>
> **Emergence of Themes:** Provides a description of the major themes emerging from the study.
>
> **Getting Started:** Provides a detailed description of how student participants commenced work on the project.
>
> **Relationships:** Describes how relationships between teacher, students, and other participants developed in the course of the study. There were two major elements of the development of relationships:
>
>> **Teacher as Facilitator** describes how Shelia acted as a guide to help the students develop the tools necessary for doing ethnographic work.
>>
>> **Students as Ethnographers** provides an account of the way students assumed the ethnographic role.
>
> **School-Community Interrelations:** Tells how students came to increase their understanding of their families and communities and relations with the school, characterizing the school as a microcosm of the larger community.
>
> **Place—The Temporal and Physical Context:** This section illustrates how *Time* and *Place* were important elements of the study. Both time and context appeared to effect other features of the study.
>
> **The Teacher's Reflections:** Reveals how the teacher developed her facilitating role in the project and, in the process, learned to relinquish control and trust her students.
>
> **An Ongoing Learning Process:** Reviews the outcomes of the project, finishing with the words "action research can revitalize the entire learning community and can aid teachers in changing or reflecting on their classroom practices."

Using People's Terms and Concepts: The Verbatim Principle

As we engage in data analysis, it is particularly important to use the terms and concepts from the participants' own talk to label concepts and categories. The temptation to characterize people's experience in terms that seem to make more sense or clarify the issue from the researcher's perspective, or to translate it into language fitted to theoretical or professional discourses, should be clearly resisted. Later, when the need for joint accounts incorporating diverse terms, concepts, and/or ideas emerges, we may need terminology that allows us to collectively describe similar elements or features with one term or phrase. "I was angry," "She made me feel bad," "I nearly cried when he did that," and "I'm just scared what he'll do next" may be elements of a feature described as "The Emotional Impact of . . . ." Generally, however, we should seek terms from within the speech of the participants themselves, adding additional words only to clarify meaning or extend understanding when the words themselves are insufficient for the purpose.

> Maria Hines is very explicit about her experience of analyzing data in the Barrios Juntos project. With a slight frown, she describes how she "never knew how difficult it was not to put my own words and meanings in. We had to really concentrate to make sure we used what people had actually said and not put in our own words. It was *hard.*"

These words remind us to focus clearly on one of the central features of action research—consciously seeking to understand the perspective of others and using those perspectives to formulate actions. This is centrally important at the stage of data analysis where the possibility of reinterpreting, misinterpreting, or colonizing people's words, concepts, and ideas—taking them and using them for our own purposes—is ever present.

Data Analysis (2): Categorizing and Coding

The previous sections presented processes for interpretive data analysis designed to more effectively represent individual perspectives and experiences. Another process of data analysis, used commonly in qualitative research, is based on procedures for unitizing data and sorting units into categories, each of which is denoted by a label—a conceptual "code" (see Figure 5.4). The process is very useful for analyzing large bodies of qualitative data, and is especially amenable to electronic data analysis software now available . It runs the risk, however, of losing participant perspectives in conglomerating data from a wide diversity of sources, and of revealing conceptual structures meaningful mainly to those responsible for data analysis. Using participatory processes of data analysis can minimize both of these weaknesses.

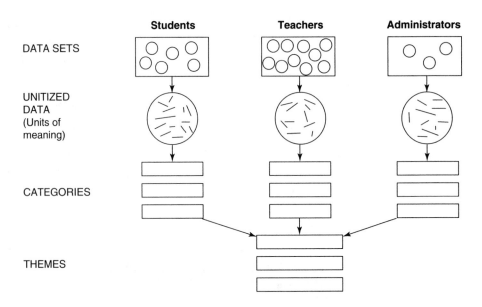

Figure 5.4
Categorizing and Coding

Purposes and Processes in Categorizing[1]

The purpose of analysis in action research is not to identify the facts, or what is actually happening, but to distill or crystallize the data in ways that enable research participants to interpret and make sense out of the collected materials. Initially this involves working with data and organizing them to make connections between events or ideas and identify commonalities, regularities, or patterns. These new ways of seeing or interpreting the information gathered sheds light on events, transforms people's understanding, and provides the means to take therapeutic action on the problem at hand.

---

[1] Harry Wolcott (1994) suggests description, analysis, and interpretation as the three purposes of data analysis—the latter being generalized theorizing not specifically relevant to the context at hand. The type of analysis presented herein makes no distinction between analysis and interpretation, as Wolcott depicts them. The purposes of action research require "theorizing" or "interpretation" that makes sense from the perspective of participants. Generalized theory, more relevant to theory building in the academic disciplines, has less relevance to our current purposes, though they often assist in framing the study. Shirley Bryce Heath (1983), for instance, used ethnographic methods for studying children's language use in different communities. Both data gathering and analysis were affected by understandings about the types of things associated with or affecting children's language, resulting in descriptions of the communities of people. The "interpretive lens" filtering information was that provided by socio-linguistics.

The process commences by reviewing interview and focus-group data and dividing them into "units of meaning"—that is, unitizing the data, then using these to construct an organized system of categories and themes. This system of categories then provides the basis for research reports and accounts and for action agendas that guide the ongoing activities of action researchers. Categories may also emerge from data gathered through observation, reviewing artifacts, or from relevant literature.

Reviewing Data Sets

Stakeholders in action research usually are comprised of groups having different roles within the context and, in consequence, experiencing events in different ways. In schools, for instance, teachers often experience and interpret events quite differently from students or administrators. Male teachers may have a different experience and perspective than female teachers, and science teachers have quite different perspectives than teachers of English literature. Experience and perspectives of students is also likely to differ according to students' age, family background, religion, race, ethnicity, and so on.

Often, these differences in experience or perspective will become apparent in the course of the study, but one of the important features of research is that we don't assume differences; rather, we must allow them to emerge in the course of data analysis. Generally, however, we formulate data sets to acknowledge the important distinctions existing between stakeholders in a setting. This allows us to take into account the differences in perspective and experience of the types of people inhabiting the context of the study. In Figure 5.4, for instance, data from students, teachers, and administrators is analyzed separately to reveal points of commonality and difference in their perspective of school events and issues.

The purpose of reviewing the data sets is to familiarize researchers with the data, and allow them to take an overall view of the information so that links between items and elements begin to emerge. Those responsible for data analysis should therefore commence by reading through all the data.

Unitizing the Data

The next step in the process is to isolate features and elements of experience and perspective; to focus on the specific details emerging from peoples' talk about events and experiences. Data recorded in interviews and focus group sessions is first printed, and then divided into *units of meaning*. A unit of meaning might be a word, a phrase, a part, or the whole of a sentence. The sentence, "I don't really like the way I organized this class because it's too one-dimensional, and I prefer to work thematically" has a number of distinct units of meaning. These include "I don't like the way I organized this class," "the class is too one-dimensional," and "I prefer to work thematically." As indicated here, it is sometimes necessary to add words to a unit so it makes sense when it stands alone.

A variety of methods are used for this purpose. Some researchers isolate units of meaning by physically cutting sheets of interview data with scissors, while others use highlighters to isolate units of meaning related to emerging categories.

Computer programs such as NUD*IST, Ethnograph, Nvivo, WinMAX, and Hyper-search are also used to engage in this process electronically.[2] Computer-assisted programs, however, provide only a data storage, managing, and searching tool. They cannot engage in analytic processes such as identifying units of meaning or formulating categories.

The process of unitizing the data results in a large pile of discrete pieces of information. From these building blocks, researchers sort, select, and organize information into a system of categories that enables participants to make sense of the issues they investigate. The next phase of the process of analysis, therefore, is to categorize and code units of data.

Categorizing and Coding

Spradley's (1979a) schema for *componential* analysis, similar in concept to analysis of *units* of meaning, provides a useful conceptualization of the process of categorization. Spradley's approach to analysis is based on the idea that people's everyday cultural knowledge is organized according to systems of meaning they give to phenomena in their lives. These systems of meaning, he proposes, are organized taxonomically and use a hierarchical structure to distinguish the different types of phenomena comprising everyday life. Category systems divide and define our cultural worlds systematically, which allows us to impose a sense of order on the multiple and complex phenomena that comprise our everyday life.

A simple set of common categories is indicated in Figure 5.5. Ingestibles—substances that can be swallowed and ingested—are comprised of food, drink, and medication. Each of these is comprised of a number of different items that make up the category. The category "food," for instance, is made up of fruit and vegetables. The category system is incomplete, but it provides an illustration of the way people organize phenomena in order to help them define objects and communicate meaningfully.

Systems of meaning are inherent in every culture, and one of the early tasks in the life of a baby is to learn to understand the different types of people with whom

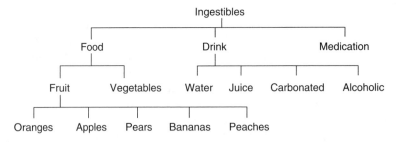

Figure 5.5
Category System for Ingestibles

---

[2]Reviews of these programs may be found on *http://www.sagepub.com.*

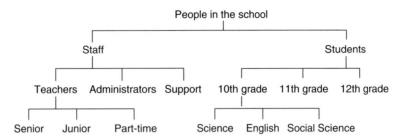

Figure 5.6
Taxonomy of School People

he/she comes into contact (e.g., distinguishing mother, father, and siblings). The research act requires participants to uncover the systems of meaning inherent in people's way of defining their experience and to formulate new ways of organizing the information that extends understanding of the experience.

Having identified the units of meaning inherent in the interview data, researchers will then identify those associated with each other, which may ultimately be included in the same category. The example in Figure 5.6 provides a way of categorizing the different types of people in a school.

In the taxonomy in Figure 5.6, two major types of people are identified from the data—staff and students. Different types of staff include teachers, administrators, and support staff. Important distinctions between teachers are made by participants according to whether they are classified as senior, junior, or part-time. As the system of categories is organized, decisions must be made about the placement of each item into a particular category or subcategory. In this example, there may be a need to decide whether a senior teacher who has administrative duties is classified as a teacher or administrator. Items are placed within particular categories or subcategories according to a system of *inclusion* and based on the *attributes* of each element. The categories senior and junior teacher, for instance, are first identified by asking *structural questions* regarding who should be placed in each category (e.g., "Can you name all the senior teachers in the school? Who are the junior teachers?").

We extend our understanding of the reason for placing people into particular categories by asking *attribute questions* that identify the reason for placing a person in a particular category (e.g., "What is a senior teacher?"). Answers to these questions would provide the criteria employed for making a decision to define a teacher as senior as opposed to junior or part-time. A senior teacher might be identified, according to the system of meanings used in this school, as one who:

- Has been at the school for more than four years
- Is a full-time teacher
- Has some leadership responsibilities

These attributes define a senior teacher and allow researchers to make decisions about which types of teacher are to be included in that category.

When we place phenomena into a category, one of the principal tasks is to name that category to identify the type of phenomena it contains. Apples, pears, and oranges might be identified as fruit, for instance. This process is called coding; therefore, the term used to name the category is called, by some researchers, the *code* for the category. Spradley (1979a) refers to this as a "cover term." Researchers should first determine whether an existing term occurs naturally in the language or talk of the people from whom the information has been acquired. Otherwise, they should provide a label for the category that clearly identifies the nature of the category. "Fooling around," "sitting still," "working conscientiously," and "talking loudly," for instance, might be identified by the code or cover term "student behaviors."

As information is placed in categories, therefore, we become aware of the need to define more clearly the meanings intended by research participants in order to understand how the word or phrase is being used, and therefore whether it should be included in one category or another. The codes or cover terms will eventually provide a structured set of categories that help us to organize and make meaning of the experiences of diverse groups of people. The system of categories also provides a framework of events, activities, behaviors, and materials that assist in understanding events and formulating actions to deal with those events.

Categorizing and coding, therefore, requires researchers to:

- Unitize the data
- Sort units into categories
- Divide categories into subcategories, where appropriate
- Code each category using a cover term expressing the type or nature of information in the category or subcategory
- Identify the attributes defining each category or subcategory

Other formats for coding and categorizing data may be found in Bogdan and Biklen (1992), Creswell (2002), and Arhar, Holly, and Kasten (2000). These provide detailed instructions for developing descriptions and representing findings.

Organizing a Category System

As researchers formulate categories, they first place them in an organized system that identifies features and elements of experience in ways that clarify the relationship between them. Categories do not fall automatically into a structure or system, and decisions must be made about which categories are given priority and where they are placed in relation to each other. In the school evaluation project featured in Figure 5.7, major categories identified included Administrator Perspectives, Teacher Perspectives, and Student Perspectives. Each contains subcategories revealing different elements of those perspectives. Teacher Perspectives includes subcategories Student Achievement, Relationships with Students, Inquiry Curriculum, and Learning Materials. Details within those subcategories are comprised of units of meaning revealing people's experiences or perspectives of those issues. Note that there is no right way of organizing the data. It might as easily have been organized with Student Achievement as a major cat-

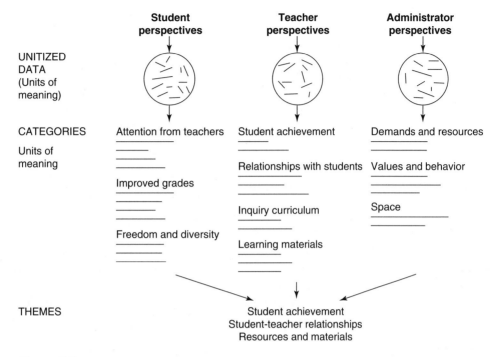

Figure 5.7
A Category System for a School Evaluation

egory and administrator, student, and teacher perspectives presented as sub-categories. The general process is depicted in Figure 5.7.

In Figure 5.7, different categories of experience and perception have emerged for students, teachers, and administrators. The first cluster of units of meaning is labeled Attention From Teachers, the next Improved Grades, and the final category emerges as Freedom and Diversity. Teacher categories (i.e., labels chosen to characterize the clustered units of meaning) include Student Achievement, Relationships with Students, Inquiry Curriculum, and Learning Materials. Categories of experience and perception associated with administrators include Demands and Resources, Values and Behavior, and Space. Although category labels provide no common elements across stakeholding groups, it is clear that some issues are related, and these have been identified as *Themes,* each identified by a code. The student category Improved Grades has been associated with teacher category Student Achievement and identified as a theme coded Student Achievement. The categories Attention from Teachers and Relationships with Students have been linked as a theme having the code Student-Teacher Relationships. Teacher and administrator categories, Learning Materials, Demands and Resources, and Space have been linked under the code Resources and Materials.

This system of categories provides useful information about the types of people whose perspective are presented, the issues concerning them, and the relationship between some of those issues. The way of organizing these categories into a framework assists to clarify the significant features of experience emerging in the process of investigation. At a later stage, they also provide the agenda for planning actions related to those agendas.

Researchers, therefore, construct a system of categories and subcategories organizing the emerging information in ways that make sense to the participants. It does so by using terms or codes they recognize as representing or encompassing their experience and perspectives, but providing new, interesting, and clarifying ways of organizing data.

Enhancing Analysis: Incorporating Non-Interview Data

Thus far, data analysis has proceeded by exploring information derived largely from interviews. A variety of other data also has been gathered, however, and this has the potential to enhance or clarify information or issues emerging in the first phases of data analysis. Information acquired through *observation, artifact reviews* (documents, records, materials, and equipment), and *literature reviews* might be used to complement that inherent in the items categorized in the preliminary analysis of data. In the example in Figure 5.7, for instance, interview information related to Student Achievement might be enhanced, extended, or thrown into question by data from student records or reports. Likewise, staff perceptions about resources and materials might be given more credence, or challenged, by information from the school inventory or after comparison with district or state records about levels of resources in schools. Once interview data has been analyzed, therefore, researchers should review other available information, focusing especially on information pertinent to the identified issues, features, or elements.

Other data also includes information emerging from the literature review. In action research, the process of investigation is driven by participant perspectives rather than those contained in the literature on the issue. Authors within the literature, however, might be viewed as secondary stakeholders since their writings have the potential to influence the research process. In this respect, viewpoints within the literature are treated as another set of perspectives having the same status and validity as those of other stakeholders.

Research participants may find it fruitful to review information within the professional, bureaucratic, or academic literature that might throw light on issues and elements emerging from data analysis. There is a broad range of educational research that challenges many of the commonly held assumptions circulating in school and community contexts or reveals the uncertain nature of many of the so-called "spray on" solutions that emerge from time to time. A thorough review of the research literature on any topic often provides a unique resource assisting people to refine their analysis of the problem investigated. Pertinent information that enhances or clarifies participant perspectives is identified and included in the process of analysis.

In the Barrios Jantos school-community study, parent participants were firm in their opinion of the need for greater participation of parents within the school. A review of the literature would have confirmed this perception since a large array of literature now signals the benefits to be obtained.

The perceptions of students and staff in the Brazos School evaluation study that student achievement had improved were verified by a review of student scores on state-mandated tests. This not only indicated increasing test scores, but showed how well the students were doing compared with similar schools in the district and state.

Non-interview data are especially important when working with young children who frequently have a limited ability to talk of their experience in abstract terms. There are many other ways, however, in which children make meaning of their experience and communicate with others. We should carefully observe the ways children enact their work and play activities, the ways they talk to others, their drawings, their songs, stories and poems, their descriptions of events, and their responses to events and activities. These "artifacts" assist us in understanding how a child makes meaning of events in his/her life and to construct accounts clearly representing the child's perspective. If we can fathom ways of making learning activities meaningful from their perspective, then our teaching task becomes so much easier and more rewarding.

Reviewing information related to children's events and activities provides richly rewarding information helping researchers, including the children themselves, to make sense of the issue at hand. It has the potential to greatly enhance the engagement of children in their learning processes and to increase the effectiveness of teaching. Analysis of these types of data require interactive processes that first identify significant features or elements of experience, then check the ways children make meaning or interpret those features of experience. Researchers should review data related to:

- Observations of children's activities, or their participation in events in the classroom, school yard, or other relevant settings
- Aural or visual recordings of their activities, including verbal interactions
- Drawings and art work
- Class written work
- Letters
- Stories, verbal and written
- Play
- Drama

Researchers should work with children to identify significant features and elements of these types of information to construct understandings on the basis of the way the children interpret the information reviewed.

In a study of bilingual kindergarten students, Cathrene Connery (2001) talks of the multiple ways in which children make meaning. She tells the story of a young boy who, hearing the teacher suggest to another student ways of drawing a dinghy, said "No, you're not doing it right. You've got to go 'Urrrr-Uuurrrrrr!! Aururrrrr-Aurrrrurrr!!—like that!', making pulling motions with his hands, apparently trying to invest the action and urgency into the sounds and motions of starting an outboard motor. The event was clear. What was emerging was the child's way of trying to capture that event—sight, sound, and words. We have a much clearer picture of his experience of a boat by combining elements of interview and observation.

Lisa Keck's (2000) eight- and nine-year-old students identified major features and elements of their classroom experience of art by discussing the issue verbally and drawing pictures to represent their experiences and perceptions. They used these features and elements to construct written accounts that resulted in a book and a mural to express their combined perspective on their experience of art in the class. As a structured research activity, it not only served to cover a number of areas of the class curriculum, but also generated considerable interest and excitement in the children.

Non-interview data, therefore, provides a variety of rich resources having the potential to enhance and clarify understandings emerging in the processes of investigation. The process is described schematically in Figure 5.8, though the cyclical nature of action research will mean that the revised analysis may be subject to further exploration using participant interviews or focus groups. This process is also incorporated in data-collection procedures (see Figure 4.6). What emerges through the incorporation of non-interview data may enable participants to extend their understanding or reinterpret their experience leading to stronger analyses that provide the basis for effective action.

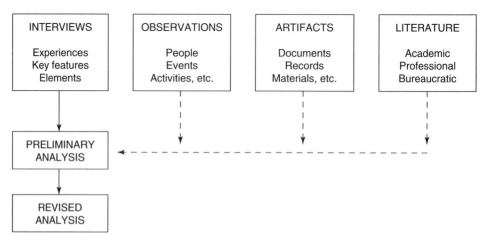

Figure 5.8
Incorporating Non-Interview Data

Using Category Systems: Frameworks for Reports and Accounts

Systems of categories emerging from data analysis provide frameworks of concepts that provide a structure for reports. The Brazos School evaluation study, for instance, (see Chapter 9) used the system of categories presented in Figure 5.7 as a framework for structuring the evaluation report:

Small Is Beautiful: Brazos School Evaluation Report[3]

Introduction
History
Student Experiences
    Attention from Teachers
    Improved Grades
    Freedom and Diversity

Teacher Perspectives
    Student Achievement
    Relationships with Students
    Inquiry Curriculum
    Learning Materials

Administration
    Demands and Resources
    Values and Behavior
    Space

Details within the report are derived from the units of meaning included within each category or sub-category. Thus, the evaluation report described here includes the heading Teacher Perspectives and the sub-heading Student Achievement and commences with the following text: "Teachers are also enthusiastic about the response of students to the school's model of education. One teacher, comparing his experience in public schools, recounted the differences he experienced. 'You have to give students at other schools tangible rewards'. . . . " The text continues to present details of how teachers are experiencing and interpreting student achievement, including the full range of elements drawn from the unitized data within the Student Achievement category. A copy of the preliminary report is presented in Chapter 8, providing an illustration of the way research materials and analysis have been incorporated.

Analyzing Data Collaboratively

Data gathering and analysis in action research is much more effective when it is accomplished as an interactive process between stakeholders. Although it is important for people to have opportunities to explore issues individually in the earliest stages of an inquiry process, continued explorations increase in power as people participate in

---

[3] The framework for this report has been simplified for illustrative purposes.

processes of collaborative inquiry. Focus groups provide a context in which individual information can be shared and further exploration engaged. Sharing may take place initially within each group of stakeholders, but eventually diverse stakeholding groups should be brought together to share their perspectives, to identify common issues or agendas, and to explore ways of dealing with issues on which they fail to concur.

Data gathering, therefore, becomes an ongoing part of the Look-Think-Act process. As information is gathered and analyzed and actions emerge, the process often leads to the need for further exploration, or the acquisition of more information in an ever increasing circle of investigation extending participants' understandings and providing the basis for strong and effective action.

Figure 5.9 represents this process. Participants share accounts emerging from individual interviews, formulate a joint account, then return to the interview phase to reflect on and extend their own accounts. There may be a number of iterations of this process during an extended study of a complex issue.

A similar process is envisaged in Figure 5.10, where focus group exploration provides the material to develop an initial account. This account provides a framework of concepts and themes that is used for further exploration of people's experience and perspectives of the issue. Again, the process is designed to help groups achieve deeper understanding and greater clarity, which provides the basis for actions that resolve the issue explored.

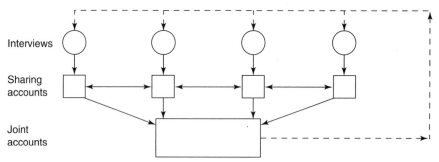

Figure 5.9
Developing Collaborative Accounts

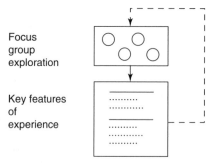

Figure 5.10
Focus Group Analysis

Analyzing data in focus groups enables stakeholders to come together to share information derived from their own perspectives and experiences. This not only extends understanding between the diverse individuals and groups, but enables them cooperatively to construct a framework of ideas for ongoing collaborative action. As these procedures progress, they trigger new ideas or memories in participants that lead to a productive extension of the research process. It enables participants to identify perspectives and experiences they have in common and assists in identifying areas in need of further negotiation or study.

Over the years, I have been impressed by the amount of energy and goodwill emerging from well-prepared focus groups. Positive and productive outcomes are never certain since a history of antagonisms or the presence of authoritarian figures may inhibit group discussions or interaction. I have experienced, however, a high degree of success in this type of activity. A recent half-day workshop with faculty within a College of Education illustrates the types of outcomes possible. Faculty explored the use of technology in their teaching and shared ways they currently use computers to enhance student learning and identifying future uses. The level of animation in their discussions and the extensive lists of useful information emerging from their discussions were testament to their enthusiasm and the extent to which they appreciated opportunities to learn from each other. It also provided clear direction for the project team who had set up the workshop—indicating directions to take in resourcing faculty to extend their use of technology to enhance student learning.

The productive buzz that continued through this workshop was not the result of idle gossip or general conversation. As I walked around the room listening to group conversations to monitor the progress of their discussion, I was taken by the intensity of their focus. In professional contexts, opportunities for practitioners to get together to discuss the broader dimensions of their work are infrequent. Group discussions focused clearly on issues of interest or concern provide a wonderful context for reaffirming the broader contexts of professional work. They take people out of the sometimes humdrum organizational trivia of everyday institutional life and remind them of the underlying nature of the work they do together.

Conclusion

Data analysis is the process of distilling the large quantities of information, and therefore revealing the central features of the issue investigated. The process of crystallizing information into a category system provides the basis for increased understanding of the complex events and interactions comprising everyday events in classrooms, schools, and other educational settings. The process is not merely a technical routine, however, since its purpose is not to delineate a relatively small number of variables affecting the focus of study. Its major purpose is to provide the basis for richly evocative accounts and reports providing stakeholders with information and understanding upon which to make informed decisions about policies, programs, and practices for which they are responsible. It also provides the building blocks for therapeutic action within the research process, and clearly delineates issues and agendas requiring attention. When engaged collaboratively, it also provides a rich field of interaction that enables stakeholders to develop productive relationships that are a central feature of a good action research process.

Summary

The *purposes* of data analysis are:

1. To reduce, distill, or crystallize large quantities of data
2. To provide clarity and enhance stakeholder understandings of issues and events

Two processes for analyzing data are presented:

Analyzing Epiphanies

1. Select key people from within each stakeholder group.
2. Review the data for each selected person.
3. For each, identify epiphanies or significant experiences.
4. Identify major features of those events or experiences.
5. Identify the elements of experience associated with each feature.
6. Use identified features and elements to formulate a framework of concepts and ideas that represent each person's experience of the issue investigated.
7. Make connections: Identify similarities and differences between features or elements in stakeholder experiences.

Use frameworks to construct accounts and/or reports.

Categorizing and Coding

1. Review the interview data for each stakeholding group.
2. Unitize the data: Divide into units of meaning.
3. Formulate *categories, subcategories, and themes* identifying patterns, connections, commonalities, or regularities within the data.
4. Organize these into a category system.
5. Complement the analysis with information from non-interview data.
6. Use the category system to provide a framework for accounts and reports.

Collaborative Data Analysis

Focus groups may be used to analyze data and share information collaboratively.

Representation: Communicating Research Processes and Outcomes

6

RESEARCH DESIGN	DATA GATHERING	DATA ANALYSIS	COMMUNICATION	ACTION
INITIATING A STUDY	CAPTURING STAKEHOLDER EXPERIENCES AND PERSPECTIVES	IDENTIFYING KEY FEATURES OF EXPERIENCE	WRITING REPORTS	CREATING SOLUTIONS
Setting the stage			Reports Ethnographies Biographies	Problem solving
Focusing and framing	Interviewing	Analyzing epiphanies and illuminative experiences	PRESENTATIONS AND PERFORMANCES	Classroom practices
Literature review	Observing			Curriculum development
Sources of information	Artifacts review	Coding and categorizing	Presentations Drama Poetry	Evaluation
Ethics	Literature review	Enhancing analysis	Song Dance Art	Family and community
Validity		Constructing category systems	Video Multimedia	School plans

Contents of This Chapter

As participants engage in research processes, they need to inform each other of their progress. At the conclusion of a project, the outcomes of research also need to be communicated to stakeholding audiences.

This chapter provides an understanding of:

- The *purpose* for reporting research processes and results
- The different means used to *communicate* this information, including written reports, presentations, and performance
- Procedures for developing *written reports*
- Procedures for preparing and staging *presentations*
- Procedures for preparing and producing *performances*

Introduction

Within the Look-Think-Act framework of action research, the first Act is to present the outcomes of analysis to research participants and other stakeholding audiences (see Figure 6.1). The purpose of this process is to ensure that all acquire a body of shared meanings emerging from the research process that can be used to work toward resolution of the research issue. Participants need to *represent* the information in a form that increases clarity and understanding for all participants and stakeholders.

This chapter presents a variety of approaches to communication. Each is intended to ensure that participants and audiences of a project acquire clear understandings of both the processes and outcomes of research. According to the desired purposes, therefore, research participants may construct narrative, ethnographic, or biographic accounts that inform various audiences and stakeholders. They may also formulate presentations or performances as alternative effective means of communication.

Communication in Action Research

As people work through action research processes, it is essential for all participants and stakeholders to be informed of the continuing progress of the study in order to take their part in bringing the project to fruition. Teachers and/or groups of students

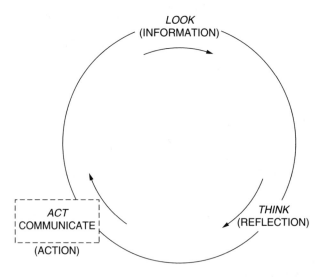

Figure 6.1
Communicating in Action Research

engaged in classroom investigations need to keep others in the class informed of their activities. If their work results in significant changes in the way their class operates, they may need to inform the school administration and/or students' parents. In larger projects, such as the evaluation of a school, the development of a new curriculum, or the institution of a new program, the work will require ongoing communication between the various stakeholders. In all these circumstances, there is a need to communicate significant features of the investigation to ensure that all parties are fully informed. Participants need, therefore, to think carefully through processes for recording and communicating their progress.

Purposeful communication provides the means for all parties—students, teachers, administrators, and parents—to understand the forces that move each others' lives, affecting their behaviors, performances, and practices. As participants become increasingly aware of the influences at work in each others' lives, they are able to take into consideration the diverse agendas and imperatives to be taken into account and to work toward mutually meaningful solutions to the problems they experience. Effective communication enables understanding.

Research participants may report to each other for the following purposes:

- To share information that keeps people informed of the processes and outcomes of the investigation
- To enable stakeholders and other audiences to understand each others' perspectives and experiences
- To check the accuracy and appropriateness of the information emerging from the investigation
- To provide an ongoing record of the project

I recently worked in a school where the issue of communication became paramount. A number of problems had emerged that appeared to result from a breakdown in communication between school and home. Teachers, parents, and administrators became aware of the need to be more clearly informed of activities pertinent to school and classroom events. The usual form of communication—sending notes home with the children—was not effective, so new processes of sharing information became a priority. Teachers and administrators began to communicate with each other and with parents in a variety of media, including written notes and memos, electronic mail, telephone trees, and verbal reports. These events emphasized the problems that arise when people are poorly informed. Many of the problems and complaints evident in early stages of the project disappeared as more effective methods of communication were developed.

Different Strokes for Different Folks: Forms of Communication

How information is shared is critical, since it is imperative not only that people acquire the so-called facts, but also that they understand the dynamic ways in which significant features of the situation impact the lives of the people involved. The "objective," formal reports so common in institutions often are inadequate vehicles for these purposes when they are framed in formalized language focusing on institutional structures and agendas.

The type of report format, therefore, needs to clearly differentiate between the research audiences and purposes since they may be pertinent to three major audiences—academic, public, and professional/organizational:

• **Academic:** University research focuses principally on the development of a body of knowledge shared with a community of scholars. The outcomes of research are reported in journals and books stored in university library collections. The knowledge is also passed on to students in order to inform and educate future professionals.

• **Public:** Research sometimes is used to inform and educate the public about significant issues. Research sponsored by government bodies, public interest groups, or community groups report their findings in the media, often incorporating their work into television documentaries or presenting it on stage or as street theatre. Thus, the outcomes of research on educational achievement levels, school curriculae, school environmental issues, school staffing, and so on, are increasingly released directly into the public domain.

• **Professional/Organizational:** Research is increasingly used for direct professional and organizational purposes to improve or strengthen programs, services, and practices. Research outcomes can be applied directly to the development of new programs and services or used to formulate solutions to significant problems in institutions, organizations, and community contexts. Teachers engage in research to better inform their pedagogical practices or to seek solutions to problems in their classrooms. Schools, school districts, or education departments engage in research to assist in the formulation of new programs, or to solve deep-seated problems, such as underachievement or excessive school drop-out rates.

The different audiences and purposes of action research require researchers to think clearly about the types of reporting that will enable them to communicate effectively with particular audiences. Examples of a range of different report formats are provided in Chapter 8. These do not cover, however, the full range of possibilities, as will become evident in the latter sections of this chapter. Depending on the stakeholders, the purpose, and the context, reporting may take the form of **written reports, presentations,** or **performances.**

Written reports provide an easy means to communicate information. They may take the form of short, informal reports providing limited information, or highly formalized reports providing detailed information about all facets of a project. Written reports provide the most common medium for maintaining a record of progress or recording the outcomes of a research process. They have great utility at all stages of research.

Verbal and/or visual **presentations** provide richer possibilities for engaging people in processes of communication. They provide more diverse and creative means of enabling people to share focused, richly textured understandings of their research activities. Verbal or visual presentations are an especially effective means for children to exchange information and reveal experience. For these groups, visual, poetic, musical, or dramatic **performances** also provide effective ways to communicate visceral understandings of their experiences and perspectives.

Reports, presentations, and performances, therefore, provide diverse means for administrators, teachers, students, and parents to convey the processes and outcomes of their research. They provide multiple methods for presenting new understandings with clarity, precision, and authenticity that enable people to contribute effectively to the ongoing development of actions and events designed to improve their situation.

Reports and Accounts: Writing People's Lives

Written reports are derived from the products of data analysis (see Chapter 5). Key features and elements identified in these processes provide the basis for accounts reflecting the perspectives, perceptions, and experiences of individuals and groups participating in the process. They may take the form of:

- Individual reports
- Group reports
- Progress reports
- Evaluation reports
- Final reports

As Denzin (1997) suggests, we are not seeking definitive or objective accounts, but evocative accounts that lead the reader to an empathetic understanding of people's lived experience. Accounts or narratives thereby provide insight into people's lives, recording the impact of events on their day-to-day feelings of well-being and their capacity to interact healthily and productively with the life-world that confronts them. They reveal the rich, densely layered tapestry of human experience, and the complex emotional world lying beneath the surface of seemingly innocuous events that breaks into view in those special moments of triumph, success, love, struggle, loss, or discord that have such a dramatic effect on people's lives.

In action research, therefore, we seek to produce evocative accounts conveying accurate insights into and understandings of the impact of events on people's lives. Writing evocative accounts entails more than the bland reporting of events. It requires report writers to find the textual means to evoke those forms of understanding. A government report that referred to the "inadequate sewage" in a school failed to evoke an understanding of the stench of excreta and the parents' ongoing fear for their children's health. Objective reports are sometimes dangerously uninformative. Extended ethnographic accounts comprised of full, richly textured narrative provide the possibility of in-depth insight into the community and/or institutional contexts in which events are played out. The accounts are inscribed with the history of the situation and reveal the interactional and emotional features of people's experience. Shorter reports such as meeting minutes, team reports, progress reports, and so on, provide more condensed accounts, but should still capture the essence of people's experience.

Life Stories: Biographies, Autobiographies, and Ethnographies

Written narrative accounts have the capacity to illuminate the often complex and deeply problematic nature of people's lived experience. In contrast to psychological case studies that interpret individual behavior from within a framework of disciplinary theory (personality, behaviorism, etc.), biographies and ethnographies provide the means to understand people's lives from their own perspective. Action research provides the means, therefore, for people to describe their lives from their own points of view.

Research processes provide the means for stakeholders to reflect on and describe their experience and to distill or crystallize salient features that may form the basis for ongoing interpretive action. This material may form the basis for biographic or semi-fictional reports revealing the history of their experience and significant features of their lives—epiphanic or defining moments—revealing the underlying dynamics of their experience. Often, the mere act of "telling their own story" is therapeutic and reveals to the individuals concerned features of their lives they had inadvertently repressed, or that they had accepted as a necessary though damaging feature of their lives. Conversely, it may reveal hidden positive dimensions of experience and enable them to see their worlds in a more positive light or become aware of new possibilities.

I have witnessed many situations where people have been greatly enlivened by opportunities to tell their stories and listen to the stories of others. In classrooms, workshops, program development projects, and many other arenas, I have experienced the joy that comes from this process. What I see is not only a sense of worth emerging from people who feel, sometimes for the first time in their lives, that someone is really listening to them; that they have something worthwhile to share with others. I am no longer surprised, but always feel gratified, when people express their appreciation in the most heartfelt terms. On more than one occasion, people have burst out in the moment, or quietly informed me later that "This changed my life!"

Something quite wonderful happens in the process. Not only does the storyteller experience the exuberance of being heard and acknowledged, but in the process they learn something significant about themselves and their school experiences. It is illuminating and sometimes revelationary. I have often seen people—storytellers and/or audience—in tears as their stories emerge. The teller does not need to be a practiced orator. Sometimes the straight recounting of events by simply spoken people—parents, old folk, children—has a dramatic impact on an audience. The presence of the people themselves can speak volumes. When people tell stories of their lives it is no small thing.

Writing personal accounts of experience as part of an action research project is not intended to reveal "the facts" or "the truth" of people's lives, but to help them look at their lives in different ways; to reinterpret events, experiences, and responses; and to come to new ways of understanding their situation. Autobiographical and ethnographic accounts provide potential useful resources that enable individuals and groups to re-evaluate their place and their interaction with others in the context; to "connect and join biographically meaningful experiences to society-at-hand and to the larger culture- and meaning-making institutions . . . " (Denzin, 1989a, p. 25).

While ethnographic accounts largely have been written by external authors, we now recognize the potential of auto-ethnographies, individuals, and groups working through self-referential processes of exploration to write accounts of their own lives. Sometimes, the stories are so sensitive, reaching into the intimate details of people's lives, that people have no desire to have them made public. In these situations, it is possible to disguise both the people and places by use of fictitious names or by providing generalized accounts revealing the major features of their experience, but not providing the means to identify particular people or places.

Joint and Collective Accounts: Connecting Stakeholder Experiences

While individual stakeholder stories sometimes reveal singular experiences relating only to one person, they often share significant experiences or perspectives with other stakeholders. Further, although they may not share the same experience, participants may be affected by the same events in different ways. We need to make connections between stakeholder experiences, therefore, in order to develop an understanding of the dynamic interactions between individuals and groups. When individual stakeholder epiphanies and features of experience have been identified, therefore, we search for connections with others:

- Focus on each epiphany or significant experience for each individual.
- Review the data for all other selected stakeholders.
- Identify features or elements of experience common to other stakeholders.
- Identify points at which other stakeholders' experiences or perspectives have been effected by the original epiphany/experience.
- Record those features or elements as a sub-list of the original epiphany.
- Take note of the number of times an experience or element is repeated for different stakeholders.

As we use this information to formulate accounts and reports, we will be able to provide information about the extent to which stakeholders share any experience or perspective. By comparing information within groups and across groups we are able to make judgments about the extent that events, experiences, or perspectives are commonly held by those within a group or shared with other groups. These types of comparison provide information that also is important at the "action" phase since it enables us to identify those common elements of experience from which productive action might be formulated (see Figure 6.2). It also enables us to identify those singularly important experiences and perspectives that may need to be taken into account in formulating solutions to the problem investigated. The terminology reveals the extent of

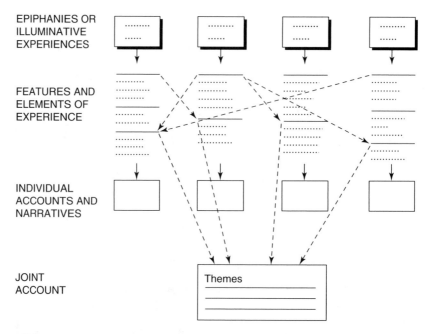

Figure 6.2
Formulating Joint Accounts

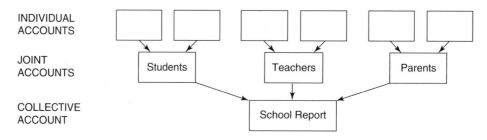

Figure 6.3
Individual, Joint, and Collective Accounts

commonality—"All teachers in this study . . . ," "Many teachers shared a concern about
. . . ," or "While some students indicated . . . others were more inclined to . . . ."

Joint accounts, therefore, provide a summary of individual accounts, but focus particularly on commonalities and differences revealed through cross-analysis of major
features and key elements. Common or similar features, in this case, may be thought
of as themes. Joint accounts provide ways of presenting the perspective and experience of stakeholding groups in a study—teachers, students, parents, and so on.

Collective accounts may present an overview of the major features and elements
of experience and perspective for each of the major groups so that a school report
may comprise features and elements drawn from each of the stakeholding groups
(see Figure 6.3). Commonalities revealed in these accounts provide the basis for col-

lective action, while points of difference suggest issues requiring negotiation (see Guba and Lincoln, 1989), so that appropriate steps can be taken to defuse or resolve potential conflicts.

> When I participated in a recent research project, analysis of data revealed that many teachers and parents expressed similar ideas about parent-teacher conferences—insufficient time, the need for more effective communication between parents and teachers, and so on.
>
> Although each perceived the same features, they sometimes expressed it from their different sides of the coin—for instance, teachers felt that parents didn't communicate effectively with teachers, while parents felt that teachers didn't clearly communicate what was expected of parents.
>
> These types of analysis provided the basis for changes the school made to parent-teacher conferences with the intent of making them more effective. More time was allocated for conferences, and individual teachers were able to implement group advisory sessions that provided parents with more detailed information. This included ways of helping parents to understand how classroom learning processes were organized and how parents could assist their children's learning.
>
> In the process, however, a number of other issues emerged that enabled the school to take steps to improve communication with families.

Accumulating Knowledge and Experience

Written reports provide the means whereby teachers may, over time, accumulate knowledge and experience that greatly enhances their capacity to deal effectively with problematic features of their professional lives. Though these processes take time and energy, and require support and resources from the institutions within which they work, in the long term, they provide resources that increase a teacher's professional capacities. They gain a stock of knowledge and skills that not only enables them to greatly enhance their teaching or administrative work, but also informs and enlivens their day-to-day work with students. The ability to listen as people tell of their experience and to provide the means whereby students, parents, and others may have the joy of telling their story and being heard is not only exhilarating in an immediate sense, but ultimately provides them with much greater status and recognition among the people who matter most—those they serve. Knowledge is power. Providing and receiving the knowledge of others' experiences is empowering for all concerned.

Written reports may, therefore, provide a historical record of significant events and projects that add to the vitality of the culture of the school. At the classroom level, many teachers provide the means for students' written work to be incorporated into "books." A written record of specific events and projects in which students engage as a result of an action research process provides the means for constructing a stronger sense of togetherness and assists in the formation of a learning community. Research reports, therefore, have the capacity not only to assist in developing solutions to particular problems, but also to contribute to the culture of the school.

Constructing Reports

Constructing effective and useful reports is an art form that sometimes requires years of practice to accomplish. By following some fundamental processes, however, most people can write a report containing relevant information and conveying emerging understandings. Those responsible for writing a report should:

- Define the *audience and purpose* of the report
- *Identify participants*
- Identify the significant *features and elements of experience*
- Construct a *report framework*
- *Write the report*
- *Review and edit* the report
- *Member check*

Audience and Purpose

Carefully define the audience and purpose of the report. Ask:

- For which particular people (or type of people) will this report be written? (e.g., students, teachers, administrators, parents, and so on; in which locations—particular classes or grades; at which schools)
- For what purposes will the report be used? (i.e., to inform people of progress on a project, assist them to understand features of people's experience, or reveal required actions?)

Participant Perspectives

Decide which participant perspectives—individuals or stakeholding groups—are to be included. Note:

- Whose experiences or agendas are central to the report
- Which people have important or significant associated experiences or agendas
- What data can be isolated for each of these individuals or groups

Review the Data

- Read the data relevant to the identified participants to become familiar with the material.
- Note particularly effective quotations illustrating key features of people's experience.
- Note the terminology and language used by participants to describe their experience.

Identify Significant Features and Elements of Experience

- Review the analyzed data to identify relevant material for the report.
- Make a copy of key features and elements of experience for each individual or group.

Construct Report Framework

Use the features and elements of experience to construct a framework for the report (see Figures 5.2 and 5.8). Note:

- Key features as headings or sub-headings
- Elements or units of meaning as the content of each heading or sub-heading

Write the Report

Write the report using the framework as a guide and incorporating the terminology and language of participants in the body of the narrative. The framework guides the writing process, but is not by itself sufficient to adequately capture people's lived experience. Authors of reports and accounts need to encompass in their writing the multiple dimensions of human experience, including emotional, physical, and interactional elements of behavior and perspective, as well as the organizational and procedural components. The framework guiding data collection is useful as a checklist for what can be included in a narrative—people, acts, activities, events, purposes, emotions, places, times, and objects. In all this, it is important for the words of participants to provide the words and language of the report. Not only should they make up the headings in the report/account, but their words should constitute the body of writing. Some writers string together sections of the unitized data to form the body of the account. Others use quotations prolifically to clearly illustrate the points they are making or the contexts they describe.

> The BSIC evaluation report (Chapter 8, p. 193) includes a heading "Teacher Perspectives" with a sub-heading "Student Achievement." The latter includes the following text: "Teachers are also enthusiastic about the response of students to the school's model of education. One teacher, comparing his experience in public schools, recounted the differences he encountered: 'You have to give students at other schools tangible rewards.'" The text continues to present details of how teachers are experiencing and interpreting student achievement, including the full range of elements drawn from the unitized data within the category.

The report should include:

- An introduction revealing the purpose and the general contents of the report
- A brief description of the context drawn from interview and observational data
- Accounts encompassing the key features of stakeholder experiences and perspectives
- Quotations capturing significant features or elements of experience
- A concluding summary highlighting the major features revealed in the report and the implications for action relevant to the issue investigated

Reports will vary widely in style, detail, and length according to the purpose of the report or the intended audience. In some instances, reports may be no more than a short summary of the key points emerging from prior stages of the research, informing participants or other stakeholders of the progress of the project. In other cases, extended reports provide detailed information for the benefit of administration or funding authorities. Formal reports for funding, professional, or academic bodies—annual reports, evaluation reports, theses, or dissertations—often require a meticulous rendering of the research process in highly structured ways.

In the "Listen to the Families" project, two forms of a final report were prepared. One, written in English and Spanish, presented parents with a one-page summary of the major outcomes of the research process in bullet form. A more extended ten-page report provided more detail for administrators and teachers at the school, revealing many details of the processes and outcomes of investigation. The former enabled parents to see that their voice had been heard, while the latter provided educators with information they used as the basis for changing parent-teacher conferences, which was the focus for the research project.

Review and Edit

Review the report. Check that:

- Its stated purposes have been accomplished: Does the report provide adequate and appropriate information to inform the intended audience?
- All relevant participant perspectives have been included.
- The language is appropriate for the intended audience.
- The report accurately reflects the perspectives and experiences of participants rather than that of the author or one stakeholding group.

Whenever I'm facilitating report writing, I continually ask the author "Who is speaking here? Whose perspective is being presented?" It is surprising how often even the most careful report writer will allow his own perspective to intrude. When we write accounts, we must take great care to ensure we don't unwittingly present material reflecting our own perceptions and interpretations of the situation. The exceptions are those situations where we overtly include our perspective as a participating stakeholder in a research process.

Member Check

Give a draft to those about whom the report is written:

- Provide time for them to read and respond.
- Talk with them in person, if possible, or by phone if not.
- Check for accuracy, sufficiency, and appropriateness of information contained in the report.
- Modify or correct according to the members' input.

Report Formats

According to the audience and purpose for which they are produced, research reports differ in length, detail, and reporting style. Reports to groups and individuals communicating progress of activities will tend to be informal and brief, while reports to organizations and institutions are likely to be more formal and detailed. They may be presented in outline or summary form; as a bulleted list; or as complex, detailed, and/or highly descriptive accounts. Chapter 8 provides a number of different forms of research reports used for school purposes. They include:

- A short evaluation report for the use of teachers and administrators
- Reports of classroom and school projects for professional audiences
- A brief report on a school project for a parent audience

Other reports, however, may take the form of:

- Meeting minutes informing participants of reports and discussions about project activities and issues
- Memoranda reporting on current activities and issues
- Formal reports for administrative and professional audiences
- Academic reports for publication in research journals
- Theses and dissertations

Presentations: Creative Communication

Presentations provide exciting ways to communicate research results to participants and stakeholding audiences. Constructed from multiple materials and using diverse presentational modes, they can captivate audiences by powerfully presenting participant perspectives and illuminating key features of the research. Presentations provide the possibility of clear and effective communication based on richly evocative accounts that accurately capture and represent peoples' experience. They may range from simple verbal presentations to complex performances incorporating multiple forms of visual and electronic media that effectively communicate with a wide variety of audiences.

Even academic and professional conferences now provide opportunities for staging a wide variety of presentations. Though direct verbal addresses from prepared papers are still common, many presentations involve creative and innovative approaches incorporating charts, overheads, or electronic materials, or roundtable interactive presentations, poster sessions, and structured dialogues. Presenters seek forms of communication that enable them to communicate information efficiently and effectively. These types of presentations are becoming increasingly common in professional and school contexts as teachers and administrators share information or report on school activities.

Such flexible formats are especially relevant in contexts where lengthy written reports may actually inhibit communication with important stakeholding audiences. Children and some adults from poorer or culturally different contexts may not have sufficient familiarity with professional or technical language to enable them to read lengthy formal reports. Further, written reports are often an inadequate vehicle for expressing the full range of participant experiences. They fail to convey the emotional, interactional features of experience, the nature of their social circumstances, or the complexities of their cultural realities. Presentations, when carefully prepared and authentically presented, provide the means for more clearly and effectively communicating the concrete reality of people's lives, and provide the elements that need to be taken into careful account when taking action. As with written reports, presentations need to be carefully and creatively planned to suit the audience, the purposes to be achieved, and the outcomes expected.

A group of Aboriginal graduate students presented an evaluative account of their experience of course work in their program. Direct verbal presentations were supplemented with role-plays, poetry, and art. Their presentations were richly peppered with Aboriginal names and terminology, and humor was an integral feature of the dialogical interaction between participants. Not only were they able to provide an enjoyable and informative experience for the audience of students and academic faculty from around the university, but they embodied the Aboriginal cultural ethos that was central to the program of study they had engaged. Derived from a preliminary focus group exploration, their presentations clearly depicted the joys, struggles, and other major features of their learning processes. It provided a dramatic counterpoint to the rather soulless, form-filling exercises usually used for class evaluations.

Audiences and Purposes

Research participants using presentations to communicate information about their research will need to identify carefully their audience and purpose in order to achieve the effectiveness of their project. The major question to be asked is, "What information should be presented, and how can we communicate most effectively with this particular audience?" In a school, audiences of children, parents, teachers, and administrators may require somewhat different presentations because different agendas will be relevant to each of those audiences, and each may have a different part to play in actions emerging from the research process. All groups, however, will need to understand each other's perspectives so that they are able to work in unison to achieve their desired purposes.

Presentations, therefore, will vary according to purposes to be achieved. Short, informal presentations help participants to communicate the progress of activities to each other, which allows progress to be monitored effectively, and ensures that all are working in unison. These types of presentations will be very different from more carefully structured and planned presentations required at key points in the research process. If participants wish to inform a key stakeholding group—administrators, funding body representatives, supporters—of the issues emerging from their inquiries to garner support for actions they wish to take, then more detailed and carefully structured presentations may be necessary.

Presentations will also be affected by desired outcomes. If participants wish to generate a clear or deeper understanding of people's experience, then participants will prepare evocative presentations designed to achieve that effect. Such presentations will be multidimensional, providing a clear picture of the context in which events occur and their impact—rational, physical, emotional, and spiritual—on the lives of participant stakeholders. This is a more emotive presentation seeking to engender understanding of the dynamics and complexities of people's experiences and perspectives. If participants wish an audience to focus on more practical issues for planning purposes, then the presentation will take a more didactic form and focus on key features and elements of the issue investigated. Presentations that keep people informed of activities in progress but require no action on their part will differ from those presentations requiring decisions, input, or actions on the part of the audience. In the latter case, the presentations themselves must be structured to make provision for audience participation at appropriate points.

In recent years, I was involved in a curriculum development project to institute a graduate program in Indigenous studies. Preliminary research with prospective students and associated audiences identified the content of the program—the skills and knowledge required by the students to achieve their educational, social, and cultural purposes. These provided the basis for content of study, teaching/learning processes, and program organization, including staffing, budgeting, space, timetable, and so on.

As we worked through developmental processes, different means were employed to inform the different audiences of program details. A charted summary of the content areas was produced and used to talk with prospective students about the program. A flowchart helped the planning team to work through organizational issues with administrative people. A series of reports provided relevant information to a variety of other stakeholders, including institutional committees and a community advisory group. These forms of presentation enabled stakeholding developmental partners and participants to maintain a clear picture of the program as it developed and ensured wide acceptance within the institution and the community.

A smaller research study at a local school developed small reports for teachers, administrators, and parents. These were presented verbally to the principal, to a meeting of school staff, and to a meeting of parents. The project was marked by high degrees of participation by parents and enabled school staff to make changes in the way they communicated with parents. The combination of written and verbal presentations provided the means to reach a wide range of participants.

Planning Presentations

Well-planned presentations ensure that stakeholding audiences are well-informed, enabling them to maintain clarity and to gain insight into the issues investigated.

Research participants will use similar processes to report writing (see p. 134) for planning presentations, defining:

- Audience—Who is the audience to whom we wish to present?
- Purpose—What is our purpose in presenting to this audience?
- Understandings—What do we wish our audience to know or understand?
- Content—What information or material will achieve this purpose?
- Format—What presentational format might best achieve this purpose?
- Outcomes—What do we wish to achieve? What outcomes are desired?

Steps in Planning

- Identify the *audience* and *purpose*.
- *Identify participants* whose experiences and perspectives are pertinent to the presentation.
- *Review the data* for each of these participants.
- *Review the categories and issues* emerging from analysis of data for each participant.
- Use categories to *construct a framework* of headings.
- *Write a script* using units of meaning and/or elements within the data.
- *Review and edit* the script, checking for accurate rendering of participant perspectives and appropriateness to audience.
- *Member check* by having participants read the script.
- *Practice* the presentation.

The basic outcome of presentation planning is an *outline* or *script* presenting the information in an easily accessible form. A bulleted outline provides a script that guides people's presentations. The script may be complemented by additional material, including quotations from people's talk or documented information to be read verbatim to an audience. For more formal presentations, people may rehearse their presentation to ensure they are clear about the material to be presented and to keep their presentation within the allotted time.

Research participants, therefore, need to carefully prepare a script that has the following basic format:

- *Introduction*
  The focus of the project—the issue investigated
  The participants
  The purpose and desired outcomes of the presentation

- *Body of the Presentation*
  Previous and current activities: What has happened or is happening
  Key issues emerging from research: What has been discovered; what is problematic
  Implications: What needs to be done (actions, next steps)

- *Conclusion*
  Review of major points covered

Presentations should be carefully scripted and directed so that each participant knows precisely where and when to speak and the material for which he or she is responsible. Practice provides both clarity and confidence, maximizing the possibility of an informative and effective presentation. This is especially important for people who are not used to speaking publicly, but their inclusion—the effect of people speaking for themselves in their own voice—dramatically increases the power of a presentation.

Only in rare situations should people read from a prepared written report. Though these types of presentations provide people with feelings of safety and accuracy, they usually detract from the purpose of the event. The written word is different in form and function than the spoken word, and people reading from a paper usually fail to convey the meaningfulness that is a necessary function of a presentation. We have all experienced presentations, delivered in mournful monotone or excited exuberance, that rattle or drone on and on. Usually, there is far too much information for the audience to absorb and little opportunity to process that information. Rarely do audiences in these situations gain appreciable understanding and retention of information. Presenting an address by reading from a prepared paper is an art that few possess.

Members of the Barrios Juntos Neighborhood Collective planned a presentation to the American Educational Research Association national conference—a rather grand event that seemed somewhat imposing to them. After carefully identifying the message they wished to present to a largely academic audience, they carefully reviewed the material they had accumulated, identifying and assessing those features that appeared central to the research in which they had engaged. These features were ordered into a framework of ideas—headings and sub-headings—and persons allocated to take responsibility for the various sections. They rehearsed their presentation a number of times, reallocating some material to different people or places, until each participant was clear on what he or she needed to say and when. The actual presentation at the conference was highly successful, providing the audience with a clear understanding of the power of community participation in a school research process. The degree of engagement of the audience was evidenced by their rapt attention and the diversity of questions they asked. The participants were highly delighted by the success of their presentation. It became an event that further heightened their research skills and feelings of empowerment.

Enhancing Verbal Presentations: Audio-Visuals

"Talk is cheap" is a common saying that has relevance to presentations. Though verbal presentations can sometimes be effective and inexpensive, it requires a skilled and practiced orator to hold an audience for an extended period. Interest and understanding is greatly extended when visual and auditory materials are incorporated into presentations. They aid clarity and enable significant quantities of factual information to be presented. Statistical summaries, numerical information, or lists of features and elements may be presented in chart form or as overheads. Charts have the advantage of providing a constantly available record of issues, but suffer sometimes from problems of size. Overheads and other electronic means of displaying information have great clarity, but can only project one sheet at a time and thus limit the flexibility of a presentation.

A variety of visual aids complement and enhance verbal information. Diagrams, maps, concept maps, symbolic representations, figures, and so on, provide effective ways for presenting information and focusing attention. Whiteboards or chalkboards also enable the active construction of illustrations and diagrams to stimulate attention and enable the structured exposition of a wide range of subject matter.

These processes can be presented using electronic media in the form of audio or video recording, or as electronic presentations created with software such as PowerPoint. It is important to ensure that these are used in moderation because extended use of videos or electronic media can be detrimental to a presentation. Their overuse can create a passive audience and detract from feelings of engagement. Judicious use of electronic media, however, can provide vivid illustrations or large bodies of information that greatly enhance people's ability or willingness to participate in ongoing dialogue. As a stimulus, they are sometimes unparalleled.

At each stage, therefore, we need to ask how we can best achieve the types of understanding we desire. Presentations can be greatly enhanced by using:

• Maps	• Figures
• Charts	• Overheads
• Artwork	• Audio recording
• Concept maps	• Video recording
• Lists	• Electronic presentations

For some years, colleagues and I have presented workshops on cultural sensitivity or race relations to a variety of audiences. The intent was to assist them in investigating ways to modify their professional work practices to ensure greater effectiveness in cross-cultural contexts. These sessions have been greatly enhanced by having participants view short segments of a video film showing Aboriginal people presenting accounts of their experiences. One popular segment presents an old man talking of the time police and welfare officers came to take away his children. Moved to tears, he narrates the way he was prevented from taking any action as his children were driven away. Returning the next day he talks of how he put a piece of old tin over his only remaining reminder of his children—their footprints in the sand. This segment, used many times in workshops and presentations, never fails to evoke rich and sometimes intense discussions. It provides keen insight into the way past events continue to affect interactions between racial groups in Australian community life. Sometimes a picture *is* worth a thousand words.

For some audiences, presentations may take on an almost concert-like appearance. Creative presentations may incorporate a variety of materials and performances (see the following paragraphs) to provide a rich body of factual information and authentic understandings of people's lived realities. Presentations, constructed from materials derived from the analysis of data, use key features and elements as the basis for a script, incorporating quotes from the data to highlight important information. Presenters may incorporate tape-recorded information derived from participant interviews, read from reviewed materials, or as appropriate, segments of video or aural recordings, poems, songs, or role-plays. The rich variety of possibilities enables audiences of children, youth, and adult participants to fully express the ideas with which they have been working.

Interactive Presentations

Presentations are more effective when they are interactive. It is difficult to stimulate interest or involvement in a research process when the audience is passive and uninvolved. Where presenters dominate presentations, other participants are likely to feel left out, marginalized, as if their perspectives and issues are less important. Wherever possible, presentations should provide opportunities for all participants to interact with the material presented. At regular intervals, audiences should have the opportunity to participate in the unfolding presentation, comment on issues, ask for clarification, or offer their perspectives on issues presented. As part of an "hermeneutic dialectic"—meaning making dialogue—these processes not only enable people to extend and clarify their understanding, but also increase their feelings of inclusion and ownership in the project at hand.

Presentations may also include small group work that enables participants to explore issues in greater depth by engaging in dialogue or perusing related documents or materials. Feedback from small-group discussions provides a further means to gain clarity and understanding, especially about points of contention or uncertainty. This points to the need for flexibility to allow participants to take advantage of opportunities arising in the course of presentations. It is possible to turn a presentation into a workshop or focus group so that audiences become active participants in the ongoing development of the investigation. In these circumstances, time may be allocated for this purpose to allow participants to take advantage of the ideas emerging from their work together.

When I work with research groups, I often have them chart the key elements of their recent activities. Each group then speaks to their chart, reporting on their progress and any issues arising. The audience is able to comment or ask questions to clarify or extend the presenters' comments. This not only informs the audience clearly, but helps the presenters to extend their thinking about the issues raised—an integral part of the process of researching.

Performances: Representing Experience Artistically and Dramatically

Performances extend the possibilities for providing deeper and more effective understandings of the nature of people's experiences. They present multiple possibilities for entering people's subjective worlds to provide audiences with empathetic understandings that greatly increase the power of the research process. Performances enable participants to report on their research through:

- Drama
- Role-play
- Song
- Poetry
- Dance
- Visual art
- Electronic media

By engaging their work through performance, research participants enable audiences to take the perspective of the person whose life is performed, to enter their experience vicariously, and to understand more empathetically their life-worlds. Using artistic and dramatic media, researchers are able to capture and represent the deeply complex, dynamic, interactive, and emotional qualities of everyday life. They can engage in richly evocative presentations comprehensible to children, families, cultural minorities, the poor, and other previously excluded audiences.

Poetry, music, drama, and art provide the means for creating illuminative, transformative experiences for presenter and audience alike, stimulating awareness of the different voices and multiple discourses occurring in any given social space (Denzin, 1996; Prattis, 1985). They provide the means to interrogate people's everyday realities by juxtaposing them within the telling, acting, or singing of stories, thus revealing the differences that occur therein and providing the possibility of therapeutic action (Denzin, 1997; Trinh, 1991). While performances fail to provide the certainty required of experimental research, or to reinforce the authority of an official voice (Atkinson, 1992), they present the possibility of producing compassionate understandings promoting effective change and progress (Rorty, 1989).

This is clearly a postmodern response, making possible the construction of evocative accounts revealing people's concrete human experience. Performances provide the means of complementing or enhancing reports and presentations by:

- Studying the world from the perspective of research participants
- Capturing their lived experience
- Enabling participants to discover truths about themselves and others
- Recognizing multiple interpretations of events and phenomena
- Embedding experience in local cultural contexts
- Recording the deeply felt emotion—love, pride, dignity, honor, hate, envy— and the agonies, tragedies, triumphs, and peaks of human experience embedded in people's actions, activities, and behavior
- Representing people's experience symbolically, visually, or aurally in order to achieve clarity and understanding

In recent years, I have been privy to some stunning performances that have greatly extended my understanding of people's experience. I have seen class evaluations include poetry, song, role-play, and art, which provided me with deep insights into the learning experiences of my students and enabled me, as teacher, to extend my thinking about the ways my classes are organized and operate. I have seen the powerful artistic work of small children provide wonderfully illuminative representations of their classroom experience. I have sat in the audience deeply moved by middle-school children's dramatic presentation of an issue touching their school lives. In all these, I have been surprised by the depth and extent of my responses to these performative presentations, feeling deeply touched by what I have seen and heard and more sensitive to the nature of the performers' experience and how the issues they represent affect their lives.

Planning Performances: Developing a Script

Performances are built from the outcomes of data analysis, using techniques similar to those of fashion reports and presentations. Key features and elements provide the material to produce a performance with participants working creatively to develop effective means for representing their experience. These may be constructed as poems, songs, or drama, or represented as symbolic or visual art. As with written and other forms of representation, performances need to be conducted with a clear understanding of the purpose they wish to achieve with a specific audience. Participants should ask: "What do we wish this audience to know or understand? And how might we best achieve that knowledge or understanding through our performance?"

- Identify the *audience* and *purpose.*
- *Identify participants* whose experiences and perspectives are to be represented.
- *Review the data* for each of these participants.
- *Review the categories and issues* emerging from analysis of data for each participant.
- Use categories to *construct a framework* of key features of experience and perspective.
- *Write a script* using units of meaning and/or elements within the data.
- *Review and edit* the script, checking for accurate rendering of participant perspectives and appropriateness to audience.
- *Member check* by having participants read the script.
- *Rehearse* the performance.

Producing Performances

As with any script, there are decisions to be made about who will perform which roles, how the setting will be designed, what clothing or costumes will be worn, and who will direct the staging of the performance (i.e., take responsibility for overall enactment of the performance).

Rehearsals are an important feature of performances that enable participants to review the quality and appropriateness of their production and provide opportunities to clarify or modify the script. People will also become familiar with their roles, sometimes memorizing the parts they need to play, though readings may be used effectively where people have minimal time for preparation or rehearsal.

Sometimes action research requires research participants to formulate on-the-spot performances so that role-plays requiring minimal preparation provide an effective means for people to communicate their messages. For this mode of performance, participants should develop an outline of a script from the material emerging from their analysis and ad-lib the words as they enact the scene they wish to represent. Role-plays are especially powerful when participants act out their own parts and speak in their own words to reveal clear understandings of their own experiences and perspectives.

Video and Electronic Media

Although live performances provide effective ways to communicate the outcomes of research, video and other electronic media offer powerful and flexible tools for reaching more extended audiences. Not only do video productions provide possibilities for more sophisticated performances, but they enable the inclusion of people whose personal make-up inhibits them from participating in live performances. The technology now available allows video productions to be presented on larger screens, to be shown on computer screens, or to be incorporated into more complex on-line productions.

Dirk Schouten and Rob Watling (1997) provide a useful model for integrating video into education, training, and community development projects. Their process includes:

- Making a recording scheme
- Recording the material
- Making an inventory of the material
- Deciding what functions the material will serve in the text
- Making a rough structure for the text
- Making an edit scheme on the basis of the rough structure
- Editing the text

Although producing a quality video requires high levels of expertise and careful production, current technology enables even schoolchildren to produce short and effective products. By recording events in the classroom, school and community students can create engaging and potentially productive works that extend the educational potential of classroom life. This type of recording enables children to provide sometimes-dramatic renderings of their experience and to engage in forms of research previously out of their reach.

Video taping also provides research participants with a variety of means for storing and presenting their material. Possibilities today include storing it in videotape form, on CD/DVD disks, or within computers. These are then viewed or transmitted through a variety of media, including video and DVD players, streaming video, and community television. These formats provide the possibility of reaching a wide variety of audiences or using video productions for many effective educational purposes.

Examples of Performances

Case Study 1: Art in the Classroom

An elementary teacher was concerned that the district was cutting funds for art, therefore restricting her possibilities for both teaching art and engaging in art-like activities for student learning processes. She worked with her elementary students, engaging in an extensive exploration of how art was part of their classroom experience. Through extensive dialogue, writing, and drawing, they mapped out the different ways they experienced art and the ways art was incorporated into their learning. By sorting through the information and materials accumulated in this experience, individual students were able to identify important features of their experience of art, and to represent them artistically and in writing. These products were incorporated into a book produced by the class, that Lisa intended to have presented to the district superintendent. The class also produced a large mural, to which everyone contributed, using similar materials to represent the class perspective on the issue.

Case Study 2: Sexual Harassment in School

Following a classroom discussion, a teacher met with five of her middle-school female students to explore the issue of sexual harassment in their school life. She facilitated a process of inquiry in which they first spoke of their experiences and perspectives on harassment, then identified key features of that experience. This was extremely helpful in keeping their focus clear and their thoughts manageable. They decided to incorporate boys into their exploration and extended their understanding of how males are affected by sexually oriented harassment. They wrote a performance piece—Speaking Out—based on what they had learned, then made a triptych—a three-paneled board—on which the audience could write down their ideas about harassment after the performance. This was performed at the school and later at the university. Three of the students also wrote an article—Students Against Harassment—for publication in the monthly school newsletter. By the end of the school year, the number of reported incidents of sexual harassment had dropped from four to five each week to one to two every two weeks.

Case Study 3: A Classroom Opera

Pam Rossi (1997) wrote her doctoral dissertation as a libretto (a script for an opera) based on her work with 31 children in a bilingual first-grade classroom. The opera, composed by the children and their teachers, describes how the children, in the course of a two-way bilingual program, came to view Spanish, English, and Chinese as three of the many choices available when creating meaning. By the end of the creation of the opera, all the students had achieved some degree of bilingualism. The libretto is comprised of a plot synopsis, a cast of characters, an overture, and a traditional act/scene structure. Rossi notes:

> The children were participants in a creating, producing, and performing community of inquirers whose interests and ideas informed and contributed to the process and product, making and sharing meaning in a variety of modes. . . . [O]pera is an awakening to multiple literacies through the facilitation of adults who were mutually engaged in a challenging project, shared their expertise and offered the opportunity for guided practice and ongoing critique in different sign systems. [It] is a vehicle for creating synergistic culture with assessment embedded in the process of doing and undergoing, acting and reflecting. (Rossi, 2000, p. 3)

Case Study 4: Transformative Evaluation

A university professor asked students in his graduate class to reflect on their experience of the class. They interviewed each other in pairs, then identified the key features of their individual experiences collaboratively. Each person used material from his or her own interview to formulate a performance representing the meanings the class had for each of them. Through poetry, art, song, drama, dialogue, symbolic presentation, and the use of a fractal, each provided a wonderfully descriptive and powerful representation of his or her experience of learning. The instructor was able to gain deep insights into the types of learning that were important for them, the extent of their feelings of competence, and the features of the class that enhanced their learning. Dialogue following these performances greatly enhanced class members' understanding of their own learning processes, providing ideas they were able to use in their own teaching. It was a dramatic and forceful indication of the way performances might be used to enhance the power and utility of an evaluation process.

Case Study 5: Quilt-Making: Understanding Teaching History

Ann Claunch (2000), an elementary school teacher, wished to understand how children learned history. Frustrated by textbooks and a curriculum presenting isolated facts along a timeline dissociated from the larger picture of social events, she moved from presenting history inductively, small to large, to a more deductive approach using narratives rather than textbooks in her teaching of history. She used a conceptual plan of a yearlong curriculum as a road map to broaden her thinking. Through reflection, dialogue, and review of literature, she recorded key features of what she learned as she reformulated her teaching, creating visual representations of her ideas and experience. "Representing my thoughts with images forced me to sort my thinking into concise statements, and the artistic representation of understanding paralleled what I had asked elementary students to do in my research." These images were fashioned into a quilt design that provided a unique and informative display of her project.

Summary

This chapter presents three main formats for presenting the outcomes of research: *written reports, presentations,* and *performances.*

These provide evocative accounts enabling empathetic understanding of participant experience. They should:

- Clearly and accurately *represent* participant *experiences* and *perspectives*
- Be constructed to suit specific *audiences* and *purposes*

Written reports may take the form of *accounts, narratives, biographies,* or *ethnographies* written as individual, joint, or collective accounts. They may take the form of *informal summary reports* for project participants, *formal reports* for professional and administrative audiences, or academic reports for research journals.

Presentations may integrate *a variety of media,* including verbal reports, charts, flowcharts, maps, concept maps, art, figures, overheads, audio tapes, video, and electronic presentations.

Performances may include *drama, art, poetry, music,* or other formats. These may be stored, displayed, and presented in a variety of visual, aural, and electronic forms.

Procedures for constructing *written reports* or *scripts* for presentations and performances include:

- Identifying *audience* and *purpose*
- Selecting participant *perspectives*
- Reviewing the *data*
- Selecting *key features* and *elements* of experience from the analyzed data
- Constructing a *framework/outline* using these features
- *Writing* the report/script
- *Reviewing* and *editing* the report/script
- *Member checking* for accuracy and appropriateness

Taking Action: Passion, Purposes, and Pathways

RESEARCH DESIGN	DATA GATHERING	DATA ANALYSIS	COMMUNICATION	ACTION
INITIATING A STUDY	CAPTURING STAKEHOLDER EXPERIENCES AND PERSPECTIVES	IDENTIFYING KEY FEATURES OF EXPERIENCE	WRITING REPORTS	CREATING SOLUTIONS
Setting the stage			Reports Ethnographies Biographies	Solving problems
Focusing and framing	Interviewing	Analyzing epiphanies and illuminative experiences	PRESENTATIONS AND PERFORMANCES	Classroom practices
Literature review	Observing			Curriculum development
Sources of information	Artifacts review	Coding and categorizing	Presentations Drama Poetry	Evaluation
Ethics	Literature review	Constructing category systems	Song Dance Art	Family and community
Validity			Video Multimedia	School plans

Contents of This Chapter

This chapter describes ways to use the outcomes of data analysis to devise systematic actions to resolve problems and issues on which research has focused. It describes how to:
- Solve specific problems in classrooms
- Formulate and implement planned activities within school settings

The chapter then focuses on the development of curricula, syllabi, and lesson plans. Two approaches to curriculum planning are presented:
- Traditional curriculum planning
- Transformative curriculum leadership

The chapter also describes how action research may be used for purposes of evaluation and assessment. Three models are presented:
- Responsive evaluation
- Action Evaluation: Open inquiry and audit review

Action research is also presented as a method for developing *professional development* programs as a means of creating purposeful *links with families* and the community and as a *strategic planning* process for schools.

Introduction

The second "Action" phase of inquiry applies the knowledge and understandings emerging from research inquiry for immediate practical purposes—resolution of the problem or issue on which research has focused. The next step, therefore, is an important transition moving from essentially reflective and communicative processes to practical actions that enable researchers to achieve the purposes of their inquiry. It is here where "the rubber meets the road," and people take specific actions to modify teaching practices, develop new classroom procedures, or engage new learning processes. Action research is used at the school, community, or district level to enhance the effectiveness of such activities as curriculum planning, program evaluation, strategic planning, and policy making.

The Look-Think-Act cycle signifies the need for research participants to "Look" at the new understandings emerging from data analysis, "Think" about the implications of that information, and plan appropriate instructional, curriculum, or evaluative "Act-ions" (see Figure 7.1).

Action research can be used to discover solutions to discrete problems that emerge in any school or classroom. This does not, however, encompass the full potential of action research as a tool of inquiry. Many of the educators' regular tasks—curriculum development, syllabus construction, evaluation, and so on—may be greatly strengthened by the application of systematic processes of inquiry. Curriculum development, for instance, is not merely a process of constructing a scope and sequence of a fixed set of topics. It is the development and application of an educational philosophy that formulates a set of educational objectives and seeks to systematically and creatively construct teaching/learning processes for accomplishing

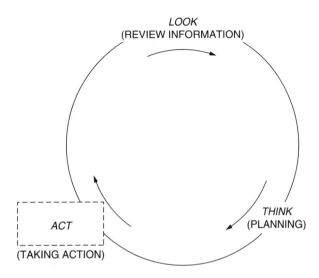

Figure 7.1
Taking Action

required outcomes. Curriculae are not arbitrary bodies of information, but complex constructions often requiring careful gathering and analysis of a large body of information. Curriculum development can be seen as an ongoing process of action research. Similarly, planning and development of classroom teaching/learning processes, or the evaluation of a program of learning, may be fruitfully engaged as a process of systematic inquiry.

The central feature of such developments is that a culture of inquiry emerges in the classroom or school so that students, teachers, and other stakeholders increase their research skills and capabilities and apply them automatically to everyday educational problems. As a culture of inquiry, action research becomes an integral part of the teaching/learning, curriculum, assessment, and planning processes of the classroom and school.

Engaging People's Passions

Education is a wonderfully complex activity requiring carefully structured and skillfully implemented programs of learning to provide for the complex needs of students. Schools are not just credential factories, but institutions whose purpose is to engage the highly sensitive task of extending human learning so that students become well-rounded, healthy individuals who live as productive, moral, and knowledgeable citizens in safe and democratic communities. Well-structured school programs are the manifestation of carefully constructed educational philosophies encompassing the physical, social, cultural, moral, and spiritual dimensions of human life.

Although programs of learning can easily become so highly routinized and ritualized that people lose sight of the underlying purposes of education, there is enormous scope for people to creatively engage educational practices that provide innovative, exciting, and effective approaches to learning. It is possible to attain any set of educational objectives in a variety of ways—to take a seemingly dull set of learning content or procedures and invest them with highly productive life and energy.

These kinds of outcome are increased dramatically when teachers, students, and/or families participate in the development of educational plans and activities. The success of a research and learning project rests as much on the development of high levels of commitment and ownership as on the skillful enactment of techniques of inquiry (See Index of Engagement, Chapter 3). When people are truly invested in activities enabling them to take action on an issue about which they are concerned, they often do so with *passion*. They take on feelings of ownership that enhance their capacity and willingness to invest themselves in the project at hand.

As a teacher, I am aware that the best classes I have taught are imbued with this sense of passion. In recent years, I have taught many courses by formulating and enacting the class syllabus in conjunction with class members, consulting with them about the aims of the class (i.e., what they wished to acquire through participation), the course content, learning processes, and evaluation procedures. I review class learning processes regularly to ensure that the content of the class is meaningful and applicable to their everyday professional and/or private lives. With few exceptions this process has produced highly successful classes; participants evincing high levels of commitment and demonstrating high levels of skill and understanding. In a number of cases the relationships nurtured through these participatory processes have endured as class participants continue to meet (sometimes over a period of years), share, and explore features of what has become a life-long process of learning (Stringer et al., 1997).

When taking action, we need to continue engaging the working principles of action research presented in Chapter 2:

- **Relationships:** Maintaining positive working relationships with all stakeholders
- **Communication:** Informing stakeholders of ongoing activities
- **Participation:** Providing opportunities for stakeholders to engage in worthwhile activities
- **Inclusion:** Including all stakeholders and all relevant issues

A key feature of this process is the need to ensure that the primary stakeholders—those principally affected by the issue—are centrally involved in the process. If student apathy is an issue, then apathetic students need to be involved centrally in the process. Where teachers and/or administrators are concerned about the lack of involvement of parents, then it is necessary to include uninvolved parents in the research process. The relationships that emerge provide the basis for extended and ongoing actions having the potential to transform people's attitudes and to energize the whole context in which they live and work. As we move from analysis to action, therefore, plans made for the ongoing work of school and classroom will be greatly enhanced by the inclusion of stakeholders in the process. From little things, big things grow.

Solving Problems: Action Planning in Classrooms and Schools

Sometimes solutions to the research problem emerge spontaneously as people see clearly what steps they need to take to work toward resolution of the issue they have studied. Often, however, careful planning is required to ensure successful resolution of the problem investigated. Solutions to problems may require actions to change any aspect of classroom or school life—teaching/learning processes, timetable, organization of the class, syllabi, parent involvement, homework, relationships, and so on. The following section delineates a simple planning process for this purpose.

Setting Priorities: Establishing an Action Agenda

Having engaged in data collection and analysis, research participants need to step back a few paces to scrutinize the information they have acquired. They will review information contained in reports, presentations, or performances and identify key issues to be addressed. From these, they will construct a set of agendas upon which they will take action.

Research participants will:

- Review the research *focus, question,* and *objectives.*
- Review the framework of *issues, key features,* and *elements* emerging from data analysis.
- From these, select *agendas* requiring action.
- *Prioritize* the issues, distinguishing those needing immediate action from those that may be handled in the medium or long term.

As part of the BSIC evaluation, the school staff reviewed the report based on the framework of concepts and issues emerging from investigation:

Student Experiences

Attention from Teachers
Improved Grades
Freedom and Diversity

Teacher Perspectives

Student Achievement
Relationships with Students
Inquiry Curriculum
Learning Materials

Administration

Demands and Resources
Values and Behavior
Space

After discussing all of the issues contained in the report, they decided that their priorities for action would focus on curriculum development, learning materials, professional development, staff orientations, and organizational planning. This action agenda defined areas in which staff would work to improve the effectiveness of the school.

Creating Pathways: Constructing an Action Plan

Carefully formulated plans enable research participants to envision the concrete steps needed to accomplish a desired outcome. Participants devise action plans for each issue identified as a priority in the action agenda. Each plan will:

- Review the *problem, research question,* and *research objectives.*
- Review the analyzed data to identify significant *issues* and *features.*

- From those issues and features, select items requiring attention.
- List items in order of priority to formulate an *action agenda*.
- Distinguish those items requiring immediate action from those requiring medium or long-term attention.
- For each agenda, devise an action plan that includes:
  - A statement of overall *purpose* (Why).
  - A set of *objectives* to be attained (What).
  - A sequence of *tasks* and *steps* for each objective.
  - The *people* responsible for each task and activity (Who).
  - The *place* where the tasks will be done (Where).
  - The *time* when tasks should commence and be completed (When).
- Make arrangements to monitor and support people as they enact their tasks.

Some of my colleagues were involved in a project focusing on "increased juvenile crime." Participants restated the issue as a goal: "To decrease juvenile crime." Reviewing the analysis from previous phases of research revealed objectives related to this goal. In a context where both parents were often engaged in the workforce, factors related to increased juvenile crime had included lack of youth leisure activities, poor school attendance, and lack of after-school programs. These were restated as three objectives: To develop youth leisure activities, to improve youth school attendance, and to organize after-school programs. Teams of relevant stakeholders developed a plan for each issue and brought them to a combined planning session for discussion, modification, and endorsement of all stakeholders. In this case, each planning group included a member from each of the primary stakeholding groups. The issue of poor school attendance, for instance, had a team that included teachers, young people, school administrators, and parents.

A simple six question framework—Why, What, How, Who, Where, and When—provides a useful basis for systematic planning. Using the previous example as the basis, it would look like this:

- **Why:** State the overall purpose of these activities—for example, to reduce juvenile crime. This *purpose* or *goal* statement should describe the ultimate end point of the project.
- **What:** State what actions are to be taken in the form of a set of *objectives*—for example, to organize an after-school program for teenagers and to develop a youth center.
- **How:** Define a sequence of *tasks* and *steps* for each objective.
- **Who:** List the *people* responsible for each task and activity.
- **Where:** State the *place* where the tasks will be done—at a school, a community center, a youth club, people's homes, and so on.
- **When:** State the *time* when work on each task should commence and when it should be completed.

PURPOSE (Why): What are we trying to achieve?							
OBJECTIVE What	TASKS How	PERSON(S) Who	START When	FINISH	LOCATION Where	RESOURCES	FUNDS
1. Establish a youth center	a. Obtain permission b. Repair and renovate c. Plan organization	Ms. Jones Lions Club Students Volunteers	6.3.02	12.6.02	Disused church	Paint Timber Tools	$1,500 School disctict Town council Goverment grant
2. Establish after-school program	a. Establish an art program b. Establish a sports program c. Establish tutoring program	Mr. Whipple Jenny Bruce Jose Venus	1.5.02	4.4.02	Youth center	Art materials Sports equipment	$350 School district Fees

Figure 7.2
Planning Chart

A planning chart may be used to clearly articulate all facets of the work (see Figure 7.2). The chart clearly defines all dimensions of the project and allows people to see their places in the broader scheme of things. It also identifies the resources required to complete the tasks and identifies the source of funds. It provides a concrete vision of the active community of which they are a part and enables participants to check on their progress as they work through the various stages of the project together.

A recent study by a classroom teacher investigated why children were not completing assigned reading for homework. The teacher assumed the children didn't like reading, which accounted for non-completion of homework—a perception reinforced by the fanciful excuses students provided for their non-compliance. A systematic investigation, however, revealed significant degrees of interest in reading, but only in certain circumstances and for certain types of reading. Having completed her data gathering and analysis, she reviewed the basis for her study:

- **Research Problem:** Students are failing to complete reading assignments.
- **Research Question:** Why are students failing to complete reading assignments?

> - **Research Objective:** To find ways of improving student engagement in reading.
>
> She then reviewed her data analysis, identifying the most significant ideas and issues emerging from her observations of student behavior and student accounts of their experience. These included:
>
> - Disinterest in silent reading activities
> - High levels of interest in group reading activities
> - High levels of interest in oral reading activities
>
> As a result of this investigation, the teacher was able to define an action agenda and to incorporate a new plan for reading into her class syllabus. She placed more emphasis on oral reading and group reading activities in class and relied less on individual silent reading in class or at home.

Reviewing the Plan

Once details have been entered on the chart, participants can review the plan to check and clarify each person's responsibilities, the sequence of activities, and the materials and resources required for each task. Questions they can use include:

- Have all needed materials and/or equipment been identified? Who will obtain them? From where? When?
- Are funds needed? Where will they come from? Who will organize them? When?
- Do people have adequate time to accomplish their tasks?
- Should other people be involved? For what tasks? Who will ask them? How will they become part of the process? Who will describe the project to them? How can they become part of our community?

Each of these elements is included in the review of the plan, with objectives, tasks, and activities carefully defined and assigned. Larger or more complex issues may require monitoring an extensive array of activities, but smaller projects usually need only limited time and resources for planning.

Sometimes planning procedures become stalled because people focus on emerging difficulties. If statements such as: "What about . . . ," "Yes, but we can't do this because . . . ," "The principal won't allow . . . ," "Parents can't . . . ," "Students aren't capable of . . . ," "We haven't the time to . . . ," "The funds aren't available to . . . ," and so on are left unanswered, people will soon become de-energized, and an air of futility will arise.

Each of these types of concerns needs to be formally acknowledged and clearly recorded, then incorporated into the planning process. It is essential that these issues be seen as problems to be solved, rather than reasons not to take action. Most statements are easily resolved, but sometimes careful and creative thinking is needed. Each needs to be reformulated from a *problem* to a statement of an *objective* or *task* which is entered into the action plan. The problem "Funds aren't available," for instance, might be formulated as an objective "To seek funds from . . . ," or "To search for sources of funding for . . . from . . . ." This objective would be extrapolated through *tasks and activities,* a *person* responsible for the tasks, and a *time-line* for beginning and completing the tasks.

Some of the previous statements point to the need to include other stakeholders in the process. If the principal and students, for instance, are included in the process, then their perspectives and agendas can be accommodated immediately. If not, then work needs to be done to ensure their perspectives and agendas are included in the plan so that "What the principal will/can allow" becomes part of the creative formulation of the plan of action.

Supervision: Supporting and Monitoring Progress

It is important that someone supervises the implementation of the plan. A designated person will confirm that people are able to carry out their tasks in the time allocated and assist them to work through minor problems. The person supervising will communicate with participants regularly, using informal conversations in staff rooms or other common meeting places or by phone messages or e-mail. In monitoring progress, the supervising person should also see himself or herself as offering personal support, especially for people working in difficult situations or carrying out difficult or complex tasks. Often, in these situations, they merely need to be a listening ear, providing a means for participants to debrief, vent where necessary, or review the work they're doing.

Progress should also be monitored at meetings of participants. These should be regular enough to ensure people remain committed to the project and to each other. Meetings should provide opportunities for people to report on their activities, to review the overall plan, to make any modifications or changes in objectives and tasks, and to celebrate successes.

Classroom Teaching and Learning

Action research may be applied to a wide range of teaching/learning processes, including the construction of a class syllabus, lesson planning, and student assessment. Essentially it enables teachers to engage inquiry learning as a tool for instruction and provides rich possibilities for engaging students in learning processes that greatly enliven and enrich their classroom life. The Look-Think-Act process applied to lesson planning enables teachers to systematically acquire and analyze information that will enable them to construct highly effective programs of learning. It provides opportunities to inquire systematically into the meanings embedded in state or district curriculum standards and extend understanding of the broader purposes and possibilities for student learning.

Engaging students in the development of class syllabi may appear time consuming, but the deeper understandings of the purposes of the curriculum and the increased levels of ownership students acquire are likely to lead to more meaningful and effective learning. Where students can make sense of the purposes and processes of the curriculum—their own learning—they are apt to engage with interest and energy.

Constructing Programs of Learning: Constructing a Syllabus

As an action research process, syllabus construction commences with a review and analysis of a mandated curriculum. Research questions investigate features of the curriculum and lead to the development of a program of learning:

- **Purpose:** What do (we) students need to accomplish? What is the goal or purpose to be achieved?
- **Objectives:** What would (we) students need to do to achieve this goal/purpose?
- **Content:** What knowledge and/or skills would (we) students need to learn in order to accomplish this goal/purpose?
- **Learning Processes:** How would (we) students learn these sets of skills and knowledge?
- **Learning Outcomes:** How would (we) students demonstrate the skills or knowledge acquired? How can (we) students apply these skills and knowledge to demonstrate accomplishment of stated goals/purposes?
- **Resources:** What resources or materials are needed?
- **Organization:** How can answers to these questions be organized into a coherent program of learning?

These questions provide the basis for exploration, description, clarifying, and construction of sections of the syllabus that may be recorded within a syllabus framework (see Figure 7.3).

GOAL/PURPOSE: Statement of broad goal or purpose to be achieved.				
OBJECTIVES	LEARNING PROCESSES	CONTENT	LEARNING OUTCOMES	LEARNING RESOURCES

Figure 7.3
Syllabus Framework

The first time I tried a truly participatory approach to construction of a syllabus was in a research class I taught at Texas A&M University in the spring semester of 1993. In the first class session, I asked students "What would you like to learn?" and "How would you like to learn it? I'd like you to help me formulate a syllabus for the course." My intent was to model a community-based approach to course planning processes. I wished to demonstrate how we could determine objectives for the class appropriate to their academic and professional needs. I also hoped to demonstrate that the content and strategies suited those objectives and were encompassed within course requirements that their schedules could accommodate.

The silence that followed was underlined by the emotions reflected in the eyes of the class members and the worry lines that furrowed their brows and wrinkled their eyes. Some kept very still. Others stirred restlessly, moved cautiously in their seats, and quietly shuffled their feet under the desks.

Eventually, someone provided a suggestion. "I would like to learn how to do observations in the real world."

"Real world observations," I wrote on the board.
"How to do ethnographic studies," a thick Texan drawl suggested.
"Applying research across the community," came another response.
As the list emerged, a spark of interest was ignited that I continued to fan with affirmative comments. As we reviewed the completed list, I commented on the variety of interests and agendas and indicated that these items would provide the basis for the syllabus and asked for suggestions about how the syllabus could be organized—what types of learning activities might be relevant, what projects might be appropriate to provide them with opportunities to practice what was learned, how they might evaluate those projects, and so on.

As we explored these issues, some people became excited as the range of possibilities emerged—presentations, debates, practice sessions, "fish bowls," group projects, discussions, ethnographic studies, journals, and more. For many, however, the levels of discomfort became increasingly evident, and some started to ask, at first obliquely, then more pointedly, when they were to get a class syllabus, when they would find out the class requirements, and what were the dates on which assignments and projects would be due.

By the end of class, the energy levels, both positive and negative, were high. Some students talked excitedly about the possibilities that were emerging, while others huddled in small groups exchanging obviously worried comments. Though I had provided a syllabus labeled "preliminary," the content and requirements of the class were described in only the very broadest of terms. By the end of the class, more detail of content had been negotiated, but course requirements had not been specified. The participants' body language spoke to me more clearly than their voices. "What are we going to do?" their worried frowns asked. "I don't know where I'm going, or when I will have to do my assigned work. How can I prepare a study schedule? How will I fit my class work in with my work requirements?" Some were unperturbed and their voices expressed excitement and interest, while others, although intrigued by the process and interested in the content of the course that had emerged, exhibited responses that ranged between consternation, concern, annoyance, doubt, disquiet, and anxiety.

By next class, I had prepared a more detailed supplementary syllabus written on chart paper and taped to the board and asked for comments and suggestions. I explained that I had crafted it, as far as possible, to fit the inputs they had provided the previous week. I sought their approval of the syllabus I had planned, and asked whether they had additions or amendments to suggest. There was some discussion and debate about the projects I had assigned, and we were able to make a number of modifications and amendments, including the times when work would be due. By the end of the first hour the syllabus had been ratified by all members of the class. Once again, the range of emotions extant in the class was evident in the participants' responses as excitement and energy competed with relief as the predominant emotions.

From the energy that emerged from the interest, excitement, doubt, and disquiet of those classes, I was able to fashion an ongoing process of inquiry and discovery that I marked as one of the most exciting I have taught in my teaching career. Such was the feeling of community generated by this process that members continue to meet on a regular basis. They stage an annual retreat where they share ideas and reflect on their professional experiences.

The experience has changed my approach to teaching dramatically. I rarely engage students, even small children, without asking them to help me construct their learning process. Teaching, for me, has become a continuing process of inquiry and discovery that continues to enhance my educational life.

Lesson Plans

In general terms, the syllabus framework presented in Figure 7.3 provides the basis for planning lessons. Students may work with the teacher, within groups, or individually to construct a plan for a learning program. By working through iterations of the Look-Think-Act process, they may identify:

- **Goals/Purposes**—the broad purpose to be achieved in the lessons
- **Objectives**—the objectives through which this broader purpose might be achieved

- **Learning processes**—the specific learning activities in which they will engage to accomplish each of these objectives
- **Content**—the particular topics, concepts, or issues that comprise the content of the lessons
- **Resources**—books and materials required in the process
- **Outcomes**—how they will demonstrate they have accomplished learning objectives

All these may be associated with state or district curriculum guidelines and standards.

Lessons may also be formulated using problem-based inquiry learning processes. Lessons emerge by focusing on an issue, problem, theme, or topic, then using action research processes—Look-Think-Act—to develop a solution to the problem and/or extend children's existing stock of knowledge. The teacher should facilitate the process by asking students:

- What they already know about the topic, issue, or problem
- What they would like or need to know
- How they can learn about identified issues or topics
- What resources they will need
- How they can demonstrate their competence or problem-solving

Exploration of any topic often elicits considerable information from children, to which the teacher contributes by assisting them to build order and coherence into the emerging body of knowledge. Information may be written on the whiteboard as it emerges, then organized appropriately (a quick form of data analysis) and complemented by reinforcing activities that assist the children to acquire a deeper understanding of the topic. The teacher may provide additional information from her/his own stock-of-knowledge to round out the lesson.

Although inquiry learning may not be suitable for all lessons, it provides the basis for rich and active alternatives to standard information transmission approaches to instruction. It is surprising how much information may be acquired from a classroom of young children who are apt to become enthusiastic and engaged as they construct a body of knowledge they themselves generate.

Outcomes-Based Learning Projects

Outcomes-based learning projects can derive from many sources, including prescribed curriculae; special events occurring in a neighborhood, town, or country; or a topic of interest arising in the children's experience. The purpose of a learning project is to provide opportunities for children to explore an issue or topic and to present the outcomes of that learning in multiple ways. Standards and outcomes from literacy, mathematics, social studies, and science curricula may be incorporated in the one project that provides students with integrated and effective learning experiences. Learning projects may incorporate many sources of information (data gathering), including library research, community visits, interviewing and observing, and materials and artifacts. By selecting and organizing relevant information (data analysis), children may formulate a coherent body of knowledge related to the desired outcomes. This body of knowledge may be presented in multiple forms—written reports, presentations, or performances (see Chapter 6). All have the potential to enrich the student's educational experience and to generate high levels of motivation and competence.

Proponents of the Reggio Emilia approach to learning provide many useful examples of the ways research can productively be incorporated into children's learning (Edwards, Gandini, and Forman, 1998). They suggest that including parents, and other adults from the neighborhood or community, even in the planning stages, can enhance learning projects. This, they suggest, not only provides rich resources for child learning, but also enables adults to extend their understanding about schools and education.

The Foxfire approach to learning also provides rich possibilities at the high school level (Wiggington, 1985). Students collect folklore in their communities by interviewing people in the community about what they do or know, sometimes also observing them at work on a chore or craft and, in some instances, taking photographs. Students, therefore, gather an extensive body of local knowledge or historical information that is then incorporated into a magazine. This "cultural journalism" is accomplished through action research routines that provide rich possibilities for engaging multiple learning experiences and accomplishing high levels of learning across the curriculum. An action research process applied to inquiry learning requires students to:

- Identify a focus, topic of interest, or problem.
- Gather relevant information through interviewing; observing; collecting artifacts, photographs, or recordings; or engaging in library research.
- Analyze the data to identify key elements of information.
- Organize those elements into a structured framework of ideas.
- Present the outcomes of their research in multiple formats—reports, art, music, dance, demonstration, drama, and so on.

I once worked with a third-grade class in Bryan, Texas, on the topic of Australia, which was part of their social studies syllabus. I was amazed at the depth and extent of information these 8- and 9-year-old children were able to provide. They spoke, of course, about the common animals—kangaroos, koalas, and so on—that are part of the international Australian image, but then went on to give me extensive details of the life of the wombat, the platypus, and other less-well-known animals. The stock of knowledge in that class was extensive; ranging from information about the climate in various parts of Australia, the rotation direction of cyclones (called hurricanes in the United States), the cities in Australia, through quite detailed information about other features of Australian life. Their questions were insightful and enabled me to complement the information they had provided. I was able to use pictures and other materials I had prepared as they became relevant. All of the children in the class were interested, excited, and engaged throughout the lesson. Participatory, constructivist processes, I have discovered, are powerful tools for learning.

Assessment of Student Learning

Assessment is an integral part of lesson and curriculum planning and is the means by which we know what students have learned. As a process of action inquiry, therefore, assessment can be built into the construction of a syllabus or curriculum, which links the statement of objectives, learning processes, and content with outcome assessment. Student learning processes are greatly enhanced where they participate in deciding how they may demonstrate their competence in a body of knowledge, or the performance of skills. Student learning may be demonstrated [and reported] in a variety of ways. Numerically graded written tests are the most commonly used procedure, but presentations, performances, portfolios, and projects also provide the means for students to demonstrate competence. These methods are especially useful ways of enabling students to demonstrate complex learning objectives not easily inscribed in written tests.

As Astin (1993) indicates:

- Assessment is not an end in itself but a vehicle for educational improvement that enacts a vision of the kinds of learning we most value for students.
- Learning is a complex process that entails not only what students know, but what they can do with what they know.
- Assessment works best when the programs it seeks to improve have clear, explicitly stated purposes and goals. It entails comparing educational performance with educational purposes and expectations.
- Assessment requires attention to outcomes but also and equally to the experiences that lead to those outcomes. Where students "end up" matters greatly.
- Assessment works best when it is ongoing, not episodic. Though isolated, "one-shot" assessment can be better than none, improvement is best fostered when assessment entails a linked series of activities undertaken over time.

An action research inquiry process provides the means to engage students in more comprehensive and exploratory processes of assessment and enables them to systematically *evaluate* the nature and extent of their learning. This type of assessment provides opportunities for them to make meaningful connections between classroom activities and learning objectives and their own learning processes.

Assessment as a cyclical process of inquiry involves:

- Reviewing learning objectives and standards
- Describing or demonstrating the types and/or levels of skills and knowledge acquired by learners
- Judging the adequacy of learning in relation to the objectives and standards
- Formulating next steps in learning or remediating weaknesses in learning

Teachers work with students to develop an evaluation framework to provide a clear process and set of criteria for judging the adequacy or level of learning. Although this may suggest mountains of grading for teachers, the reverse is actually the case, since it is possible to incorporate self-assessment, peer assessment, on-line grading, and a variety of other assessment tools and procedures into the process. The teacher, in other words, is not the only person who may assess student learning, though she bears overall responsibility for checking the veracity and authenticity of the results obtained.

Traditional classroom assessment procedures often provide a numerical estimate of the *degree* or *extent* of student learning. This information is also sometimes used to *rank* students to show how well they have performed compared with their peers. Assessment procedures also may be used *diagnostically* to indicate points of weakness in student learning.

Curriculum Development

Action research provides a process for developing a rich, engaging curriculum, relevant to the lives and purposes of students, engaging their interests and abilities, and serving the broad human needs of the community, society, and planet. Creative construction of curricula or syllabi provides the means whereby the needs, perspectives, and/or interests of diverse stakeholders can be incorporated into vital, creative, and effective programs of learning.

Participatory curriculum development is not a new idea. It emerged in the early twentieth century through the ideas of John Dewey (1930, 1916/66). As Lois Christensen reminds us (1997), John Dewey thought that "Learning should be approached in an integrated and participatory fashion to enable learners to construct and continually reconstruct meaning from authentic experiences." In exploring the processes of curriculum planning, Peter Oliva (2001) notes, "To varying degrees, the democratic process is accepted more and more in school systems across the [United States]. Nowhere is its presence more clearly felt than in the participatory procedures that seek to involve the major constituencies of the school in curriculum development . . . . Administrators and their staffs, teachers, students and the citizens of the community."

Participatory action research provides an authentic context in which teachers, learners, and other stakeholders develop a shared culture of learning through the collaborative development of common meanings and purposes. Where educational professionals engage in curriculum development without engaging other constituencies or stakeholders they run a grave risk of incorporating agendas derived from organizational pressures or their own social and cultural perspectives into the curriculum. In doing so, they are likely to construct curricula deeply imbued with values and meanings that have little meaning or are contrary to the social and cultural context of parents and students. In such circumstances, teachers are likely to face cohorts of disinterested and sometimes antagonistic students, searching to find ways of coaxing or making them engage the content of the curriculum. While the speedy formulation of a curriculum may seem pragmatic and efficient, the outcomes of such a process are likely to be a lack of ownership and engagement by significant segments of a school population.

As a young teacher, I taught a state-prescribed curriculum to children in an Aboriginal community. Having only recently emerged from the desert into contact with the modern world, people in the community still lived a life-style of the hunter-gatherer. Living in closely bonded and carefully interrelated family groups, they enacted an economic life based on sharing and a rich spiritual tradition manifested through song, dance, and ritual. From this context, the children came to school to confront a curriculum derived from the ethos of a materialistic, capitalistic, European, suburban society.

I now look back in shame at the inadequate and possibly destructive learning processes in which I engaged those children. Teaching them that "Captain Cook, the English navigator, discovered Australia," and the delights of a "nutritious, balanced meal comprising the five major food groups," the curriculum failed to incorporate the difficult but necessary task of helping them to deal with the changes that were necessarily part of their experience as their community came to grips with the "modern" and "civilized" world.

I fear that similar processes still operate in many similar contexts where the social and cultural experience of communities and students diverges significantly from those who operate the school systems. This is certainly true of many U.S. schools in which I have worked, where predominately African-American or Hispanic students confront a curriculum with little relevance to the ongoing realities of their social and cultural lives.

Two approaches to curriculum development are presented next. The first—curriculum planning—summarizes a traditional approach to curriculum construction based on a model developed by Tyler (1949) and modified by Oliva (2001). The second approach—Transformative Curriculum Leadership (Henderson, Hawthorne, and Stollenwerk, 2000)—presents a more collaborative, constructivist approach to curriculum development.

Curriculum Planning

The complex task of curriculum planning may be engaged as an action research process with participants investigating input from diverse sources (data gathering), distilling and selecting desired content and outcomes from that large body of information (data analysis), and formulating these key features and elements into a coherent curriculum framework (action).

A well-developed curriculum provides the blueprint for learning that incorporates a wide array of purposes or goals, including those derived from descriptions of human, national, social, and individual need and inputs from diverse sources—the academic disciplines, the human and behavioral sciences, and the community. A curriculum plan provides the means to envisage how these diverse agendas might be incorporated into programs of classroom learning at all levels of a school system.

Oliva (2001) presents a widely used model, based on a curriculum framework initially developed by Ralph Tyler (1949), that incorporates the following elements:

- **Needs Analysis:** Statement of *personal needs* of the learner and *social needs* of the community/state/nation.
- **Goals and Objectives:** Broad *goals* derived from those needs, together with *specific objectives* to be attained by learners, and filtered through a screen of philosophical assumptions.
- **Learning Processes:** What *learning activities* will enable learners to accomplish the objectives?
- **Content:** What *subject matter* will be associated with those learning activities?
- **Assessment/Outcomes:** How will learners *demonstrate* they have accomplished the learning objectives?
- **Evaluation:** To what extent does the program of learning enable learners to *accomplish purposes/goals?* Do they fulfill the *personal needs* of learners and *social goals* of the community?

Action research engages relevant stakeholders in formulating each of these stages of production. They describe and analyze student needs—personal needs, future employment needs, and social needs—that will provide for the development of a healthy, harmonious citizenry. A statement of needs provides the basis for a set of broad goals and more specific objectives describing how these goals are to be attained. Learning processes and curriculum content comprised of specific skills and knowledge are then incorporated into a well-organized program of learning.

Transformative Curriculum Leadership

Henderson, Hawthorne, and Stollenwerk (2000) provide an interesting alternative to the standard curriculum processes described previously. Their framework contains many of the elements of the standard model, but is much less mechanistic and takes into account the human dynamics that are an integral part of the curriculum. Their process is directly linked to action research as a process of inquiry incorporating multiple stakeholders. Speaking of the evaluation component of the curriculum, they suggest:

> Transformative evaluation assesses both the quality of school life and the quality of student learning to give students information about their own learning and ability to create meanings. This complex process must allow for multiple personal expressions. Thus, while standardized tests are part of transformative assessment, they do not dominate it. More important is a spirit of inquiry and critical analysis that takes the form of action research. (Henderson, Hawthorne, and Stollenwerk, 2000)

Thus, teacher researchers provide "curriculum leadership" and guide others to construct a curriculum, rather than constructing it themselves. They describe five fundamental principles for enacting a transformative curriculum leadership (the five Cs) that requires participants to be:

- Creative
- Caring
- Critical
- Collaborative
- Committed

Working within the ambit of these guiding principles, a transformative curriculum process moves through four phases: deliberating, building a vision, assessing student learning, and planning a classroom curriculum. Each of these may be envisaged as a cycle of the action research process.

Deliberating About a School-Based Curriculum

Stakeholders, including teachers, administrators, students, and others, have an active voice in reviewing, critiquing, and revising standards. They build a curriculum design platform containing the goals, criteria, assumptions, and principles by:

- Describing and analyzing the current curriculum, as currently expressed in plans, policies, and materials and experienced by students in classrooms
- Sharing personal stories of meaningful and exciting curriculum experiences and reflecting on beliefs and values related to living in a democratic society
- Analyzing projections about national and regional economic, ethical, cultural, political, technical, and interpersonal futures
- Examining state and national standards, outstanding curriculum plans developed by others, and alternative forms of student assessment

Building a Vision of the Curriculum

Using the curriculum design platform as a guide, stakeholders construct an overall vision or structure for a curriculum. They:

- Identify problems, issues, and themes to focus student engagement.
- Describe the content: Big ideas, perceptions, values, skills, and ways of knowing.
- Identify key forms of student inquiry.
- Identify supportive materials and equipment.

Again, the process is participatory and draws together teachers and community members to visualize imaginative, exciting, and appropriate learning events in which students are actively engaged and highly interested.

Assessing Student Learning

Assessment procedures are designed to determine what students have learned and gain insight about how students can use what they know. Students become active agents in their own learning and assessment processes. In this phase, participants identify:

- What students have learned
- How students can use learning
- How they are becoming active agents in their own learning
- Information about the quality of student learning
- Information about the quality of school life

Assessment may be accomplished through:

- Standardized tests that are used for assessment processes but don't dominate them
- Performance assessment that tests a student's ability to apply knowledge and skills
- Portfolio assessment using a variety of materials to demonstrate the nature and extent of learning

Planning the Curriculum in the Classroom

In this phase, teachers apply the curriculum in their classroom—in conjunction with students and community members, where appropriate—by creating:

- Specific objectives
- Learning activities
- Materials
- Learning contexts
- Assessment procedures

At all stages of curriculum development, therefore, stakeholders engage in participatory processes of inquiry through which they build shared understandings and commitments to the curriculum.

Evaluation: Assessing the Value and Quality of Educational Programs and Services

This section presents three models of evaluation concomitant with participatory action research—*responsive evaluation* (Guba and Lincoln, 1989) and two orientations to action evaluation: *open inquiry evaluation* and *audit review evaluation* (Wadsworth, 1997). Readers engaged in the evaluation of large and complex projects would do well to consult these sources in detail.

The forms of evaluation presented here are *formative* (Scriven, 1981a) insofar as they focus on the ongoing processes of teaching and learning, rather than describing or measuring learning outcomes, which is a *summative* (Scriven, 1981b) process of evaluation. Formative evaluation, in other words, speaks to a broader set of criteria attempting to understand the more complex processes through which learning takes place and the types and qualities of learning occurring, rather than solely measuring or describing student performance on a specific set of learning outcomes.

Responsive Evaluation

Responsive evaluation is clearly aligned with the underlying principles of participatory action research revealed in this book. It has an action orientation that defines a course to be followed and requires evaluators to interact with people in ways respecting their dignity, integrity, and privacy.

> Responsive evaluation . . . signal[s] the idea that all stakeholders put at risk by an evaluation have the right to place their claims, concerns, and issues on the table for consideration, irrespective of the value system to which they adhere. It was created as the antithesis of preordinate evaluation, which assumes that the evaluator and client together possess sufficient information and legitimation to design and implement an evaluation completely, without the need to consult other parties. (Guba and Lincoln, 1989)

These features make it an especially pertinent tool in action research, since the processes of evaluation are not only responsive to participant stakeholders' views and perspectives, but become the basis for assessing action to be taken. The principal audiences of an evaluation are stakeholders, who Guba and Lincoln define as:

- Those put at risk by the evaluation
- Agents who contribute to the development of the evaluand (the instrument of evaluation)
- Putative beneficiaries that are expected to profit from the evaluation
- Secondary beneficiaries (e.g., parents of students)
- Victims—those injured or deprived by the implementation of the evaluand

Guba and Lincoln speak of the need to provide stakeholders with insights about the roles they might play and questions they might ask as well as their right to become full partners in the evaluation.

The Flow of Responsive Evaluation

Since action research processes incorporate participatory processes, much of the following activity has already been accomplished by participants. Sometimes, however, an external evaluator is a required part of funding. Where an evaluation is set up separately, however, evaluation facilitators will move through the following steps:

- **Contracting:** Initiating contract with client/sponsor
- **Organizing:** Selecting/training a team of evaluators and making logistical arrangements
- **Identifying Stakeholders:** Identifying agents, beneficiaries, and victims, and formalizing conditions agreements
- **Developing Within-Group Joint Constructions:** Establishing hermeneutic circles (focus groups) and shaping emerging joint constructions
- **Enlarging Joint Stakeholder Constructions:** Incorporating new information from documents, interviews, and evaluator constructions
- **Sorting Out Resolved Claims, Concerns, and Issues:** Identifying and resolving claims, concerns, and issues
- **Prioritizing Unresolved Items:** Submitting items to prioritization
- **Collecting Information/Adding Sophistication:** Collecting further information and utilizing further hermeneutic circles to add sophistication to stakeholder constructions
- **Preparing an Agenda for Negotiation:** Defining and elucidating unresolved items and testing the agenda
- **Carrying Out the Negotiation:** Selecting a representative circle from all stakeholding groups, shaping the joint construction, and determining action
- **Reporting:** Providing reports on the activities to stakeholding groups

Guba and Lincoln's responsive evaluation process is very similar to those involved in action research, though the terminology they use is somewhat different. Hermeneutic circles, for instance, are comprised of groups of stakeholders and are designed to enable participants to make meaning together in a fashion similar to those described for focus groups in previous chapters. Nevertheless, they provide a sophisticated process for enabling stakeholders to work together to assess the ongoing progress, accomplishments, and deficiencies of their work. Responsive evaluation provides the basis for evaluating school programs and services and may be incorporated into the evaluation phase of a strategic planning process.

Action Evaluation: Everyday Evaluation on the Run

Yoland Wadsworth (1997) presents two approaches to action evaluation—open inquiry evaluation and audit review evaluation. Like action research, action evaluation works through reiterative processes of inquiry enabling participants to collaboratively explore their work, gain greater insight into their activities, and identify ways to solve problems or enhance the outcomes they seek. Participants build or extend their common understandings of the worth of their activities and test the value of what they are achieving. This is done through:

- **Reflection:** Observing their own actions in the world and reflecting on what is being experienced.
- **Design:** "Naming the problem" and systematically answer questions arising:
  - Who or what is to be researched?
  - Who are to be the researchers?
  - Who is it for? Whose lives will be improved (the critical reference group for whom services are provided)?
  - Who is it for? Who provides services, funds, and so on, for the critical reference group (primary stakeholding group)?
- **Fieldwork:** All relevant parties reach an effective understanding of what different people think, value, and what things mean to them.
- **Analysis and Conclusions:** Identify themes, trends, or understandings to develop conclusions, explanations, and theories.
- **Feedback:** Check with the researched or evaluated and the critical reference group that we "got it right" and that findings are understandable, plausible, or convincing.
- **Planning:** Realistic, practical, and achievable recommendations for changed and improved practices are prioritized, planned, and put into practice.

Open Inquiry Evaluation

An open inquiry approach to evaluation, through its focus on identifying and solving problems, increases the chances of improving educational programs and services. It enables innovative, creative, and dynamic ideas and perspectives to emerge and provides participants with a sense of enthusiasm.

Open inquiry evaluation examines existing practices in the following ways:

- **Starting with general questions:** How are we going? What are we doing? What's working? What's not? How do we know?
- **Asking problem-posing and problem-solving questions:** How could we improve things?
- **Asking what the community needs**
- **Repeatedly asking "opening up" questions:** Why are we doing this?
- **Starting with immediate problems**
- **Revealing existing assumptions and intentions**
- **Developing new and improved evaluative criteria**

For some people in some contexts, open inquiry is not sufficiently systematic and comprehensive and risks overlooking important matters. The uncertainty involved in the emerging construction of evaluation criteria and foci, with the consequent possibility of lack of clarity, disagreement, and conflict may create some anxiety. Generally, however, the essentially anthropologic, interpretive approach to inquiry makes it particularly relevant to participatory processes of inquiry.

Audit Review Evaluation

Audit review evaluation uses a more focused approach, though people sometimes see it as complementary to open inquiry. The sense of this approach is signaled by the word audit—to check. The audit starts with different questions and has different endpoints. The audit review focuses on:

- **Objectives:** It starts with questions based on an existing set of objectives— Have we done what we set out to do? What are the signs we have done this?
- **Gaps and Irrelevancies:** It asks questions about gaps and irrelevancies— What are we not doing? What are we doing that we shouldn't?
- **Needs:** Assumes community needs are known
- **Distilling Information:** The questions are "narrowing down," and check activities on the bases of pre-existing understandings
- **Revealing Problems:** Systematically problematizes all existing activities— that is, checks to see if they are problematic
- **Reviewing Practices:** Examines practices in light of existing objectives

An audit review has the advantage of checking all matters previously planned for; thereby reassuring participants that much has been done and matters not yet attended to will be. The comprehensive nature of this approach is especially advantageous if the prior research base was strong and enabled participants to affirm previous agreements and strengthen a collective sense of direction. The fixed nature of the exploration also can feel very comfortable and provide a sense of stability and unity.

The audit review, however, does not always discriminate between still-valuable activities and those that have become outdated. It does not identify what needs to change or how changes might be accomplished. The attention to detail enabling a comprehensive review of activity may also be tedious and wastefully time-consuming.

An audit review provides, however, a useful approach to evaluation especially loved by those responsible for administering or funding educational activities. The sense of a fixed universe and clearly defined objectives provides an illusion of expertise and "best practice" often at odds with the complex realities of educational environments. In the end, however, it can provide more concrete evidence of the extent to which a set of objectives have been achieved, though lacking insight into whether those objectives are appropriate or relevant.

Professional Development

Action research provides the means for formulating relevant and effective professional development programs. The need to improve teacher professional development has been clearly acknowledged in recent explorations (Darling-Hammond and McLaughlin, 1995; Feiman-Nemser, 2000; Hawley and Valli, 1999; Little, 1993; McDiarmard, 1994; National Commission on Teaching and America's Future, 1996). The National Board for Professional Teaching Standards (1994) has established a set of assumptions they consider as necessary conditions for sound professional development. These acknowledge that:

- Teachers are committed to students and their learning.
- Teachers know the subjects they teach and how to teach those subjects.
- Teachers are responsible for managing and monitoring student learning.
- Teachers think systematically about their practice and learn from experience.
- Teachers are members of learning communities.

Stein, Smith, and Silver (1999) suggest that meeting the ambitious school reform goals and standards put into place in the United States over the last decade will require a great deal of learning on the part of practicing teachers and those responsible for professional development. They advocate a new paradigm of professional development that supplies teachers with assistance and resources to develop a community of practice. They suggest a professional development design process enabling teachers to engage in thoughtful, conscious decision-making to create, implement, reflect on, and modify their teaching practices. Effective professional development processes have the following characteristics:

- **On-site Development:** Development within professional work environments
- **Resources:** Organizational resources—time, space, expertise
- **Learning Community:** A practice-based learning community of practitioners
- **Networks:** Links to appropriate people and organizational resources in the community
- **Planning:** Areas of professional development linked to organizational plans

Systematic processes of action research enhance the design and implementation of an effective program of professional development. The research framework presented in this book provides a resource enabling teachers and other professionals to:

- Identify professional development needs.
- Identify issues related to those needs—pedagogical, curricula, administrative, and so on.
- Set goals/objectives for professional development.
- Plan strategies of professional development.
- Implement and evaluate professional development strategies.

Systematic process of inquiry will enable teachers to plan sustained and substantive learning opportunities, built into their ongoing teaching work, tapping their collective wisdom, and gaining access to other sources of expertise. Through processes of reflection and dialogue inherent in action research, they may work with colleagues and other stakeholders to determine:

- Their current strengths
- Problematic issues in their work
- What is to be learned by whom?
- How will these things be learned?
- Who will facilitate and support the learning process?
- Who will provide expertise?
- How will time and resources be allocated?

- How will new learning be supported, reinforced, and extended?
- How will new learning be assessed and reviewed?
- What financial resource will be allocated?

Where mandated administrative requirements are part of this process, they may be incorporated into an holistic program of professional development. Professional development programs will be further enhanced if they are aligned with educational planning processes in the school or district and integrated into their ongoing organization. As Figure 7.4 indicates, the strategic directions of the school or school system have implications for the organization of schools and classroom teaching/learning processes. Professional development processes need to incorporate new knowledge and skills to be acquired by school staff in order to enact required changes.

Linking School, Families, and the Community

Realizing the potential of children's home and community is not always easy or straightforward. It requires systematic processes of inquiry over time to reveal the strengths of the families and to integrate them into the curriculum and ordinary day-to-day life of classrooms. By starting with small projects that link home, community, and classroom, teachers are able to build relationships with parents and their students that gradually reveal the ways home and community life can be incorporated as an integral part of the curriculum. As McCaleb says:

Figure 7.4
Strategic Professional Development

> Through participatory research, parents can be invited to engage in dialogue, either by the teacher or by their own children, the students. When family words and experiences are turned into the printed word, the thoughts of the participants are validated. . . . Parents begin to realize that their words and experiences merit a valuable place in the education of their children. . . . Through their participation, parents and community members get a concrete view of how they can contribute to their children's education. (1997, p. 58)

The learning, however, is multidirectional as teachers gain deep insights into the cultural, community, and family life of their students (Petty, 1997), and students begin to learn from each other about the rich diversity of their own communities (Baldwin, 1997). Over time, action research projects engaging families and the community provide a wonderfully engaging context for education. They affirm the multiple forms of cultural life existing in the community and provide the basis for engaging the academic life of students.

Action research is particularly effective in situations where students come from culturally diverse families and communities. As teachers, we work from within the experiences and perspectives we derive from our own upbringing and social experiences and cannot fully comprehend the quite different worlds from which our children come. We may sometimes need to modify both the content and processes of instruction to ensure that our students' learning is accomplished in ways acknowledging, respecting, and celebrating the social and cultural strengths of home and community life. McCaleb (1997) suggests that "The school's failure to acknowledge and value the family's learning and knowledge has a detrimental effect not only on the children's image of their parents but also on the students' appreciation of themselves as members of their home culture."

McCaleb's experience led her to appreciate the following benefits of engaging in research with families:

- Co-authorship produces increased communication, dialogue, and sharing within the family and community.
- Student family voices are heard.
- Personal histories are validated.
- Self-identity and self-esteem are strengthened.
- Parents discover the validity of their own experience.
- Through the negotiation of meaning, adults and students achieve new levels of understanding and self-knowledge.
- Children's respect for their parents and parental respect for children grows.
- The teacher comes to know the family and community better.
- The building blocks for creating a culturally relevant curriculum are laid.
- Teaching becomes easier.

Research processes presented in previous chapters provide the basis for engaging inquiry with parents, families, and other community members. Initially informal interactions enable school staff to establish effective communication and to develop working relationships with parents. Home visits, or meetings in community centers or cafes, provide a better context for talking with parents than school, since many of the parents teachers most need to engage have had poor school experiences.

Meeting on the parent's "turf" enables them to speak more comfortably. Small, informal lunch or coffee meetings also provide a more natural context and enable teachers to set up other meetings with individuals or small groups as issues worthy of further exploration emerge.

As parents become interested in exploring solutions to problems, teachers can engage them in processes of inquiry and exploration to seek solutions to small problems that concern them. From these beginnings, other agendas will emerge so that, over time, parents, students, and teachers may engage in more extended investigations about increasingly significant issues.

Sometimes, however, moments of crisis may generate the conditions where groups of parents or students are willing to invest time and energy in working toward a solution to the problems confronting a school or class. A community research project with students (Baldwin, 1997) emerged from racial problems that had erupted in a school. Student researchers initially focused on issues within the school, but they discovered the need to extend their investigations in the community, which lead to significant understandings about the relationship between racial dynamics in the community.

Engaging families, students, and community members in research entails:

- Communicating personally with individuals (Notes sent home with children are usually insufficient)
- Identifying issues of concern to parents and students
- Engaging other stakeholders related to the issue
- Planning a research process
- Implementing research activities
- Planning actions to solve the problem
- Evaluating outcomes

The multiple possibilities for reporting on the outcomes of action research presented in Chapter 6 are particularly pertinent to research with families and the community. Many adults in poorer or ethnically diverse communities feel inhibited by formal written reports, but the use of creative and dramatic presentations provides the means for individuals and groups to communicate comfortably and effectively. Journals, magazines, books, or other printed materials constructed within the school or community allow family and community members to present their perspectives, experiences, and knowledge. Informal presentations in classrooms, schools, or to community groups likewise provide the means to communicate research processes and outcomes. In some instances, students or family and community members have been able to use performances—poetry, music, art, and drama—to communicate research outcomes that both entertain and inform their audiences.

The "Listening to Families" project (see Chapter 8) describes a community-based research process. Representatives of the Barrios Juntos Neighborhood Collective met with the principal of Reginald Chavez Elementary School at a local community center to discuss ways in which relationships between parents and families might be improved. After preliminary discussions, the group focused its attention on ways of improving parent-teacher conferences, and at following meetings decided to survey parents and teachers on the issue.

A framework of questions, initially framed by a university professor as "Listening to families" and "Listening to teachers," was re-formulated by Barrios Juntos members using language more appropriate for the community. A group of parent volunteers enlisted by Barrios Juntos attended a preliminary preparation session during which they practiced interviewing techniques in conjunction with the school principal.

During parent-teacher conference week, a table of food was set up in the school library and parents leaving conferences with teachers were invited to snack as they were interviewed by members of the interviewing team. A total of 120 out of 200 parents with children at the school attended the parent-teacher conference. Of the attending parents, 88 were interviewed.

The research team met in the school at a later date to analyze the results of the survey. Responses were written on charts, tabulated, and categorized. The resulting outcomes were incorporated into a one-page summary and presented to parents at a school function. Teachers were interviewed separately, and their perspectives used as the basis for a teacher report on the issue. This research has been used by the school to improve the way parent-teacher conferences are organized, but potentially provided participants with insight into the more general processes of interaction between school and families.

The indirect outcomes of the process were as important as the direct outcomes. Parent participants indicated they felt empowered by opportunities to work collaboratively and listen to the views of other parents. They also gained greater understanding of the perspective of the principal and the teachers. Community participants were able to include their own cultural elements into the process—the place of food, and the language of survey questions.

Strategic Planning: Building the Big Picture

Although action research is often associated with small scale, local studies, it is a viable tool that may be applied to the management of large organizations. Action research, therefore, may be used at the level of school, school system, or state educational system as a means for accomplishing large-scale developments. The collaborative strategic planning processes described in the following paragraphs are implicit in such popular processes as Total Quality Management (Huffman, 1997; Tennant, 2001), but they are relevant to more generalized processes of planning and administration (Block, 1990; Coughlan and Brannick, 2001). Action research processes enable school administrators to systematically gather and analyze the large array of information required to produce strategic plans for the operation of the systems for which they have responsibility.

Schools and school systems describe the "big picture" of their educational intents within policy documents incorporating *vision* and *mission* statements that are the manifestations of an *educational philosophy*. They include broad statements of *purpose* and *value* defining an educational philosophy. Such statements may cover fundamental issues related to democratic social and community life and underlying moral and ethical principles. The following statements provide examples of common types of issues incorporated into school policies:

Purpose

- All students have an inherent right to an education that will enable them to reach their highest possible potential.
- The responsibility of education in a democracy is to make it possible for all citizens to understand themselves and the world about them so that they can live effectively in the world of expanding experiences and constant change (Omaha School District, quoted in Oliva, 2001).

Value

- All students are treated with dignity and respect.
- Learning is unique to each individual.
- Parents are partners in the education of students (Orange County Public Schools, quoted in Oliva, 2001).

A coherent policy provides strong degrees of association between broad policy statements and particular educational programs enacted at all levels of the system. Broad vision statements, which are essentially philosophical in nature, are specifically linked to particular programs, services, and educational activities. Carefully articulated links at each level of planning provide guidance for practitioners to move from *vision,* to *mission,* to *operational,* and *action plans* detailing how these programs and services are to be instituted.

A school district may construct a vision for education through the following types of statement:

- The provision of a quality education for all children, regardless of race, ethnicity, class, gender, or sexual orientation, that
- Provides for their intellectual, emotional, and physical well-being at all levels of the school system.

Mission statements describe how this vision is to be achieved. For example:

- Provide pre-school, elementary, middle, and high school education programs in all districts of the system.
- Design and implement appropriate curricula at all levels.
- Provide special services (curriculum, special education, physical plant, etc.) in support of those schools.
- Supervise and monitor teaching, administration, and special services.
- Provide funds and resources required to implement programs and services.

Each school in the district would articulate an operational plan that describes a set of specific objectives related to each of these mission statements. For example:

- Provide a fully developed program of education in all classes of the school.
- Organize and coordinate the ongoing operation of those programs.
- Provide supervision and support for those programs through the school administration.

- Provide resources—equipment and materials—and special services in support of school programs.
- Evaluate the effectiveness of school programs.
- Link the school effectively to families and the community.

Action plans at the classroom level establish syllabi and lesson plans enacting the educational philosophy established in the vision. Classroom plans derive, therefore, from curricula emerging from operational plans and incorporate philosophical guidelines delineated in the school/district vision. The beauty of action research is that it provides the means for the integrated development of programs and services at all levels of the system. Opportunities for school and classroom stakeholders to review and re-envision their work in this way provides the impetus for thinking "outside the box," maintaining their focus on the real purposes of their endeavors, and enhancing their educational life.

The strategic planning process depicted in Figure 7.5 is a nominal version of an actual planning process. It shows the levels of planning that need to occur and signals the interconnection between the different sections. The figure illustrates how classroom learning is linked to larger social and educational issues and agendas. Action research provides the means for educators to systematically acquire and analyze the complex array of information required to formulate educationally effective classrooms and schools.

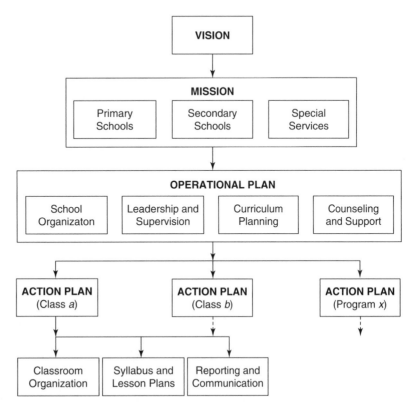

Figure 7.5
Strategic Planning Process

Summary

This chapter outlines ways action research can be applied to common school educational processes. It presents frameworks for:

- **Solving Problems:** Action Planning in Classroom and Schools
  - **Setting Priorities:** Establishing an Action Agenda
  - **Creating Pathways:** Constructing an Action Plan
  - **Reviewing the Plan**
  - **Supporting and Monitoring Progress**
- **Classroom Teaching and Learning Practices**
  - **Constructing Programs of Learning:**
  - **Creating a Syllabus**
- **Lesson Plans**
- **Learning Projects**
- **Assessment of Student Learning**

- **Curriculum Development**
  - **Curriculum Planning**
  - **Transformative Curriculum Leadership**

- **Evaluation:** Assessing the Value and Quality of Educational Programs and Services
  - **Responsive Evaluation**
  - **Action Evaluation:** Open Inquiry and Audit Review
  - **Professional Development**
  - **Linking School, Families, and the Community**
  - **Strategic Planning:** Building the Big Picture

Case Studies: Action Research Reports, Presentations, and Performances

8

Introduction

Examples of action research projects in schools and other educational contexts are proliferating rapidly. The extent of interest in this form of investigation is demonstrated by expanding audiences at action research sessions at conferences and reports in educational and professional journals. It is becoming a recognized tool of classroom teachers and a regular part of pre-service preparation and in-service professional development.

The following case studies, therefore, represent but a few of the creative and productive ways teachers, students, and parents have applied action research in their school and community contexts. They are real-life studies that provide some indication of the diversity of forms participatory investigations take and, particularly, applications of frameworks similar to those described in this book. They differ in style and quality and do not necessarily represent "best practice" in report writing. They do represent, however, the diverse means the authors used to communicate information to different audiences according to the purposes they wished to achieve.

1. A Study of Sexual Harassment in the Lives of Middle-School Students
2. Small Is Beautiful: Internal Evaluation Report, Brazos School for Inquiry and Creativity
3. Listening to Families: Improving Communication Between the School and the Community
4. Students and Teacher as Co-Researchers: Developing Multicultural Awareness in a High School Class
5. Creating a Dialog for the Role of Computers in the Classroom
6. Doggerel: An Elementary School Children's Research Project
7. Classroom Chaos
8. Class Evaluation: Something
9. Ode to Denizen
10. Children's Construction of History: A Quilt

1. A Study of Sexual Harassment in the Lives of Middle-School Students

This paper was written by Alex Scott, a middle-school teacher who reported on a research project carried out by a group of middle-school students. It describes details of the research process, as well as the "actions" in which students engaged. It details the methods they used to explore the issue—gathering information by dialoging about their experiences of harassment, including other "stakeholders" in the process, and distilling the data to reveal key features of their experience. It describes actions taken by students, including the writing of an article for their school newspaper and a poem that became the basis for a play. The paper also demonstrates how to produce an empathetic text that speaks clearly and movingly about participant experiences.

FRAMING

Students in my eighth-grade language arts classes were excited about working on a research project concerning a school issue. In a class discussion, they had no hesitation in identifying sexual harassment as the number one issue facing them on a daily basis. My first period class felt that sexual harassment was so pervasive that most of the 850 student body had experienced sexual harassment in the hallways, in class, locker rooms, the cafeteria, and on the buses. "Nowhere is safe at school," said Moira, one of the eighth-grade girls who became a participant in the study.

Students shared that sometimes sexual comments created such anxiety that it was hard to focus on class work. Some students had stayed home from school to avoid being a target. They felt that physical abuse of peers was much less of a problem than verbal sexual harassment. In fact, sexual harassment was a way of life, "You get used to it, 'cause there is nothing you can do about it," said Katie, and many students nodded in agreement.

"Like it happens when teachers are around," reported Moira. When teachers heard name calling in the hallways, like "faggot," nothing was done about it. Moira went to her desk in science to find her name written across two desks. It said, "Moira gives me a boner." When Moira asked for the names of the students who sat in those desks, the teacher said he didn't know. The following day the graffiti had been removed, but when she again asked for the names of

the students from the seating chart, the teacher replied, "What do you want me to do? Write a research paper about it?" In fact, there have been many research papers written about sexual harassment, and it appears that some of them need to be presented to the faculty at my school.

In *Hostile Hallways,* a survey carried out by the American Association of University Women and released in 1993, the overall national picture is revealed. Of the 91% of students who reported some experience of harassment in school, 68% said they had been harassed at least once in the hall; 55% reported the classroom as the site of harassment; 43% reported occurrences outside school but on school grounds; 39% reported harassment in the gym, playing field, or pool area; 34% indicated the cafeteria as the location; and 23% named the parking lot as the site of the harassment. Students said locker rooms (19%) and rest rooms (10%) were also locations for sexual harassment. Overall, 83% of the girls and 60% of the boys reported experiencing unwanted sexual attention in school. When this study was shared with the class, there was relief that our school wasn't the only one with the problem of sexual harassment. There was also anger and confusion as to why sexual harassment is such a prevalent issue among teens. We started a research group.

METHOD

Five girls volunteered to meet after school every Tuesday afternoon to explore how they had experienced sexual harassment. We began in October of 1999, and continued meeting through May of 2000. Their level of concern and commitment shown in the fact that they never missed a single meeting. The first step was to write letters to parents explaining the project and asking permission for their daughters' participation. Letters were also written to the principal, assistant principal, counselor, and our on-site police officer explaining the nature of the study.

The girls were interviewed individually using the Ethnographic Interview Questions (Spradley 1979a). I took notes during the interviews and collected articles that the girls brought in from their own research in magazines and from the Internet. The group was extremely involved and self-motivated. At times, our meetings were very intense—a natural response to such a sensitive issue. And I wrestled with my own ignorance of what a school day is like for an eighth-grade girl. The pressure to look pretty, to not appear smart, and to defend oneself against verbal attacks takes a huge amount of energy. Going into the project, I had no idea the extent of the issue. One of the girls suggested I interview the counselor and the police officer, as many students sought out their help after they had been sexually harassed. I made appointments and followed through with interviews. One of the mothers volunteered to be interviewed.

The group also decided to ask other students in our language arts classes to anonymously write down their thoughts about sexual harassment. We saved these writings and later incorporated them into a performance piece.

After the individual interviews were completed, we began by discussing the official stance on harassment: "Arnet Independent Schools are committed to providing all members of the school community with a safe, supportive and harassment free environment. Members of the school community are expected to treat each other with mutual respect. Harassment is a form of disrespectful behavior that is intended to intimidate, creates a hostile environment, unreasonably interferes with an academic or working environment, adversely affects academic and employment opportunities, or seriously alarms or terrorizes another person. The conduct to be harassing must be such that it would cause a reasonable person to suffer emotional distress, or deprive victims of access to educational opportunities or benefits provided by the district."

This policy was sent to all AIS schools as a direct result of *Davis v. Monroe County Board of Education* where a student had sued the school district for failing to protect the student from sexual harassment. The district was found in error and had to pay damages to the student for emotional distress. The students in the study wanted to know why the school had not told them of the policy to protect them. It made me think about the importance of sharing information, especially when harassment drains so much energy from learning. They have the right to be protected from harassment.

ANALYSIS

Moira had said that she was only just now recovering from a traumatic seventh-grade year. During most passing periods she was harassed on a daily basis. Boys taunted her with comments about her appearance, "You have a nice butt," "You are so hot," and "I heard you sucked everyone at Bellamy." During science class, a boy next to her masturbated. Moira tried to avoid going to science class by asking the teacher if he had any errands. At no time did she tell the teacher what was going on because she believed nothing would be done about it. She also said she didn't want to be known for getting someone in trouble.

At the same time, Moira was being harassed in the bathroom by girls who were calling her slut and whore, or saying, "You want to do it with Jeff." Moira said that the girls hate her because she is popular and pretty.

"Students tell me that teachers have a crush on me. Teachers like me for a lot of reasons, but being pretty adds . . . a guy has never called me a slut to my face but girls have. I don't take what girls say seriously. . . I discovered I had power over men."

I read my notes back to Moira at the end of the interview. It was a moment of insight for her because of the word power. "Oh, wow, I really said that didn't I? I like that they appreciate me. But, I don't think it's good about the power stuff."

Toward the end of seventh grade, a male student in science class leaned over the desk and told Moira, "I'm going to your house tonight to rape you." This galvanized Moira into action because she was really afraid. She went immediately to Officer Meredith who talked to the boy in his office. Soon after that, the young man was expelled for bringing a toy gun to school, so she didn't see him again. Moira added that she wasn't really scared because "I didn't think he would do it." And again, she didn't want the boy to know "it was me who narked on him." Moira did report that she felt better after she had sought out help, and that a grown-up had listened to her. For her, anxiety stemmed from inertia.

Katie and Leslie, two of the other participants, shared their anger at not being harassed. They both perceived themselves as unattractive, fat, and "way too smart." They also believed that "only cute, popular girls get harassed." Both girls heard others being verbally harassed on a daily basis, but felt powerless to do anything about it, or too scared of reprisals. "I keep my head down so no one will talk to me," said Katie, "but I don't think it is right that everybody is calling each other names." Leslie said, "It's just a joke, they don't really mean to hurt anybody." But this was counteracted by Moira who vehemently responded, "Yeah, they say mean things, then say 'oh, I'm just joking' when they really mean it."

Rose, the fourth student in the study, left six weeks into the study. She joined the group because she wanted to represent the students who had not been harassed. Rose's reason for leaving was that she was overwhelmed by the others. She felt "no one is listening to me," and yet she rarely said anything in the group meetings. There had been an ongoing competition with Katie about grades and sharing a best friend. The group talked it over with her and tried to problem solve, but in the end, she decided to leave. She didn't feel her voice was being heard. This had a huge impact on what the group decided to do with the presentation of our research. We decided to write a performance piece in which everyone's voice would be included.

Adult Input

Our school counselor said he dealt with sexual harassment on a daily basis. Students came to talk to him about awkward situations, but often the students didn't know if it was harassment or not, they just felt bad. He talked about the lack of awareness of what harassment is, but that in coming to him with feelings of confusion, he could help clarify why they felt very uncomfortable when called "faggot" or "lesbo." Most of the verbal harassment he dealt with was between girls: sexual name calling and rumor spreading about who did what with whom. Most of the inappropriate physical harassment was from boy to girl. This included unwanted full body hugging, pinching, and grabbing of girls in the halls. Girls were more likely to report incidents of harassment than boys. The counselor said he rarely had boys in his office who wanted help with being called gay. In his experience, girls report harassment more often than boys, even though the counselor observed sexual harassment as being gender equal.

When parents were called about their child harassing another child, the parent often was at a loss as to know what all the fuss was about. Two girls had gotten into a fight because one had made remarks about the size of the other girl's chest. The girl didn't think it was cruel. When her mom was brought to school, she supported her daughter by saying, "It's no big deal." It is clear we need to do more for our students and parents to increase awareness of what sexual harassment is.

The parent who volunteered to be interviewed had requested a transfer for her daughter from the neighborhood school to Bellamy. This meant her daughter had to travel an extra 45 minutes on public transportation. She felt strongly that her daughter had been seriously harassed at her home school by gang members and teachers. "White teachers discriminated. They gave more freedom to white kids. The administration would not do anything about it. Here they listen." She felt her daughter would feel safer and more challenged academically at our school.

DISTILLATION OF DATA

At the beginning of each Tuesday meeting, we reviewed the key elements from the last meeting. This was extremely helpful in keeping our focus clear and our thoughts manageable. Then we shared any insights or research we had during the course of the week. This gave everyone a chance to be heard. Rose brought in an article about the restrictions placed on girls in Afghanistan. In that country, girls are denied an education and are physically mutilated if they show ankles or wrists.

Leslie was vehement that we invite boys to join us. This proved difficult. None of the eighth-grade boys showed up even when they said they would, until Leslie hit on an idea. She thought we would have more success if we asked high school boys. This proved to be the key. Two tenth-graders showed up and told us of their experiences in high school. They said it was much worse for boys because, "everything was gay, and about how you looked and which group you fit in." They wanted to start a group like ours at their school so students would think about what they were doing to each other. "It's not right to treat people bad, and what if they are gay? They must feel worse. There's too much stress on sex in high school."

At the end of the year, we took all of our key elements and distilled them down into these issues:

1. Harassment is not just a boy/girl problem.
2. Harassment happens between girls.
3. Harassment is not just a middle-school problem, it's world-wide.
4. Harassment causes long-term damage.
5. Harassment can be dealt with.
6. Each person is responsible for his/her own behavior.
7. We can do something about harassment.

We decided to write a performance piece based on what we had learned from our own experience of sexual harassment, incorporating the writings of other students and interviews of other adults. We decided to integrate suggestions of how to contact help, as well as suggestions of what to say to protect oneself when harassed. The group felt that sometimes students were so frozen by humiliation they could not respond verbally. They felt this lowered self-esteem and confidence. We decided that we needed an art piece to accompany our performance, "Speaking Out." After looking through many art books, we came across the work of Keith Haring. He had a huge canvas of the Statue of Liberty on the floor of a museum in New York. Students who came to visit were able to write on the canvas about what liberty meant to them. This was what inspired us to make a triptych, a three-paneled piece, where students could speak out about harassment by writing down their ideas after the performance.

COMMUNICATION

1. *Drama: "Speaking Out"*

   Framing

Voice 1:	After being harassed, I get a knot in the pit of my stomach That lasts all day.
All Voices:	I can't think!
Voice 2:	Middle school is about how I look How many boys like me?
Voice 3:	Yeah, and if the girls like my butt
Voice 4:	Who are you going out with?
Voice 1:	Am I a slut?
Voice 3:	Am I a player?
1:	Names ringing in my ears So what did the teacher say?
All:	I can't think!
3:	I want to hurt someone Please don't let it be me.

   Method

4:	You started with questions.
5:	"Tell me about school."
4:	Do you have a few weeks? I can tell you about fourth grade When I felt the power Of my body. That's when I smiled in a different way

	To get boys near me. The rush of being popular The joy of being manipulating I liked their eyes on me Now it's more than eyes And I can't give up that power.
1:	So, you want to start a meeting Like I have to talk to those girls Who look down their nose at me Because I'm a pretty slut Yes, I know I'm beautiful But don't hold that against me.
2:	Yes, she's pretty and popular If I were that pretty I would be popular too, But I'm not, so I don't get Harassed. Why doesn't Some one pinch my butt?
5:	OK, we'll meet on Tuesdays after school
2:	Anything to figure out why I feel so bad all the time.

   Analysis

5:	We talk and cry and then laugh Now what are we gonna do?
1:	Enough talking already!
2:	Well, who can we tell?
All:	We start to speak in surer Voices.
4:	"Don't you ever speak to me that way!"
1:	"You're harassing me. Quit it"
All:	Speaking out and feeling Power of a different kind Strong, united, together.
2:	For a moment that frightening Isolation is gone.
All:	We can think.

   Communication

1:	Writing begins with Clear words and offerings Of what to do if what happened To me happens to you.
3:	We explore the safety of the Written word together.
4:	But images pound us Memories of powerlessness Recur and recur.
2:	Words fail and we begin To imagine a canvas

Full of color, bright and
Potent, to catch eyes and thoughts
Perhaps to change those ugly slut
Words into kinder conversations.

3:     Looking at other artists'
       Work inspires and energizes us
       Now we talk of
       Images and shape and form and
       Composition of creating
       An interactive piece where
       Others can add their wisdom.

5:     Adrenalin of hope replaces
       Tears and powerlessness.

Action

1:     Now Tuesday afternoons are full
       No time for questions
       About past inertia
       It's voice and art and speaking out.

3:     Guests who drop in from
       High school, helping out with
       Loud discussions and talk
       Of beginning another group
       In my school.

All: At times, we catch each others'
       Eyes and remember
       There is a different way.

2. *Newsletter Article:* We also agreed that we needed to write an article about our group for the school newsletter in an effort to let students know they could join. The newsletter would reach parents about the issue of harassment. We checked beforehand with the administration, and they agreed to publish the article.

STUDENTS AGAINST HARASSMENT: ARTICLE FOR THE MONTHLY BELLAMY NEWSLETTER

By Katie Dupont, Moira Rodriguez, and Leslie Junette

Since October of 1999, a group of eighth-grade students have worked collaboratively toward making positive changes in the issue of harassment at Bellamy Middle School. Recently, they were joined by a concerned group of Francisco High School students. Together, the groups have worked on ways to identify different types of harassment and how to stop it.

The Merriam Webster dictionary states that harassment "is to annoy persistently." The official policy of Arnet Independent Schools states that "harassment is a form of disrespectful behavior which will not be tolerated. Harassment consists of knowingly pursuing a

pattern of behavior that is intended to intimidate, creates a hostile academic working environment . . . or seriously alarms or terrorizes another person." It is also stated that harassment could cause substantial emotional distress. From a survey taken by eighth-graders, distress caused by harassment is seriously interfering with the educational process at Bellamy Middle School.

"I have personally been harassed and I know how it feels. The pit of your stomach turns, and the rest of the day, I feel horrible," says an eighth-grade boy at Bellamy. Several girls report harassment from girls, as well as harassment from boys, making learning in the classroom nearly impossible.

Based on the student survey and interviews with parents, students, teachers, and a counselor, as well as high school students from Francisco, the Students Against Harassment concluded that harassment could be dealt with positively.

First, any unwanted actions or comments from an aggressor should be addressed immediately. Phrases like, "Don't ever talk to me that way again," and "Stop! That is harassment and I don't have to take it," are examples of proper responses because they state your demands to be treated with respect. Your voice must be clear and firm.

One way adults can help is to gain more knowledge on the topic of harassment and how to prevent it. Teachers need to teach students that harassment is unacceptable. Secondly, victims should report any incidents to the proper authorities. Officer Meredith at JMS reports, "When harassment is dealt with quickly, students realize that there are boundaries which cannot be crossed." Officer Meredith conferences with students and parents to clarify appropriate boundaries. Individuals who are being harassed must take action as soon as possible.

So remember:

1. *DO NOT IGNORE HARASSMENT*
2. *TELL THE HARASSER, "STOP! THAT IS HARASSMENT!"*
3. *IF THE HARASSMENT DOES NOT STOP, TELL OFFICER MEREDITH. IT'S CONFIDENTIAL.*

Students Against Harassment have written a performance piece to be presented at Manzanita Center at UNM on May 10. This is the beginning of extending public awareness of the issue of teenage harassment. The group will also perform on Friday, May

12, at 6:30 in the gym at BMS Student Forum.

Please contact Katie Dupont, Moira Rodriguez, or Leslie Junette if you are interested in joining Students Against Harassment. Working together, students can reach the goal of ZERO tolerance of harassment at Bellamy Middle School.

The article was submitted well ahead of the deadline. It was never published in the newsletter. When we asked about the omission, we were told it was too long to be included, even though we had prior approval. It will be resubmitted next year.

ACTION

Katie arrived for the performance at UNM. She addressed the group with confidence, describing the creation of Students Against Harassment and what the experience had meant to her. She stood alone, as the other participants could not attend due to a hectic schedule of end-of-school activities. For a 14-year-old, Katie appeared very comfortable speaking to a group of adults. University class members filled in the remaining voices and performed "Speaking Out," while standing in a "theater in the round" formation. This was our first, official "engagement," and it moved people enough for them to write on our triptych, "Speak up against what is wrong," "Walk in Beauty," and "Right the Wrongs." Katie reported back to the group the next day that she saw how "it got to people." She didn't think it odd that grown-ups were performing it because they had been teenagers themselves once and that they probably remembered what it was like to be harassed.

When we performed "Speaking Out" during Student Forum there was a standing ovation. Students filled the triptych with comments such as: Yeah, you said right; it happened to me too; have courage and speak up; never again; we can stop harassment; no more silence. Some students chose to write the names of family members who had experienced harassment. Three panels were covered with statements of strength and affirmation. It is a permanent, artistic reminder that we can find courage together to right the misuse of power.

Sexual harassment is an issue of power. In *Confronting Sexual Harassment* (1997), Judith Brandenburg states that sexual harassment is "a manifestation of deeply held beliefs, attitudes, feelings, and cultural norms. In its most prevalent forms, it is predicated on sociocultural views and sex-role stereotypes that males are active dominant, and entitled to power, while females are passive, nurturing, submissive, and powerless."

These attitudes and beliefs shape the socialization of children and the development of gender identity. The meanings we attach to gender are the basic underpinnings of what society expects from a girl instead of a boy. In our study, we found that boys use physical contact and verbal comments about body parts to harass girls. But girls use rumor and speculation about sexual activity to isolate one another. Boys who are assumed to be sexually active are "hot," while girls who are assumed to be sexually active are "sluts."

Throughout childhood, sex-role stereotypes are reinforced by the media and society. Television, sports heroes, and books tell us males should be active, independent, and aggressive. In spite of some increased sensitivity in the media over the last decade, girls and women still appear less frequently than men, and they are shown largely in stereotyped roles. In ads and music videos, women are objects, a collection of body parts. Women are valued for how they look: thin and pretty and sexual. Moira talked about feeling the power of being pretty and planning how to get boys to notice her because she liked being beautiful. At age 13, she would not go out of the house without make-up. "I don't know how I could live, if I wasn't pretty." By fourth grade she had formulated the belief that her worth lay in her outward appearance. In middle school, she found boys responded to her looks, vying to sit next to her in class, but girls saw her as a tremendous threat. She was labeled a "slut" because she was popular with the boys. Thus, girls learn to compete against each other for the label of "prettiest". It then becomes easy to attack self-esteem with epithets of ugly and fat. Similarly, teenage boys are inundated with media images of male virility and sexual prowess with girls. How easy it is to threaten this image with insults of "queer" and "faggot."

As educators, we can talk and talk about equality and respect. When students themselves speak out about their experiences and when students are courageous enough to offer alternative ways of being, the balance of power will be impacted. In October 1999, Officer Meredith reported dealing with four to five incidents of sexual harassment every week. At the end of the school year, he said the numbers had dropped to one every two weeks. When students know harassment will not be tolerated, behaviors change. Change can happen.

BIBLIOGRAPHY

American Association of University Women (AAUW). (1993). *Hostile hallways.* The AAUW survey on sexual harassment in American schools. Washington, D.C.

Berman Brandenburg, J. (1997). *Confronting sexual harassment: What schools and colleges can do.* New York: Teachers College Press.

Denzin, N. (1997). *Interpretive ethnography: Ethnographic practices for the 21st century.* Thousand Oaks, CA: Sage Publications.

Eaton, S. (1995). Sexual harassment at an early age: New for schools. In E. Miller (Ed.) *Ready To Learn: How schools can help kids be healthier and safer.* Cambridge, MA: Harvard Education Letter, Reprint Series 2.

Hassenpplug, A. (2000). Courts and peer sexual harassment: School district liability for damages. *Brigham Young University Education & Law Journal,*

Morewitz, S. J. (1996). *Sexual harassment and social change in society.* San Francisco, Austin & Winfield.

Shakeshaft, C., & Barber, E. (1995). Peer harassment in schools. *Journal for a Just and Caring Education, 1* (1) 30–40.

Stein, N. (1999). *Classrooms and courtrooms: Facing sexual harassment in K-12 schools.* New York: Teachers College Press.

Stein, N., & Sjostrom, L. (1994). *Flirting or hurting? A teacher's guide on student-to-student sexual harassment in schools.* West Haven, CT: NEA and Wellesley College Center for Research on Women.

Tangri, S. S., & Hayes, S. M. (1997). Theories of sexual harassment. In W. O'Donohue (Ed.), *Sexual harassment: theory, research and treatment.* Needham Heights, MA: Allyn & Bacon.

2. Small Is Beautiful: Internal Evaluation Report

Brazos School for Inquiry and Creativity

By Dr Ernie Stringer

This document was written for the Brazos School for Inquiry and Creativity, a small charter school in Bryan, Texas, as part of an internal evaluation process mandated by the State of Texas. It resulted from a five-day review process in which school staff, students, and administrators were interviewed and the school observed by the evaluation facilitator. An interim report was presented to teachers on day five of the process, enabling them to discuss the findings and identify actions they could take to improve the quality of the school's operation. These actions are included as an appendix to the report. Information included in the report was obtained from interviews, observations, and a review of school documents and records. It was produced as an internal document for the information of school staff and administration. Statistics related to student achievement levels, "at risk" classifications, and so on, were included in another report produced by an external evaluation team.

INTRODUCTION

The Brazos School for Inquiry and Creativity sits on the outskirts of downtown Bryan, surrounded by older and slightly worn houses, redolent of a past and more prosperous era. Housed in six rather cramped classrooms and nestled at the rear of a large Catholic church from which it leases the building, the school seems rather cramped for space, considering the nearly 100 children and numerous teachers, administrators, and adjunct faculty working within. It is an impression reinforced by teachers, administrators, and students at the school who almost with one accord spoke of the inadequacy of the buildings and the desire to move to larger quarters.

The physical surrounds, however, belie the energy and movement that envelopes visitors as they walk through the busy main corridor and pass classes scattered with children that would, in other venues, be classified as "noisy." In some rooms, the children sit listening to a teacher working through material written on a blackboard. In others, children laze across desks, lounge in beanbags, or talk animatedly with each other within easy reach of one of the adult figures, teachers,

or adjunct faculty who appear in surprisingly large numbers for such a small school. In still other rooms, usually housing older students, individuals or small groups work in concentrated fashion through their work, oblivious to the surrounding buzz and the ever-attentive teachers who move between them. "Chaos theory best describes us," says one teacher, referring to the patterns apparent in seemingly random sets of events, eventually emerging for the visitor, as he becomes more understanding of the nature and the purposefulness of the multitude of events happening simultaneously in this small, but busy school.

Order emerges from the chaos through the ministrations of two administrators busily coping with a multitude of tasks and issues as children, teachers, parents, and the telephone intrude on the one small administrative space. It takes shape in the excited talk of teachers as they describe the way they attempt to turn an educational theory into the ongoing practice of a school. It reaches greater clarity in the sometimes hesitant, but always clearly articulated, perceptions of the students as they mull over their experience attending a school quite different from those they've previously attended.

With around 95 students, two part-time principals, five full-time core teachers and 30 part-time adjunct faculty, known within the school as Aggies, the school operates on two campuses. K–2 is housed in a kindergarten facility a mile or so away, while grades 3–12 operate in the main campus, facilities complemented by those of a nearby Boys and Girls Club used for Physical Education, and a local swimming pool.

The brain-child of Dr. Robert Slater, whose passion for the children is acknowledged by teachers and administrators at the school, Brazos School for Inquiry and Creativity enacts a theory of education focused on a balanced curriculum to implement democracy. Its educational philosophy/principles, carefully elucidated on a Web site and espoused by teachers and administrators, focuses on the need to balance both the aesthetic and logical/rational capacities of students. It is an experiment in democratic schooling that appears to have enormous potential to provide a productive and relevant education for the children who attend.

HISTORY

The school, now seven weeks into the second year of operation, is still in its early days. Both administrators and staff recognize they are still in the process of formulating, working through, clarifying, and improving many aspects of its operation. A recent meeting of teachers and administrators clarified details of a discipline plan, for instance, and the school is in the process of investigating the extent to which it has been able to achieve academic excellence within the framework of the democratic freedoms central to the school's philosophy. It is, in other words, still a school in process.

But the comparative constructive, productive, though jumbled, order that characterizes its operation was achieved only through the determination and hard work of the people who initially gave it life. Those staff who remain from the first year of its operation tell of the difficulties and disorder arising from the growing pains of the school—the lack of order, the inability of some students to realize the implications of responsibility that went with the freedom they enjoyed, and the lack of facilities taken for granted in a fully operational school. As one administrator said, "I wasn't prepared for Inquiry and Creativity. It seemed like chaos to me. The children were eating and drinking, listening to music. They didn't have books. They had a lot of freedom, but they were used to a structured environment and couldn't use their time wisely or productively."

Coming from traditional models of schooling, it was hard for teachers and administrators to adjust to the demands and practices of the inquiry/creativity model, though a period of orientation allowed them to come to grips with the model. Dr. Slater talked with them at length and gave them papers to read explaining the theory of the school that enabled them to better understand the task before them. As one said, "As time went on I began to see the vision, and I bought into it."

Some students, likewise, found it hard to adjust to the atmosphere of the school and some left of their own volition or were asked to leave as their behavior, responses to traditional school environments, threatened to disrupt the school too severely. Most, however, adjusted to the demands of this different school environment and settled into more productive routines. "Kids went through a metamorphosis. . . . But it took a lot of repetitiveness for them to understand what we're about. Some still don't [get it]. . . . We had a ton of discipline problems. . . but this year we've seen very little of children we saw repeatedly last year."

The school, therefore, though only in its second year of operation, has gone through a period of development characterized by adjustments and changes and leading to a more settled and productive atmosphere. It has discovered, to some extent, what it can and cannot do, which students are capable of sustaining themselves in the atmosphere of "freedom with responsibility," and the minimal rules required to ensure an educationally functional environment. It is a school still in process, with administrators, staff, and students working through issues and problems as they appear and gradually building the structures and processes that enable them to enact the inquiry/creativity model.

At this early stage, however, it is apparent that much has been accomplished and both students and staff tend to look back with feelings of accomplishment as they see the early reward in student academic achievement for their efforts. As the following report reveals, there is much to be celebrated, but there is also much work still to do. Though the pains of birth have passed, there is still much growth to achieve.

STUDENT EXPERIENCES

A visitor to the Brazos School for Inquiry and Creativity cannot help but be impressed with the responses of students. They express almost unanimous approval of their experience at this new institution. Almost all indicated that they much preferred this to their previous school and were intent on continuing at the school. The one exception indicated that he'd like to have experienced a middle school after elementary school instead of coming directly to the Brazos school. His, however, was a divergent opinion—all other children provided responses ranging from quiet approval to excited or wholehearted enjoyment of their experience. One girl, obviously almost ecstatic at her progress, indicated in heartfelt tones, "The school is a blessing."

The reasons for this extended vote of confidence by the students relate to their comments during interviews. They felt that:

- They received more attention from teachers.
- The teachers were nicer.
- They were learning more.
- Their grades were improving.
- They had increased freedom.
- They appreciated the diversity of activities.
- They liked the small size of the school.

Students were almost unanimous in voicing their approval of the school. With very few dissenting voices, they asserted that they preferred the BSIC to the school they last attended and spoke positively of their experiences here.

More Attention from Teachers: The Teachers Are Nicer

It was clear that the students appreciated the close attention made possible by the small student-to-teacher ratio in this school. They commented on the nature of their relationship with their teachers and the fact that teachers knew them personally, knew their needs, and were available to help them with their work. One said, "They give you more attention and do things with you." Another indicated, "Teachers know you, work with you, know what you need. They're approachable, you can ask them things." Others compared this with the situation in their old schools, where much of the teacher's time was spent focusing on disruptive students. "At my old school, teachers spent their time giving attention to students acting up. They didn't give their time to students who wanted to learn." Another commented, "I really like my relationship with the teachers. They're, like, your friends!" The informality and friendliness of relationships between students and staff is notable to a visitor and acknowledged by all. It clearly is a significant factor in maintaining the ethos of "inquiry and creativity" that is at the heart of the school. As one faculty member indicated, "We're like a family. If something happens to someone, we all know it."

Learning More: Grades Improving

Many of the children came to BSIC as underachievers, either well behind in their schoolwork or on the point of failing or dropping out of school. Some would be classified as "at risk" from an educational viewpoint. The low student-to-teacher ratio, however, and the individualized learning processes ensure that children who are failing to achieve do not escape attention. In these circumstances, it is unsurprising that students felt that they were learning more at school and that their grades were improving.

Although this varies from student to student, even students who did not evince much interest in their schoolwork clearly indicated increases in achievement. While observation of classrooms suggests that some still have difficulty in remaining focused, the constant attention of teachers ensures that all achieve at least a minimal amount of productive engagement with their work—something they are apparently able to avoid in mainstream classrooms. For some children,

attendance at the school has been a transformational experience. One student, a low achiever at her previous school, spoke enthusiastically of her progress: "I was well below my grade level, but since I've been here, I've been making great progress, working my way back up. . . . I feel as if I can really learn here!"

Like other children in the school, she works by herself doing exercises based on the TEKS. "Aggie" tutors assist her to set up assignments and projects based on the TEKS materials, and she works through them, asking assistance from teachers and tutors as she requires. Individualized work is required of some students, especially at higher levels, or where they are well behind the requirements for other students at their grade levels. The flexibility of the curriculum and instruction allows each student to formulate a program of work that fits his or her grade or ability level. Tests indicated that one 15-year-old student was achieving at only grade fifth- to sixth-level, so she was allowed to start working at that level. As one administrator said, "She realized there was a gap and wanted to go to that level so she wouldn't miss any information. . . . She's really excited because she's learning." Her progress has been quite dramatic, and she appears truly engaged in her learning. She leaves work for tutors to review when she goes home and communicates with teachers via e-mail.

Although this case dramatically illustrates the potential of the flexibly organized teaching/learning processes at BSIC, it is not unique. Almost all students indicated increased learning, a fact borne out by the high TAAS scores achieved by children in this school. Figures indicate that BSIC TAAS scores are two standard deviations above the state mean, a fact made more laudable by the at-risk status of much of the student population.

Freedom and Diversity

Most children commented positively on the greater freedom they experienced at this school. It manifested itself in the choices available to them in the schoolwork, in their freedom of movement in the school, and in the activities available to them. Almost all students commented positively on this aspect of the school; one noting particularly that, "We can work at our own level, at our own rate [pace]." Another noted the impact of this on his learning—"When I came here I was behind. Now I'm achieving at my grade level." He indicated that the students in the school liked working at their own rate.

The freedom that comes to the children through the enactment of the Inquiry/Creativity Model is matched by the flexibility of instructional arrangements. As noted, a number of children indicated that they appreciated the opportunity to formulate their own learning levels and activities, but they also commented on the diversity of activities available in their school program. They enjoyed physical education activities, including swimming, exercises, weights, and games—activity not available at their previous schools. They were particularly enthusiastic about the field trips from which they learned much. This type of activity helps the school stand out from the education received at public schools in the region and provides diverse and active learning experiences that engage the children and provide a positive focus of attention on their schooling.

The difficulty of maintaining a model that provides freedom while expecting responsibility, however, is still evident in some of the children. With years of experience in traditional classrooms, some still maintain the attitude toward their schoolwork and behavior redolent of an authoritarian approach to schooling from which they were alienated and that they resisted through their behavior. One boy indicated, "We can get away with a lot more," referring not to misbehavior, but to the ability to make choices about work to be done, leaving the classroom, and so on. He still interpreted these freedoms as "getting away with things."

As one might expect in these circumstances, some children still require persistent attention to keep them focused and do not appear particularly interested in their work. This seems a greater problem for older male students whose educational experience appears to have alienated them from the productive possibilities available to them. The larger picture of the school, however, is that most students evince an interest in their work and are actively engaged in the activities and projects emanating from the TEKS formats. Even a cursory walk through the school provides evidence of energy and engagement that pervades the school and shows through some of the seeming babble that occasionally erupts when the schedule changes from one period to the next.

Small Is Beautiful

Almost all children remarked favorably on the small size of the school. Asked about their experience of the school, they noted that: "Its smallness is good," "I like the small size," or "It's tight, cool." They obviously like the attention they get that is not available in the more anonymous, larger schools they previously experienced. Their comments on the attention they get from their teachers and the fact that teachers are aware of their presence, their needs, and the gaps in their work all reflect the outcomes of the small size and the low student/teacher ratio. It is clearly, from the students' perspective, one of the benefits of attending the BSIC.

It does, however, have its downside. One student mentioned that she was "a social person," and would like to have more students with whom to interact. It also creates difficulties for students at higher levels of high school who have few fellow students with whom to share their work. One noted that it took some adjustment, but that she was now able to enjoy being self-motivated and organized, though she would like to have a teacher or mentor in eleventh and twelfth grade who was more focused on college preparation.

ADMINISTRATION

Administration is a demanding occupation for the two part-time principals of the Brazos School for Inquiry and Creativity. They have all of the administrative and organizational requirements of a larger school being necessary, but fewer facilities and human resources available to complete the work. The smaller number of students does not necessarily lead to less work, though the ability to ignore the large number of rules, regulations, and requirements of large school systems is a bonus, a fact noted also by teachers. Administrators are responsible for the general organization of the school, must monitor the development of class curricula, facilitate the development of a variety of school plans, order and distribute textbooks, engage in extensive disciplinary activity, formulate and complete a variety of forms, maintain school documentation, organize report cards, and assist in the construction of the complex scheduling required by the flexible instructional arrangements in the school. Because the school is so new, much of this activity is developmental and being engaged in an ongoing way as a need arises. It is demanding activity requiring after hours work by both part-time principals and the head of the school board.

One of the ongoing difficulties is to provide organization and structure in ways that are consonant with the values and principles of the school. As one principal says, we try to deal with things on an individual basis, focusing on values rather than on a fixed set of rules. Only when a problem becomes school-wide, with, for example, tardiness and absenteeism becoming wide spread, are rules defined. In many instances, however, individual children are given counseling to help them understand the purposes of the school and the need for them to be responsible for their own work and behavior.

This focus on individual counseling of students has paid off. Behavioral and disciplinary problems having decreased dramatically over the past year, though some older students continue to have problems taking the Inquiry/Creativity Model on board. As one administrator noted, "Older male students, especially, tend to come with too much baggage. They're products of the existing system." It is clear that systematic talking through of issues and focus on individual child responsibility for behavior is having an impact. Students understand and conform to the routines laid down for resolution of problems and disputes. A sense of order and responsiveness prevails amongst the students, despite the sometimes-high levels of activity and movement.

Administratively, therefore, the school has much to celebrate. As levels of conflict and associated disciplinary problems have decreased, the students appear much happier, a facet of their experience most evident in interviews. Many children who were "at risk," that is, on the point of being suspended from their previous school, are becoming more settled as they get used to the way the school functions. Attendance has improved—the school attained a rate of 98% for the first six weeks of the school year, and children are increasingly engaged in productive work. As one administrator noted, "We're now starting to see the Inquiry/Creativity Model coming in." It is not easy, however, and she continues to find it hard not to fall back into a traditional mode of operation. Although it is relatively clear how the model works at a classroom level, it is more difficult to imagine how to run a school accordingly. Nevertheless, the school evinces a comfortable, laid back, harmonious ethos in tune with the spirit of the Inquiry/Creativity Model that gives it life.

Although administrators focus on the needs of the children and the instructional processes to implement this innovative educational model, it is apparent that they work under difficulties. Even a short period of observation reveals the lack of space, furniture, and facilities to establish an efficient administrative system. As the school develops, it will need to acquire the resources necessary to provide space for the multitude of interactions occurring at all times, facilities for information storage and retrieval, an efficient system of records, facilities for preparation of documents, and the many other tasks and functions required to administer a school effectively. The administrative staff does a surprisingly effective job in the circumstances, but as the school grows, these issues will become more pressing.

TEACHER PERSPECTIVES

The dedication and vision of the teachers at the Brazos School for Inquiry and Creativity is admirable. All have a focus that speaks clearly to the principles enunciated by the Inquiry/Creativity Model, which forms the central theory at the core of the school's operation. As Dr. Slater notes, "Without that theory, there would be no school." It is a statement pertinent to the perspectives of all teachers in the school. Though some of the teachers initially found the transition from traditional schools somewhat difficult, all are in accord with the fundamental principles of the Model and enjoyed the equality they experienced as staff members. One teacher indicated, "I found it difficult at first, but after about three months I liked it a lot. I find there's more will and more desire to learn than in the public schools. I like that the kids can work at their own level; they're excited, interested."

Teachers also enjoyed the flexibility and freedom allowed by the small size of the school. They enjoyed the ability to take field trips to ground the children's learning in real-life events and phenomena and to be able to take advantage of the children's interests. They spoke enthusiastically of past field trips and those planned for the future. Further, the less rigid structure enabled them to get the kids involved in activities related to careers in which they expressed interest and to get them in contact, through visits and visitors, with their own culture.

Student Achievement

Teachers are also enthusiastic about the response of students to the school's model of education. One teacher, comparing the experience of public schooling, recounted the differences from his previous experience. "You have to give students at other schools tangible rewards. I'd buy things like games and disposable cameras. Here, the rewards are more intangible for these kids. They know they're advancing faster than they would at other schools. [That motivates them]."

Relationship with Students

The staff also appreciates the low student-to-teacher ratios, at some times of the day being reduced to 2:1 or 3:1 when Aggie tutors are in attendance. They comment on the attention it is possible to give to individual students and the relationships that develop in the process. "You get to know your students. You become part of their environment, you become a friend, a part of their community. They have a lot more confidence asking you questions and showing you work. As a teacher, that's rewarding."

An Inquiry/Creativity Curriculum

The staff also approve of the more balanced curriculum with its emphasis on an aesthetic as well as academic curriculum. Teachers are also aware, however, of the challenges before them and of the need to improve the quality of the curriculum as well as academic achievement. As one noted, "We have to build character and self responsibility in kids and enduring knowledge, not just passing the TAAS test like the public schools. . . . I'd like the kids to be able to say that moving to the Brazos school changed their lives. I'd like it to enable them to go to their maximum capacity, to make them critical thinkers, not just pass the test or go to the next grade level." Another indicated, "The real power is to have the children review their portfolio. I'd like them to be able to critique their own work, to review their achievement and progress, and assess the quality of their work in terms of goals and purposes they've set themselves." Currently, kids don't understand why they're learning what they're learning, except insofar as it is part of the TEKS.

This raises an important issue that points to an underlying tension in the implementation of the Inquiry/Creativity Model: How to build a curriculum that enables students to formulate learning activities and focuses within a state stipulated curriculum framework. A number of teachers and administrators spoke of the difficulty in coming to grips with this issue. One indicated that she would like to see more innovation, with the students more involved in the process of developing learning projects and less lecturing by the teachers. She'd like to hear the kids talking more about what they're doing in classrooms and getting to the point where they could work independently for a whole day. On reflection, she realized that the kids were achieving much more than they had been able earlier in the school's history, but she was still concerned to see the better implementation of the Inquiry/Creativity Model.

Most teachers who indicated a desire to more clearly enact in the child's learning the model they advocated echoed this perspective. As one indicated, "The potential is there, but we're not achieving it yet. If we can get the kids natural curiosity and apply it to the work in hand, it'll be a wonderful thing. Rather than setting up [material from a state curriculum] and teaching to it, I'd like to start with what the kids are interested in

and start with that." She also saw the need to learn techniques to deal with the multiple interests and levels that would be involved in such an approach to teaching. Currently, she was not sure how to handle a situation where other students were passive as she worked things through with one of the class. "I need to think of a way to deal with this." Though the current structure revolving round the Texas Essential Knowledge and Skills has served the school well at this stage in its history, a more creative, innovative approach to curriculum processes may be required to enact the school's preferred Model.

Planning and Professional Development

It is evident in speaking with teachers that all have the desire to upgrade their skills and knowledge. They are searching for ways to more effectively implement the Inquiry/Creativity Model, incorporating more diverse types of activity, working in an interdisciplinary way, formulating a more integrated, thematic curriculum, and/or constructing learning programs more clearly centered on student needs and interests. As one said, "We need to look more clearly at what we're doing academically; whether we're really and Inquiry/Creativity school; whether the kids are asking good questions and producing a creative product."

This points to the need for the school to make provisions for staff professional development—to provide regular times, on a weekly basis and/or each semester, for teachers to work together and/or in concert with people with relevant curriculum expertise and experience; to extend their skills and build a repertoire of appropriate techniques, activities, and approaches to learning. They may also need time and assistance to formulate a more systematic, structured curriculum process reflecting the principles of the Inquiry/Creativity Model. Individual teachers have some ideas and access to limited resources, but it is likely they will need an extended and systematic planning process to collaboratively plan and develop a more clearly structured and integrated curriculum.

Equipment and Materials

These issues are made more problematic by the lack of equipment and materials; a fact clearly evident to the eye of an experienced visitor. A dearth of storage space, a lack of general teaching equipment and materials and a paucity of books, including textbooks and other resource materials, spoke to the realities of a school in its early days of operation. One teacher noted that he had heard it took 5-7 years for a school to become fully operational. It is evident that to fully implement the chosen model the school will need to increase teaching/learning resources, especially in light of the highly individualized instruction required. An increase in computer numbers will alleviate this problem to some extent, as students will be able to access knowledge and information available on the web. It will not solve the problem, however, and as the school moves toward a more clearly articulated Inquiry/Creativity curriculum, required resources should be identified. It may also need to institute a process for regular planning and ordering of teaching/learning equipment and materials.

Achievements

Despite the obstacles they face—the limited resources and the rather crowded conditions—there is a real air of achievement amongst the teachers at Brazos School for Inquiry and Creativity. They enjoy their relationships with students, and the feeling of having achieved something significant in the process is evident in student accomplishments and engagement and in the mere fact of having *survived.* "The school has a lot to say about how at-risk kids can learn. Most of these kids weren't making it in the public schools. A lot of people said it couldn't be done. We've done it!" Staff are also clear in their desire to maintain themselves in this type of school. As one indicated, "I couldn't go back to a public school. I couldn't overlook the structure, the kids that didn't make it, the general acceptance of that." Despite the problems they face, most indicate that they "love working in this school," and are intent on maintaining the momentum toward achieving the vision that has given new meaning to their professional lives.

CONCLUSION

Dr. Slater's vision of an innovative school, an integral part of preparation for participation in a democratic society, is manifest in the operation of the Brazos School for Inquiry and Creativity. His drive and passion for this model can be seen daily in the dedicated and enthusiastic work of staff of the school and in the quiet and productive achievements of the students. The school is far from a finished product, but has already achieved significant gains in providing an effective education for the students who attend. A steadier and more orderly educational environment has supplanted the hard work and seemingly chaotic events of the first months

of the school. Those responsible should take heart in the clear achievements already evident in the lives of their students, noting carefully the results they have achieved, not only academically, but also emotionally and socially. While there is still much work to be done, the principles of the model are clearly in the minds of all who work in the school, and stand as a beacon guiding future developments. These principles will become increasingly manifest as staff and students continue to develop the structures and strategies that give form and coherence to their educational life. The successes experienced should be applauded and celebrated and the strengths built upon. Brazos School for Inquiry and Creativity is a testament to the idea that **"small is beautiful!"**

APPENDIX

ACTION AGENDAS

Administrators and teachers reviewed this report and discussed issues within it. The following major agendas derive from this discussion:

Curriculum Development

There is little doubt that children within the school have increased their learning dramatically. At the moment, however, learning is still based on a linear movement through the TEEKS, and school faculty are still grappling with ways of enacting an inquiry-based model of instruction. They are concerned about standards students have for themselves and the possibility that student learning is somewhat superficial. They seek a curriculum that is more oriented to the interests and experiences of the children and towards enduring knowledge and life skills. Action agendas include:

- The systematic development of an integrated school curriculum more clearly reflecting the Inquiry/Creativity Model
- A block of time (4–5 days) put aside for school staff to formulate an initial curriculum structure and a process for its ongoing development
- Although school staff are well equipped for this process, it would be enhanced by inputs from people with relevant curriculum expertise

Resources

As a new school, the BSIC is relatively poorly resourced for the rich array of materials and equipment required by the model of education it espouses. There is need for the school to:

- Systematically review current equipment and material needs related to teaching and student learning
- Acquire resources as indicated by the curriculum development process

Professional Development

Teachers and administrators indicate a desire to extend their understanding of practical ways of implementing an Inquiry/Creativity curriculum. They may upgrade their skills through:

- Regular, structured opportunities to exchange ideas and information
- Reviewing individual staff professional development needs
- A program of workshops or short courses to extend skills

Staff Orientation

Over time the school will experience continuing changes in staff, particularly the student tutors who provide an important resource. To ensure that people working at the school engage their work appropriately, the school will require:

- A process for orienting and training staff in appropriate teaching/learning and behavior management processes

Organizational Planning

In the early days of school development, staff were called on to engage in a variety of activities as needs emerged unexpectedly. With the increasing stability of the school's operation, staff expressed the need to:

- Engage a long-term planning process to ensure a continuity of staff and a continuing engagement with the Inquiry/Creativity vision
- Clearly define the roles and responsibilities of staff so that school needs were met systematically

3. Listening to Families: Improving Communication Between the School and the Community

A Collaborative Project of: Barrios Juntos Neighborhood Collective, the University of New Mexico, and Reginald Chavez Elementary School

This report describes a collaborative project insti-gated by women in a neighborhood collective and de-veloped by them with the assistance of the school principal, a university professor, and graduate stu-dents. It presents details of the research process, in-cluding the process of data collection and analysis, together with a report on results of the survey. It also indicates the way the school used information emerg-ing from the study.

I. PROJECT BACKGROUND

The focus of the research project on parent-teacher conferences can only be understood if we present the people behind the project. The project was formulated and implemented by participants from the Barrios Jun-tos neighborhood collective, Reginald Chavez Ele-mentary School, the University of New Mexico, and volunteers from the community at large.

Barrios Juntos

The project was initiated by Barrios Juntos, a group of concerned community people dedicated to ad-dressing the many problems that exist in the locali-ties in which the live. They believe that because of their deep commitment to their community areas, and their intimate relationship with the residents of these neighborhoods, they have a first-hand knowl-edge of the problems that exist. Their combined ex-perience and successes as community activists in addressing these problems, even without financial sponsorship, places them in the best position to identify, address, and help correct many problems that exist in their identified areas. In their planning and strategy-development sessions, they have at-tempted to identify all of the major problems in their community, while selecting specific problem areas where their work will begin.

II. PROJECT INTENTION

Barrios Juntos' plan to improve children's educational experiences by changing the role of parents and im-proving opportunities for parents to participate in their children's education. The first step was to bring to-gether a core representation, which included neigh-borhood parents, children, residents, principals, teachers, and key school administrators, to discuss these issues and to decide what could be done to im-prove parent inclusion.

III. PROJECT PROCESS

Surveying Parents

Preparations for conducting the survey began with the identification of neighborhood volunteers who were brought together for an initial evening and subse-quent training at the Reginald Chavez site. Volunteers included parents and grandparents, neighborhood as-sociation leaders, former teachers and UNM graduate students, and service corps members. Information cov-ered with the training session included background on the subject, the thinking behind the survey ques-tions, and considerations of different ways to gather survey data. During parent-teacher conference time, volunteers were carefully stationed around the school to intercept post-conference traffic and then either survey on the spot, or more typically, find a quiet place, such as the library, to sit and talk. To make parents feel more at ease with this process, Barrios Juntos provided food and drink for all those who answered survey questions. Of the 200 families affiliated with Reginald Chavez, 120 of these at-tended parent-teacher conferences, with project vol-unteers surveying 88. Many of those not surveyed attended conferences organized before the start of the school day.

Analyzing Results

Six survey questions were identified prior to the par-ent-teacher conferences. After the conferences, Pro-fessor Stringer from UNM suggested that follow-up work with parent answers focus on three questions: 1A, 3A, and 3B, with answers to other questions often proving repetitious. The Barrios Juntos/University group went through collected surveys recording parent responses to each question on large sheets of paper for all to see and discuss. Where responses were repeated, a check mark was added to the first response, with additional information added alongside in a different color.

Documenting Findings

After responses to a question had been listed, they were then all grouped by theme into four headings. The questions were reviewed by the Barrios Juntos/University group, with Professor Stringer leading the discussion. Responses were woven into a written report by the university group, who sought to maintain documented voices as much as possible. The report was later brought back to the entire Barrios Juntos/University group for review and revision.

IV. PROJECT RESULTS

Question 1A–How did you feel about your parent-teacher conference?

Introduction
The following results were derived from an analysis of parent responses to this question. It drew responses that were grouped under four headings: communication, how parents feel about the conference, the school and the teachers, and what parents learn from the conference:

Communication
It was interesting to see that many of the parents stress the importance of "ongoing communication" with the teachers. "Open communication" and "constant contact" are identified as key to not only the success of the conference but also the overall progress of the child. The information flow, which includes to and from the child, is "useful for the teacher as well as the parent," and one parent stated that this affects "how openly I can discuss anything with the teacher" and "how well the teacher knows the children."

Almost one-third of the parents were pleased with the way teachers "explain everything clearly," "answer questions," and "explain the child's progress and what's coming up." One parent put it concisely, stating that "the information is useful for the teacher and the parent, and ultimately for the child."

How parents feel about the conference
Most parents felt that the parent-teacher conferences "went well." They said the conferences are "thorough, yet quick," and a "very positive" experience. Some expressed that they "feel comfortable," "enjoy the conference," and that the "teacher is great." They feel they are "treated with respect," they have a "good relationship" with the teacher, and have "confidence in what the teacher is doing." On the whole, parents expressed that the "conferences are important" and "useful" for their child's progress. A couple of parents said they feel "free to express any concerns" they have.

A few parents have some concerns about the conferences. One parent mentioned how she was "not happy with the (child's) grades." Another was distressed because "there was someone else in the room" during her conference. This turned out to be another parent waiting for his/her conference. Although the teacher apologized, the parent found this "distracting." A couple of the parents said that the teachers are "not around to meet during the school year." One of the parents said they "wish the conferences were longer."

The school and the teachers
Almost half the parents made general comments about the school and the teachers. The overwhelming opinion of teachers is positive, with parents stating that "the teachers are great," and they are "happy" with them. One parent explained how the teacher "knows the (child's) strengths and weaknesses" and "is doing extra to help" both the parent and the child. The only concerns the parents have are that some "teachers don't speak Spanish," are "not around to meet during the school year," and "don't give enough help on how to help (the children) out of school time."

With regard to the school, some of the parents said they believe "this is a good school" with a "good atmosphere in the classroom." A few parents are concerned about their child being placed in special programs such as Title 1.

What parents learn from the conference
Parents leave with "more information" about their child then when they came in. For example, some parents found out that their child is "having problems of low grades," and others learned that their child is "having no problems." Some discovered that their child "is doing well," "progress was good," and the child's "reading and learning is better."

Summary

The majority of the feedback from parents was positive. However, there were some concerns, which revolved around the length of conferences and the availability of teachers during the year for more frequent communication and progress reports.

Question 3A: How can teachers improve parent-teacher conferences?

Introduction

This question drew suggestions later grouped under four headings: scheduling, communication, life in school, and the total child. At the time, many parents had positive comments they wished to record. Some noted that their conference had been "good," and a number said the conference had been "great", while others said that the conference was "perfect." Parents who were specific about aspects of the conference that they appreciated made the following comments: "Everyone was ready to start the conference," and "the teacher used a form, which explains the child's performance." Teachers were also praised for being "accommodating" and "answering questions."

Scheduling

One parent noted, "one of her child's teachers did not give her a conference date," while another asked for "more advanced notice, at least a week." Yet another commented, "bringing problems up at a conference is too late. I want to take care of things right away," and one went so far as to ask for "weekly reports; nine weeks is too long without talking." A few parents recommended that conferences be held later in the day "at a time convenient for parents." However, by far the largest concern among parents is that there be "more time available" for conferences.

Communication

While one parent made a point of talking about "good communication in giving positive feedback," another talked of the need to "establish good communication," and yet another—speaking out of frustration—said simply that the teacher should "tell the truth." Some parents asked for "a translator/interpreter," and one asked specifically for "help with interacting with my daughter in English so she would feel better communicating with her (English speaking) teacher." One respondent stated that "the parent shouldn't have to ask all the questions," while another requested that the teacher have "questions

ready for the parent to ask." One parent hoped that the teacher would have "more to say about my child" and "be consistent in the way they go though the forms." It was also suggested that parents be encouraged to "bring the child" to the conference. Some feedback focused on teachers making parents more comfortable. One mother said, "They ignored me"—as the teacher focused instead on her husband. She therefore requested that the teacher make "eye contact with the person asking the question." A suggestion to make parents feel more at ease was to "have snacks" in the classroom.

Life in school

Some parents would like teachers to take time to go beyond talking about their child's progress in the last nine weeks and explain other issues relating to life in school. One parent asked that the teacher "talk about ways they deal with discipline," while others hoped that teachers would "explain math" and "talk in depth about the grading system." Yet another needed to "know more about the gifted program so I can make a decision." Other suggestions focused on helping parents better understand what is going on in the classroom, including asking for "a walk through the classroom to get an idea of what a child experiences" and for a "child's progress to be posted in the classroom."

The total child

When surveyed, one parent had only a single problem at the conference. "I disagree with putting my child on violation." This and other parent concerns that teachers "take an interest in the child" and "be aware of other needs of the child" might begin to be met through one parent's suggestion that the teacher make "home visits." Another parent went further, suggesting that her teacher "take ideas from families on how to work with children." As part of attending to the total child, one parent asked that the teachers "research and understand more about problems such as dyslexia," while another asked that school and home communicate over "hearing and eye tests."

Summary

While many parents have positive comments to share regarding their conference experience, they also have some concerns and a number of suggestions for teachers to consider. Scheduling and communication issues dominate critical conference feedback, but parents also express interest in broadening the parent-teacher interaction to cover a range of issues affecting the lives of children both in and out of school.

Question 3B—How could parents make the next conference better?

Introduction
This question drew suggestions later grouped under four headings: communication, parental involvement/showing concern, preparation, and showing up.

Communication
A parent noted that "parent and teachers should be on the same page." Some parents felt there was no need for improvement. Suggestions from parents on improving communication include: "receiving information from the teacher before the next conference," "communication with teachers outside of conference," and the "need to inform parents on an ongoing basis." Teachers also need to create the space for "parents to have the opportunity to ask teachers if they don't understand." Parents on their part need to "inform teachers of their child's needs" and "share history of family," if needed. This also includes listening to teachers and solving problems together and "pay attention to teachers throughout the year."

Parental involvement/showing concern
Overall, parents felt the need to "get the parents more involved." The methods of involvement included: spend more time in school, volunteer more, know what your child is doing, and know what is expected of them. One of the responses was that each parent needs to "pay more attention to (his/her) children, including ways to help them." Another added, "make education a priority" and "learn about their child's education and how it affects the child and (his/her) life." Parents emphasized that they need to make time for their children and let them know they really care.

Preparation
Parents emphasized the importance of "knowing your questions and concerns going in." Parents should "always be prepared," which includes requesting to see the child's work and communicating with the teacher before the conference. One of the parents suggested that parents need to go in "feeling good about what you are going to discuss."

Showing up
Suggestions by the parents include the advice that parents should "attend the conference—it's important." One couple also noted the importance of "going in as a team." Other suggestions include keeping your appointment and to "be prompt and leave on time."

Summary
While many parents have positive comments to share regarding their conference experience, they also have some concerns and a number of suggestions for parents to consider. Suggestions include the importance of attending and showing concern, being prepared, and keeping the time commitment. The importance of ongoing and effective communication was once again a high priority.

Executive Summary

One hundred twenty parents attended the parent-teacher conferences; of that number 88 were surveyed for this project. The general themes of the findings were communication, scheduling, the school and teachers, the children, and what parents learned from the experience.

While many parents had positive comments to share regarding their conference experience, they also had some concerns and a number of suggestions for teachers to consider. Scheduling and communication issues dominated critical conference feedback, but parents also expressed interest in broadening the parent-teacher interaction to cover a range of issues affecting the lives of children both in and out of school. Some concerns revolved around the length of conferences and the availability of teachers during the year for more frequent communication and progress reports. Suggestions included the importance of attending and showing concern, being prepared, and keeping the time commitment. The importance of ongoing and effective communication was by far the highest priority.

The results were summarized and presented to the community in the following document, produced in both English and Spanish on either side of a single page.

PROJECT SUMMARY

Undertaking the project has proved significant in three regards. Firstly, it has demonstrated that neighborhood organizations like Barrios Juntos are capable of designing and developing a collaborative endeavor involving community members, school and district personnel, and university faculty and students. Secondly, this project has demonstrated that neighborhood organizations such as Barrios Juntos play a significant role in developing and deepening home-school relations through their ability to organize the collection of large numbers of parent surveys. Finally, the project has demonstrated to a neighborhood organization such as Barrios Juntos that through their

"LISTENING TO FAMILIES AT REGINALD CHAVEZ ELEMENTARY SCHOOL"

The purpose of this project is to improve children's education by improving relationships between parents, children, and teachers.

Members of Barrios Juntos Neighborhood Collective talked with the school principal and teachers about parent-teacher conferences. During the week of March 20, Barrios Juntos interviewed 88 out of 200 parents about their parent-teacher conference experience.

Many parents were generally satisfied with the conference; however, they suggested that conferences should be improved in the following ways:

Parents could:

- Attend the conference and be on time. This shows that parents care and are interested.
- Be aware of what your child is doing in school and what is expected of your child.
- Get more involved in your child's classroom, volunteer at school, and request to see your child's work.
- Meet with the teacher before the conference and ask for follow-up meetings.
- Inform teachers of your child's needs.
- Time and thought into the questions to allow them to get more out of the conference. Be ready with questions and concerns.
- Show your children you care by making time for them; ask children about their concerns and ways to help.

Teachers could:

- Research and understand more about problems such as dyslexia, hearing, and eye tests.
- Keep parents informed on an ongoing basis and especially before conferences.
- Take ideas from families on how to work with children, problem solving, and parents.
- Be proactive bringing problems up at conferences is too late. I want to take care of things right away.
- Need a translator/interpreter, if the child needs more support understanding directions.
- Provide homework plans so parents can encourage and support the child at home.
- Explain more about the grading system and ways teachers/schools deal with discipline.

---

ability to develop action research agendas, universities have a potentially valuable role in strengthening community-building endeavors in school settings.

DISTRIBUTING FINDINGS

A one-page summary of project findings was distributed to the Reginald Chavez community during the school's annual celebration. It is anticipated that a more detailed report, perhaps based on the documents, will be made available to parents upon request. Findings from the research process to date have also formed the basis of a research class presentation made by university partners, while Barrios Juntos partners have made a presentation to a University Family Literacy class.

ADDENDUM

Since completion of this project, Reginald Chavez School has instituted changes in the way parent-teacher conferences are conducted, including extending the time available for each. The principal indicated that school staff were continuing to explore ways to incorporate suggestions from the research project.

---

4. *Students and Teacher as Co-Researchers: Developing Multicultural Awareness in a High School Class*

By Shelia Baldwin

This paper, produced as part of a dissertation study, describes a process by which a high school teacher facilitated a study of the school and local community by a group of her students. It describes the largely ethnographic methods used by students to gather and analyze data, including the innovative use of video. Of particular interest is the way major features identified by students and the teacher were formulated into tables to assist in clarifying information emerging in the study.

INTRODUCTION

This paper reports on ways in which I, as the teacher of a multicultural student body in an American Culture Studies class, instituted collaborative, community-based approaches to pedagogy in response to the multicultural realities of my classroom. It reveals how the development of a community of learners through use of participatory decision-making and students as researchers enabled students to affirm their cultural identity and make powerful connections between their homes and the school. In the process, we were able to engage a curriculum that was more relevant to students' lives, that provided students with opportunity for critical thought in questioning existing school practices, and led them to take positive action in response to the outcomes of their inquiries.

THE GENESIS OF THE AMERICAN CULTURE STUDIES CLASS

My concern for why many high school students appear to lack interest in learning led to the pilot study that preceded the major study. I conducted an informal inquiry with a group of high school student volunteers who were encouraged to do an ethnographic study of their own cultures and the culture of the high school (Baldwin, 1997). The nine students (six seniors, two juniors, and one sophomore) of White, African American, and Hispanic backgrounds were members of the Action committee—a group that was formed as an answer to the high school's problems with race relations.

The students and I met in the mornings before school several times during the spring semester of 1993 to learn about ethnographic methods and then to discuss observations that they had made in the school setting and in their home settings. The outcome of this inquiry was their recognition of a need for raising student awareness about cultural diversity.

So successful were our efforts that the student ethnographers encouraged me to continue with the inquiry with another group of students the next year (most of this group was graduating) or to offer a course in multicultural awareness. The course, American Culture Studies, became a reality because of the suggestion of the nine students.

Being a part of this study with students acting as ethnographers had a great impact on my teaching philosophy. The subject of the study—an inquiry into school and community culture—was relevant to them. The student ethnographers were interested and committed to this project because they were learning about themselves. They became involved and took ownership. Their desire for this project to be perpetuated through a course or a continued study emphasized the importance they placed on it. I realized that inviting students to participate in decisions that affect their learning is motivational and empowering as was demonstrated by the student ethnographers.

A CONSTRUCTIVIST APPROACH TO AMERICAN CULTURE STUDIES

Raul announced to me one day in our American Culture Studies class, "I can't believe this class is so noisy so early in the morning. Nobody's sleepin'! Everybody's so lively!" He was one of 21 high school students who assembled every morning at 7:25 a.m. for 90 minutes of cultural awareness. Of the 21 sophomores, juniors, and seniors, 14 were African American (six girls and eight boys), four Hispanic (three girls and one boy), and three White (two girls and one boy). Raul's comment is indicative of the high levels of student engagement and reflects their response to the constructivist approach to teaching/learning I had instituted for this class.

In response to student requests described previously, I had formulated an American Culture Studies course the previous semester. After gaining approval for the course outline that I wrote and submitted to the school district curriculum coordinator, the first class was offered as an elective the fall semester of 1994. I introduced the students to the course outline that would serve as a framework. I emphasized that I intended for the course to take a direction based on their own inquiries into and curiosities about cultures.

The course was divided into three-week units: World—learning about our own heritage and other world cultures; America—identifying and discussing sociocultural issues that permeate American society; and Community—exploring our school/community cultures. We began our semester together with community building activities in order to become better acquainted and more comfortable with each other. Several of the students were well acquainted, some good friends, and others unknown to each other. Also, the students cooperatively devised classroom rules in order to ensure a comfortable environment in which everyone's opinion would be respected.

The requirements of the course included a reflective journal in which students wrote about anything that might relate to the course, a book to read that pertained to some aspect of culture, and participation in class discussions. Other activities evolved with the unfolding nature of the curriculum. What happened each day led us in a direction within the framework of the course outline. For example, during the second week of class, one student raised a question about her self-identity. "I'd like to know why I do some things the way I do. Like where'd they come from?" I took that cue to ask them to write down some questions they had about culture. They posed questions about their own unique heritage, cultural traits, or about the American culture: What do some of my features mean? Did my father's family originally come from Mexico? How did a particular culture start? Why do White people think they own America? Why did the pilgrims take America away from the Indians?

Another activity that evolved from a student's question became the creation of a survey about cultural relations. While we were reviewing the course outline, a student asked, "What's this survey?" I told the class that I had intended to give them a pre- and post survey to determine attitude change, but I couldn't find one and didn't have time to construct one. Another student suggested, "Why don't we write one and survey the student body?" So, we did. We worked collaboratively compiling questions that related to our school and community. After it was approved by the principal,

the 18-question survey was distributed to approximately 10% of the student body. Because the results came back after the end of the course, 13 volunteers (11 class members and two friends) tallied and interpreted the results during two after-school sessions and had them published in the school newspaper. The results were better than the students thought they were going to be. "It's not as negative as we thought, but there is still too much negative. We need to get to know each other." The action they took was to organize a volleyball tournament as a get-acquainted activity.

Another major project the students selected was to study cultures. The class determined which cultures they would like to study and worked individually or in groups on the culture of their choice and then presented what they learned to the class.

To further our knowledge about different cultures, we invited guest speakers to our class. Our foreign exchange students from Finland and the Slovak Republic informed us about life in their countries. Another guest was a visiting professor from Australia whom they immediately dubbed the "Crocodile Man." Each class member had prepared some questions to ask our visitors. "We got to hear what *really* goes on in their countries, and we stop believing only what we hear. . . ." The students' attentiveness toward our foreign visitors and toward their classmates' culture project presentations indicated their interest in different countries and cultures.

A field trip, an event they talked about from the beginning, became a reality. We visited an art museum that had a special photography exhibit of the everyday life of African Americans. At another museum, we enjoyed the Imax presentation of *Serengeti* and a live butterfly center. Finally, we experienced lunch at a Chinese/Vietnamese restaurant. Several mentioned that the trip brought them closer together, which was exemplified in a student's comment: "I basically enjoyed everything, *especially being together.*"

Although the aforementioned were all praised and enjoyed, the highlight of the class was discussion. When I interviewed the students individually about the class, one activity that was mentioned over and over as a favorite was discussion: "We talked about things that we never talk about in other classes." The discussions stemmed from readings taken from the Anti-Defamation League of B'nai B'rith's *A World of Difference.* They talked openly about societal issues such as alternate lifestyles, prejudice, racism, and discrimination. Students provided stories, personal experiences, and opinions, all of which prompted further discussion. One student commented, "We could go on and on." We never had enough time.

On our last day of class, I asked them to interview a classmate whom they didn't get to know well during the semester. After they had completed their interviews with each other, they wrote their personal accounts of the interviews and shared them with their partners. Not only had they learned some things about each other that they didn't know but also changed some assumptions they had made. For example, Clifford wrote, "I thought Rosalia was just a quiet person, but the reason she didn't talk a lot is because she doesn't speak English that good." Raul wrote about Bonnie, "I never thought she was this way. Now, I know it doesn't matter who you are, color, or background, we are all humans and have feelings and needs." After the sharing, students spread out to other classmates to comment about their interviews or just to visit. It was an appropriate way to close the semester. Instead of saying goodbye, I said, "I'll see you all later!"

The semester passed quickly. None of us were ready for our time together in a most meaningful learning community to be over. Students offered suggestions for continuing what we had started: "How about a Culture Studies II," "Can we make this a year class?" or "Can I take this again?" Bonnie wrote in her final evaluation of the class, "If this class were a person, it would be an open, talkative, interesting person."

REVIEWING AND EVALUATING THE CLASS: TEACHER AND STUDENTS AS CO-RESEARCHERS

Toward the end of the semester, I moved toward evaluating the class. In doing so, I planned to use the participatory processes that had been central to the operation of the class. It not only fit my current educational philosophy, but was consonant with educational theories of multicultural education, constructivism, and critical pedagogy, which suggests people learn by being actively involved and by thinking about and being articulate about their learning. I was concerned not only to reflect on my own teaching processes, but to engage my students in exploring the nature and extent of their own learning.

True to the democratic, participatory intent of my pedagogy, therefore, I instituted a collaborative

process to evaluate the outcomes of the class. Of the 21 students in the class, 8 to 10 students accepted my invitation to be researchers. The student researchers and I met after school on four occasions and during lunch one day. After socializing over pizza, sandwiches, or spaghetti and soda, everyone settled down to the task at hand.

Before we began the analysis of the videotapes, I provided the student researchers with Spradley's (1979) nine major dimensions of every social situation as a means for guiding their observations, and then we proceeded. First, they viewed a videotape of some of the class sessions. As they viewed the video, I asked them to write down words or phrases that identified what they saw happening in that classroom. From their individually written notes on their observations, they compiled a list of descriptors that a student researcher wrote on a piece of poster paper attached to the chalkboard.

The audiotape analysis proceeded a little differently because the students chose to read the transcription out loud, as though they were reading a play. They verbalized their observations at three different intervals that I recorded directly on the poster paper hanging before them.

Next, they organized the list of descriptors [from the video and audio tapes] into categories and labeled each category. This process was repeated in each of the four analysis sessions according to which elements they agreed went together. Finally, they placed the categories from each session into a final set of categories, which became their key elements that framed the account of their experience (see Table 8.1).

I identified key features from recurring themes that became evident in the students' analysis, together with my own journal, student journal writings, interviews, and final class evaluations (see Table 8.2).

CO-RESEARCHERS' PERSPECTIVES AND INTERPRETATIONS

The result of our inquiry reveals the impact of complex human relationships, curricular decisions, and pedagogical practices on a learning environment. "Getting to know each other" was mentioned numerous times in reference to different situations. The student researchers recognized the importance of getting acquainted in order to develop cultural understanding before being able to become a viable learning community. One of the student researchers commented about this as they were categorizing the data during

Table 8.1
Student Researchers' Categories and Key Elements

Communication	Individualism	Feelings	Involvement
Discussion Items	*"Doing Our Own Thang"*	*Emotional Feelings*	*Class Participation*
Different lifestyles	Focusing on camera	Serious, digging	Discussion—lots, good
TG has most to say	Finally settled down and	Own experiences	Interested in visitor—
Interested but afraid to	started reading	Everyone involved	asking questions
comment because of	Took Mrs. B long time to	BO upset	Certain times—all
others' opinions	get us to settle down	Heated—LL, TM, CA,	paying attention
Blurting out	Class liked CW's idea of	TG, JC	Hoodrats paying
Some students silent	cultural dancing	Feelings hurt, Quiet	attention with Ernie
Not involved in discussion		Pointing the finger	All getting along
but listening		African American/White	
Maintaining an image		issue	
		Interesting	
Class Coming Together	*Stand Outs*	*Feelings of Loss*	*We Were Serious*
More positive	TG lots to say	Missing people missing	Serious, digging, Best
Got to know each other	LL got serious with report	Missing Mrs. B	discussion
better	Those who never got		Storytelling, Own
	into class		experiences
	TM and TG "ganging up"		Everyone involved
	on LL about pep rally		Everyone talking
			Hoodrats involved
Communication		*Letting Go*	*Interest*
Communication, Flirting		Relief from class	Interest in animals
No fighting, Fun all around		Students off task	Awe
Discussion, Laughter		Calm—relaxed—chillin'	Involvement
Loud—quiet			Hyperactive
Mixed groups			
Beverly Hills took over			
"ghetto"			
Everyone associating			
true feelings			

the second session. "We're starting to come together." As we became better acquainted, the learning atmosphere changed. Discussions became more open and serious. We were able to discuss sensitive issues and share personal experiences.

The students' friendships extended beyond the classroom. They spoke to each other outside of the classroom, which was not common in other classes. One student explained, "When I see people from this class in the hall we speak to each other. I know them. It's not like that in other classes." First impres-

sions of students changed after they got to know each other. A young man told me during his interview, "I would a thought they would offer this course before now . . . . Maybe we wouldn't a had all the trouble before. Just being in the class with other kids. Getting to know them. I think differently about people. Everyone should take this course." The students identified a solution to improving cultural relations as getting to know each other. The stress on getting to know other students extended beyond the classroom to the student body after the student

Table 8.2
Teacher Researcher's Categories and Key Elements

Emerging Community	Effect of Class Makeup	Curricular Decisions	Pedagogical Practices
Students getting to know each other Teacher getting to know students "Sitting with friends" Varying levels of student involvement	African American issues African American/White issues Subculture issues	Evolving nature Students involved in curricular decisions Student criteria for good reports Involvement • Interest in other countries • Everyone should take this course	Course design and content Process vs. product Teacher perspective on student behavior Missed opportunities Missing Mrs. B

researchers analyzed the results of the survey on culture relations. They surmised that the feelings and understanding they developed for each other in a classroom context extended beyond those walls; they had a rippling effect. Our recognition of the complexity of human relationships warrants the need for more effort to be made to build social communities in our classrooms and in our schools. Providing time in our school day for students to get to know each other is a critical aspect of education in today's world of diversity.

Not only is it important to build understanding among the student body but also among all school personnel. I got to know my students better than any class I have ever taught because I let them bring their lives into the classroom. I learned about their home cultures, families, the dreams their parents have for them, and the respect they have for their families. I developed a greater appreciation for the pride that the students have in their cultural heritage. I learned about their painful experiences. I caught a glimpse of life from their perspective. This experience has affected the way I view my classroom, students, my school, and my community. My own socialization had caused me to have a naïve, narrow perspective and a "that's the way it is" acceptance. That has changed as a result of being involved with this class in cultural awareness, taught from a constructivist, critical perspective.

The makeup of the class had an effect on the direction it took. The predominance of African American students in the class steered the discussions. Discussions centered on how negative behavior of

some African Americans reflected on the population as a whole, resulting in stereotyping. One student talked about "getting real embarrassed by some of the things that my African American people have been doin,' and it upsets me." Another wrote, "One thing that really bothers me is the lack of respect the African American culture has for themselves." The students shared their own experiences with White prejudice. This class offered them an opportunity and a comfortable environment in which to discuss with their peers how they felt. The lived experiences they shared were an acknowledgment of how deeply rooted racism is in our society. The experiences they have had in our school and community reflect the way it is and the failure to discuss racism is problematic (Tatum, 1992).

The students' observations drew attention also to the lack of acceptance by other students and school personnel of students who represented different subcultures, such as "kickers," "headbangers," and "skaters." They were becoming more critically aware of the lack of acceptance of difference in our school.

The students in the class were of varying levels of abilities, interests, and motivations. Therefore, my emphasis was on the process of learning about cultural awareness rather than the products. This created a cooperative learning atmosphere rather than a competitive one. I incorporated their perspectives into the operation of the class so that their own explorations and the reality of their community and school became the "content" of the class rather than a fixed content that I dictated. The classroom reality was transformed through their questions, their discussions, presentations, reflections, and actions toward themselves as learners and toward each other.

Alternative assessments such as self-evaluation, group evaluations and peer evaluations, and performance-based assessments provided serious, reflective assessments of their learning, of the value of different activities, and of the strengths and weaknesses of the course.

CONCLUSION

This class was a new teaching experience for me. I was learning about multiculturalism and how to respond to it. The cultural balance in this class was unique for all of us. When the semester ended, we had become a group of people who were comfortable with each other. It was a community in which everyone had a place. As Freire (1990) discussed, we had created a dialogic community. Through dialogue, we established a climate of trust. Everyone became a partner in learning, serving as both teacher and learner. This is what happened in 7½ weeks.

What might have happened if we had had another 7 weeks? I think we could have begun examining why some things were happening in the class. For example, we needed to talk about the different relationships in the class, such as with the two groups that existed within the African American students in the class. They had referred to one group as the "sisters" and the "pretty boys" and their seating area as "Beverly Hills." This group consisted of students who were involved in school activities and were academically motivated. The other group, the "Hoodrats" located in "the ghetto," would be described as marginalized students who lacked motivation and interest in school. Unfortunately, the significance of these two groups, the former representing conformity and the latter alienation, was never a point of discussion. Why did some students participate in discussions and others did not? What kind of community was emerging? We could have explored our feelings of discomfort and what we could do about it. We should have presented our findings of the importance of building a community of learners and the importance of critical dialogue in classrooms today to our faculty.

The process of theory building, reflection, and action is recursive. Through my critical reflection on

my own teaching practices, transformation was the result. The questions I ask continually about accepted practices of learning and teaching come from the theoretical perspectives of multicultural education, constructivism, and critical pedagogy that are reflected in the following description of our class:

> The classroom was a dialogic learning community in which teacher/learner and students/teachers were guided by a negotiated dynamic curriculum whose permeable boundaries accommodated students' inquiries as they explored, discovered, and critically questioned their world. Education was viewed as a democratic, social experience. Participants were actively involved in a cooperative partnership in which all voices were respected and afforded an opportunity to be heard in a collaborative search for understanding.

IMPLICATIONS FOR EDUCATIONAL SETTINGS

My approach to teaching this class was nontraditional. My students and I sought to change existing classroom practices through collaboration and community-based pedagogical processes. The following are suggestions for responding to multiculturalism in educational settings:

1. Build a community of learners through cooperation and collaboration, not competition. We need to recognize the complexity of the classroom as was illuminated in this study. The student researchers emphasized the importance of students getting to know one another. What happens in our classrooms is dependent on pedagogy, class makeup, and curriculum, all of which affect the building of a learning community. A critical focal point in teacher preparation and ongoing inservice for veteran teachers should be classroom dynamics. A positive, cooperative environment will have an effect on the learning that happens.

2. Invite students to participate in the decisions about their learning and their school community. The importance of students having a voice was demonstrated in this study. It was empowering and had an effect on their interest and motivation. Let's not assume students don't know what they want to know. The curricular framework identified the course content. My students and I collaborated about how to study it and

what we do to evaluate what was learned. Allowing students to have a voice will affect the climate in the classroom.

3. Affirm students' cultural identity by making a connection between the knowledge they bring to school and school knowledge. Schools tell children that the knowledge they bring to school is not important. Many of the students we teach have a home culture different from the school culture. What is validated is the White, Western European perspective, the dominant culture. As so many of us come from the same perspective, we take for granted that "that's the way it is." We need to be more critically aware of our own socialization and how it has shaped our perspective.

4. Make curriculum relevant to students' lives and flexible to fit the diversity of learners. With each new year (new semester), we get new students. Our tendency is to teach content not students. It is necessary to re-evaluate our curriculum with each new group of students to make adjustments. The diversity of classrooms today demands that we be more flexible in order to provide equal educational opportunities.

5. Involve students in critical thought and action. Democracy should be practiced within the walls of our schools. Students should be encouraged to question existing practices and to take action if possible. My students' discovery of the need for students to get better acquainted through their survey led them to take action by organizing a volleyball tournament. Students need to know that they have insights and are a source of valuable information that can make a difference.

6. Support teachers as reflective practitioners. Teachers should be provided opportunities and support to conduct research in their classrooms and schools. This study has demonstrated how research has contributed to my developing educational theory and has informed my practice.

7. Provide teachers with ongoing professional development to help them cope with the changing demographics they are experiencing in their classrooms and schools. Teachers need to know how they might do things differently, but also they need support groups when contemplating and implementing change.

8. Incorporate ways to bring students in the school together in meaningful activities to facilitate getting to know one another.

REFERENCES

Baldwin, S. (1997). High school students participation in action research: An ongoing learning process. In E. Stringer and Colleagues (Eds.), *Community-based ethnography: Breaking traditional boundaries of research, teaching, and learning.* Mahwah, NJ: Lawrence Erlbaum Associates.

Freire, P. (1990). *Pedagogy of the oppressed.* New York: Continuum.

Spradley, R. (1979). *The ethnographic interview.* New York: Holt, Rinehart & Winston.

Tatum, B. D. (1992). Talking about race, learning about racism: The application of racial identity development theory in the classroom. *Harvard Educational Review, 62,* 1–24.

5. Creating a Dialog for the Role of Computers in the Classroom

Shepherd Lutheran School

By Bill Miller

This study demonstrates how novice researchers can engage in productive studies having real relevance to the schools in which they work. Produced as a requirement of a research methods class, it explored the issue of the use of computers in the school. The study provided the school board with useful information that helped them to make decisions about the allocation of resources in the school.

SCHOOL HISTORY

Shepherd Lutheran School offers K–8 classes and is located at 3900 Wyoming NE, in what is known as the North East Heights of Albuquerque, New Mexico. Shepherd Lutheran School (SLS) is associated with Shepherd Lutheran Church, of the Wisconsin Evangelical Lutheran Synod (WELS), at the same address. SLS was started in 1982 as a two-room school housed in the church building. During the first few years, the classrooms had to be disassembled every Sunday morning and reassembled each Sunday afternoon. Over the years, more space was created and allocated for the classrooms. In 1994, an ambitious project of constructing a three-classroom building with a library and principal's office was completed. The school now has over 60 students and three full-time teachers with several part-time teachers for subjects such as music and art. The student body comes from a wide economic distribution of families. There is a much less diverse mix of religious beliefs—most are Protestant.

By all accounts, the level of caring and instruction are considered exceptional. Parents responded that the moral influence and Christian teachings were a deciding factor in placing their children there. When asked what was important to them, most parents replied, "The Christian education." Features such as small class size and interaction between the different ages are unique to Shepherd Lutheran and recognized as valuable to a child's development. Parents also felt that a good secular education was a consideration. "The secular education is important and I think that the principal has worked hard to improve the material." A school board member added, "I think the most important thing is offering a quality education." Another parent replied, "I love it—the small class size and the big kids helping little kids." There is a concerted effort to make the students feel like part of a family by involving their families in activities and displaying family photographs on bulletin boards. While there are not the extensive programs of public schools, Shepherd Lutheran offers more than many other parochial schools. Shepherd Lutheran has the ability to change its curriculum much quicker than a larger school. Without exception the teachers are seen as dedicated and hard working. The fact that "The teachers are approachable and easy to talk to" was stated several times. The students consider the school fun and safe and consider the small size a positive influence. Shepherd's school board understands that the tuition costs must be competitive and that a quality education must be offered. Not only must the parents and students be satisfied but also the teachers are seen as the most important part of the school.

INTERVIEWS CONCERNING THE USE OF COMPUTERS: PARTICIPANT VOICES

Parents' Points of View

Most of the parents spoke of using a computer in their work not just occasionally but all the time. "Today's jobs require them. The sooner they start learning the better so that there is no fear." One parent said, "This is a very serious thing. The future is in computers. I want my children to know how to use computers." More than one parent said, "It should be second nature to them." Some could not imagine their work without a computer. "Kids learn by poking around and by being exposed so they will learn to not be afraid of computers." When asked, "How do you feel about computers in the classroom?" one parent said, "They are a must." All of the parents interviewed were in favor of computers in the classroom, but there were varying degrees of what that involvement should be.

Teachers' Points of View

The teachers, depending on the grade level, had a slightly different response. Comments ranged from "Computers are very important" to "My room would function with or without a computer." One teacher said, "There is one computer in my classroom that we use, and I wish I had three or four computers so that more children could work at one time." Computers are seen as an important tool that can add to the classroom. "It's like having unlimited knowledge and could be used for research." New and different teaching methods can be explored. One arrangement could be a computer pod dedicated to teaching keyboard skills and word processing plus classroom computers for research and educational presentations. There is a need to update the SLS resources: "Our current encyclopedia is 10 years old and not very good." Individual classrooms would have computers based upon need. The upper grades might have more machines numbering anywhere from three per room to one for each student's desk.

New teaching materials offer exciting and the most up-to-date knowledge for use in research. The lower grades would have a few computers for the students to use during their free time and, if the appropriate software is available, learn some computer-related skills. By having computers in the school, those children that don't have one at home can gain experience. Also the congregation could have access to the machine at certain times.

School Board Point of View

Members of the school board feel that there are many components to a quality school. The reason for creating a church school was so they could "Integrate Christ-like living into every aspect." At the same time, it is recognized that "No matter what other things we stress it doesn't work unless the education component is good." School board members were more skeptical of the value of computers. "The problem with computers is they are used for the wrong reasons." Some good reasons to use a computer would be, "If a student had trouble with penmanship or to use National Geographic material." One member felt that research should be done from a book rather than a computer and that those sources should come from outside the school. There was some concern about learning a technology that is constantly changing. "It doesn't take very long to learn how to use a com-

puter." However, it was also recognized that "There is a lot to be gained with technical savvy. It's kind of the way we teach science these days, there aren't as many details, but the purpose is to develop an interest and keep an awareness."

Students' Point of View

The students liked the smallness of the school and thought that it was harder to get good grades than in public school based on what new transfer students would tell them. They felt that some resources were rather limited, such as playground equipment. When asked about computers most said there was little or no activity with computers now. They indicated that there had been more software in the past. "There is nothing worth doing on the computers any more. There are only three programs—a painting program that we just use to make funny drawings, an encyclopedia that doesn't have very many pictures, and a writing program." I asked what a computer could be used for, and one student said, "To look things up for the dailies." "Do you have enough computers?" I asked, and several said, "We don't need more computers, we need ones that work."

PROBLEMS WITH COMPUTERS

Some of the participants spoke of sources like *High Tech Heretic* and *Snake Oil Silicon* (Stoll, 1999, 1995), *Fools Gold* (Cordes & Miller, 1999), and *The Computer Delusion* (Oppenheimer, 1997), but no one had actually read these books. There are some people who have become disillusioned with all the hype about how computers can solve many of education's woes, including a teacher that said, "I have been where it wasn't for the best. We had to teach children how to program a computer, and that was a waste of time." There is a backlash from technology programs that promised great gains but failed to deliver. With resources being finite and having to be shared with so many mandatory expenses, computers and the associated upkeep are seen as unnecessary.

What about how quickly computers become obsolete? Are we teaching our children skills that will be of little value in the future? "The children are not interested in reading long clues and directions. They spend their time destroying robots."

Most people thought that some form of the technology will be around for a good while—the keyboard and video screen, for example, have been around for generations. "It's the generic knowledge that is part of the evolution of technology that's important. It was the exposure to older technology that paved the way for learning the new."

Several people had stories about how their fathers or coworkers had been afraid of computers and at the very least didn't trust them to handle their business transactions. Each of the groups recognized certain problems that come with computers. People were divided about controlling the Internet access. One teacher felt that it was a personal responsibility of the student and teacher as to what was downloaded from the net. One teacher complained, "The trouble with politicians is that they say they want government out of our lives but then introduce legislation to control what we do." All interviewees felt that some form of restriction should be employed but were divided over whether it should be the teacher, software, or both. The jury is still out on the most effective method, according to a recent article in the Sioux Falls, SD, **Argus Leader.** "Written policy to keep South Dakota State Library computer users from accessing obscene material seems to work better than electronic filtering software."

There was some concern about relying on the Internet to do research and allowing programs to automatically check and correct for spelling. Turning off features in a word processor would reduce this dependency but also eliminate some of the power of the computer. One teacher said it is "just another tool that if used correctly can be of value." The Internet really does bring the world onto a screen just inches from your face. This could be threatening to some as it is unfiltered and contains many wildly different points of view.

SOLUTIONS

There must be common ground that all the stakeholders feel comfortable with. The parents see computers in the classroom as a natural part of the curriculum. Teachers, depending on grade level, see value in having the technology available. Students seem unsure of the value of a computer in the classroom. They know how much fun they can be and how to use the available software but, in general, don't see them as being valuable in schoolwork. Some recognize that the current machines are very old and slow. The school board is more cautious because they are wary of what it brings into the classroom as well as the added expense.

How to handle the added expense of a new program is perhaps the biggest stumbling block. One teacher felt that, "Given a reasonable amount of resources we should have one computer for every three or four students in the classroom." Parents all agreed that it would be reasonable to increase either the registration fee or tuition by $40 per student, per year. One parent remarked, "I think it would be worth twice that." Other sources would be required, as $40 per student would bring in about $2,000. Some of the expenses, such as Internet access, would require consistent funding. Donations are a good way to purchase additional items that are a "one-time expense," but they cannot be depended upon for a program that hopes to build and maintain a high level of reliability.

One school board member remarked that "more teacher involvement with the school board, and maybe even a female school board member" would be desirable. The PTO was also mentioned several times as a possible major player. Another school board member suggested, "We need a model and to look down the road because there is no plan or plan to create a plan."

A PLAN TO CREATE A PLAN

A joint plan created by representatives of all interested parties: parents, teachers, students, school board, and members of the congregation.

REASON AND METHOD

The purpose for conducting this ethnographic research was to produce a qualitative look at how these different groups of participants viewed the use of computers in the classroom. By recording these voices and weaving them into a report so that each of the groups could hear themselves speak, it is hoped that a discussion will be initiated and action taken to create a clear vision of how Shepherd Lutheran wants to proceed with introducing its students to the technology of today.

During the course of interviewing Shepherd's stakeholders, I asked each group to tell me about Shepherd Lutheran School. The questions were intended to get the participants talking about their feelings. Other questions varied from "Tell me about your classroom" to a more direct "How do you feel about computers in the classroom?" Rather than build a survey and have the results displayed in graphical format, an Action Research project provides for a qualitative analysis for the facilitator and participants to interpret.

METHODOLOGY OF STUDY

The use of computers in the classroom was not so much in doubt; rather, it was the extent of use. All of the classrooms currently have computers. There is not a policy in place that all the interested parties can refer to in order to achieve a desired result.

To determine what Shepherd Lutheran School might desire to do about technology in the classroom, they could look at what other schools are doing. Valine (1995) is one example of several studies and inventories that have been done in similar schools locally and around the country. Rather than cite statistics and make comparisons to other schools, SLS can take this opportunity to find out what the various stakeholders desire in their school.

Members from each stakeholder group were interviewed at least once over the course of two months. A second interview with selected participants helped to clarify statements and cover new ground opened up by the first interview. Many of the interviews were conducted in the participants' homes. All of the teacher interviews took place at school, either in their classroom or in the administrative office. Several people wanting to be interviewed chose to do so in a public place, such as a restaurant, because they could do so during a lunch break or felt more comfortable in a neutral setting. Most of the interviews were one-hour long, except those with the students that were 15 to 20 minutes. I found that the younger participants required a great deal of interaction to get a response of more than three or four words. I selected four teachers, seven parents, two school board members, and four students. This gave about an equal ratio of participants for three of the four given group sizes. The teachers were over-represented because I felt they would be impacted the most by any changes in the classroom. My role in this study was to be a facilitator in making the various opinions known to each group. I am not a member of the Shepherd Lutheran Church congregation. My two sons have attended SLS for a combined total of 15 years. For three years, I served as chairman of the Technology Committee. It was during this time that I realized there was a significant difference between what the four groups wanted to do about computers in the classroom.

I used the concept of descriptive questions as formulated in *The Ethnographic Interview* (Spradley, 1979). Stakeholders were asked to engage in dialog, which required them to reveal feelings rather than facts about their situation. I used what is known as the unstructured schedule interview and the unstructured interview as outlined in *The Research Act* (Denzin, 1989c). This allows for a more flexible series of questions that can build on the answers to previous questions. The differences in people interviewed and their backgrounds and roles made it desirable to enter into the interview from different points. Most of the questions remained consistent in content, but the order was changed. In a few situations, some questions were not asked or were modified to take advantage of a particular person's knowledge about some aspect that they were involved with. The process evolved much like that described in *Action Research* (Stringer, 1999) where there was constant reevaluation and modification to the process. New questions evolved from the interview process. Each phase of the project had an impact on all the others and forced changes to be made all along the way. The processing of information was not nearly as complex as that reported in *Pedagogy of the Oppressed* (Freire, 1974). However, the intent to give a voice to the participants and allow their experiences to influence the reality their children will be molded by in the school environment was the same.

The sense that I got from this project and the study of several forms of participant research seems to be shared by Guba when he discusses alternative paradigm dialogs in *The Paradigm Dialog* (Guba, 1990). There is a synthesis of theories that can be made by a newcomer that blurs the boundaries defined by various schools of thought.

All of the interview material was transcribed from hand notes or tape recordings into typed written documents. These notes are available upon request as both raw field notes and transcribed Microsoft Word® documents. Answers to similar questions from each participant were grouped together and reviewed for division into units of meaning. From these categories and sub-categories, a narrative was written to give each group of stakeholders a story created and organized by the data.

FINAL MEETING

The final meeting with participants took place on the evening of November 28, 2000, at the Parent Teacher Organization (PTO) meeting. I presented the details of what was required for this study. I asked the participants to put together a puzzle for me, which was well received and required them to work together for a few minutes.

A couple of additional comments were made as follows:

"We as a school board have to be wary of what is known as 'gifts that eat'."

It was explained that money was in short supply and that the school was in no position to commit itself to an expensive program.

A parent came up to me afterward and expressed support for a use of computers in the classroom because she had worked for a construction company during the summer and said, "No one at this company knew how to use a computer and had a terrible time completing the project."

The outcome was to form a committee that would meet early next year to discuss how to formulate a plan that would get Shepherd Lutheran on the road to implementing a modern computer project. For the short term, it was agreed to gather the existing computers and create a computer lab in the old church building. One person volunteered to contact an electrician to install the required extra electrical circuit.

An indication of the commitment to improving the school was the approval later that evening to spend $6,000 on new playground equipment. This showed, at least to me, that though money is scarce there is still the ability to obtain funds and gather support for big projects. Installation of playground equipment requires a lot of sweat equity on the part of the parents.

REFERENCES

Cordes, C., & Miller, E. (1999). *Fools gold.*

Denzin, N. K. (1997). *Interpretive ethnography.* Thousand Oaks, CA: Sage.

Freire, P. (1974). *Pedagogy of the oppressed.* New York: Seabury.

Guba, E. G. (1990). *The paradigm dialogue.* Newbury Park, CA: Sage.

Oppenheimer, T. (1997). The computer delusion. *The Atlantic Monthly,*

Spradley, J. P. (1979). *The ethnographic interview.* New York: Holt, Rhinehart & Winston.

Stoll, C. (1995). *Silicon snake oil.* New York: Doubleday.

Stoll, C. (1999). *High tech heretic.* New York: Doubleday.

Stringer, E. T. (1999). *Action research.* Thousand Oaks, CA: Sage.

Valine, D. (1995). *Lutheran school computer technology survey elementary schools.* AAL.

6. Doggerel

An Elementary School Children's Research Project

By Michael LaFlamme

This piece was originally produced as a poem by a teacher to record a project engaged by children and teachers in a kindergarten class. It records the way they explored then developed solutions to a problem experienced by the school and its community. The poem was later modified and put to music.

This is a story about children and dogs,
In Ojo Amarillo Elementary
In a town called Fruitland on the Navajo land,
A land where dogs run freely and their hearts are free.
It happened in a school with 300 kids
With freedom to walk around,
A school in a town with 300 dogs
With freedom to roam the ground.

Refrain

They said,
Don't let 'em run loose,
Keep 'em tied up all day,
In a yard where they'll always be found.
Take care of your dog,
Or the dog catcher will,
And she won't live long at the pound.
Every day the dogs roamed over to school,
And waited for the kids at the school front door.
Every day when children walked out of their school,
The dogs at the door scared 'em a little bit more.
One day the principal cried, "Dog catcher

Catch these 300 pets."
The next day the children cried for their dogs,
Numbered a few hundred less.

The kindergarten brainstormed what they could do,
And decided to visit the city dog pound.
The kids asked some questions and they thought of a plan,
To care for the dogs who live in their town.
They counted the dogs that were fenced in or chained,
They counted the dogs that were stray
They met with a vet with her stuffed dog and cat,
And molded their pets out of clay.
They opened a veterinary clinic in school
And learned how to keep their pets well.
They read all the books that the library had,
And decided it was time to tell.

They wanted to share all the knowledge they had,
And thought that some posters might help dogs the most.
They posted them up at the grocery store,
And posted them down at the trading post.
The posters told grown-ups to take care of pets
A message from kids of age five.
They published their research in posters' round town,
To save a few hundred more lives.

7. Classroom Chaos

By Margo Jones

This study enabled a special education teacher to explore a difficult class situation to which she had been assigned. The purpose of the study was to help her understand the nature of the difficulties she experienced. By observing the class systematically and interviewing students, she was able to gain greater clarity about the dynamics of the class and the history of the situation. She commences with a poem as a means of evoking an understanding of her experience, then reflects on the information she had accumulated in the course of the study. Much of the account mirrors her interpretation of her own reflections rather than a description and analysis of events. It might be seen, therefore, as auto-ethnographic.

Entering into a world of yelling and anger,
A place where screaming and noise abound—
I don't feel like staying here for long
My world is spinning, whirling round and round.

There are children in this chaotic place
Have they been like this for long?
How can they stand the fighting and bickering?
The unrest that keeps going on and on and on—

A piece of this and a grain of that—a word said
Here and there
Not much makes sense at the present time.
Is there any one insider or out that cares

By themselves and alone they slowly come
Waiting to listen to strange questions of sorts
Like none they have expected to hear
    Faces that show no happiness, faces that are
      alone.
      Faces that have learned to hide some kind
        of fear . . .

Do they have so much anger?
What has made them like this?
Can it be just one solid reason?
Can it be answered in one quick list?

The major components that seemed to emerge from my analysis of data—observations of the class and student interview—were student anger and frustration and negative relationships that had existed during the time that the previous teacher and the substitutes had been in charge. Although the students made many negative comments, I do not think that they knew exactly what was causing their discontent. I do know that they all told me they did not like their other teacher and thought she did not like kids. Though most of their anger appeared to be directed toward the previous teacher and the educational assistant, it was carried over to me when I took the position. When interviewed, the students were definitely unhappy with the classroom situation and did not have any sense of wanting to cooperate with each other or to develop a positive relationship with the teacher or the assistant.

Since the approximate age of the students was 11, I think part of their anger originated from a sense of helplessness and confusion in the classroom situation because they did not have an established safe atmosphere. The students had many learning difficulties as well as emotional problems, and this factor, combined with many changes in their daily routine, created an even larger sense of frustration and helplessness. Since they did not know who would be there from week to week, or exactly what they would be learning, emotions became more inflamed, and they directed their anger at the teacher and the assistant as a way to vent their unhappiness.

The previous teacher indicated she did not leave because of a wish to leave teaching, but a number of substitutes had been called in, which contributed to a continuing lack of consistency. This factor probably accounted for the children's sense of instability and laid the foundation for insecurity in the environment and the way they were dealing with the situation that had developed in the classroom. According to the students, there was much vocal activity from the teacher, which appeared to be focused both toward individual students as well as the class as a whole.

When I arrived in the classroom, I was not prepared for what was taking place. After the first day, I was convinced that there had been no follow through on rules, and that whatever had happened previously must have been an absolute disaster. This first impression was also colored by the actions and words of the students and the educational assistant. None of the students had anything good to say about the previous teacher, and many were constantly complaining about the educational assistant. The classroom was a total mess! Students were up and down constantly, none raised their hands to speak, and if one tried to tell me something, others were constantly making rude comments. If the educational assistant tried to intervene, students told her to "shut up" and would not listen to anything she had to say. All I heard for the first few weeks was talking out, rude comments, and students who were complaining, crying, and very disturbed.

After providing some ground rules and trying to establish some kind of relationship with the class, I decided to interview the students in order to find out as much as I could about why there was so much chaos and discontent. Although I saw a difference in the class after I had been there for a few weeks, I wanted to try to find out what was the cause of so much anger and discontent. Even though I did take information from formal interviews as well as informal discussions with students and the educational assistant, I needed to do more interviews after more time had passed. My situation and the dynamics of the class were so "out of wack" that my main time and focus was on working directly with the students, with limited time to work on

formal interviews. I was able to gain insight over the next several months because I stayed until the end of the year. I do not think that the students actually understood clearly why they were so angry, but from their perspective, they appeared to be feeling unsafe and unsure because of the lack of consistency in teachers and in rules. They appeared upset because the previous teacher had told them she did not want to be a teacher any longer, which added to their anger when confronted by numerous substitutes.

When I arrived in late September, they had already established patterns of classroom behavior, perceptions of what constituted teacher effectiveness, and opinions about who should be respected. This was a great wall to overcome, but by March the students gave me a surprise party! I did have some changes in my class roster, but the main contributor to the success of the class was that I stayed and established some sense of respect and relationship with the students. At the end of the year, many asked if I was coming back, and they hoped they would be in my class! I would like to have seen more educational learning accomplished during the year, but felt the majority of my time and effort went into building trust and security. Formal learning took a back burner to creating a safer and more peaceful environment.

8. Class Evaluation: Something

By Denise Baccadeutre

Written by a teacher as part of a group presentation for a conference, this paper includes the sung rendition of the author's experience of a graduate class. It demonstrates the way performances may powerfully evoke a person's learning experience, though much of the impact is lost in this print version. As a means of evaluation, it provides concrete evidence of the meaning of her learning experience and enables the audience to understand how learning research enters her inner personal life and her more public professional life. As an evaluation, it focuses on student outcomes rather than instructional processes.

The class assignment at the end of the Qualitative Research semester was to pair off with another person in the class and, using Spradley's questioning techniques, focus on the other person's experience in this class, identify the key or important elements of the other's experience, and put it in a framework to create a presentation—an evocative account, a performance assessment—that would enable the others in the class to understand your experience. Elliot Eisner (1999) states, "Despite the lack of a single definition, performance assessment is aimed at moving away from testing practices that require students to select the single correct answer from an array of four or five distractors to a practice that requires students to create evidence through performance that will enable assessors to make valid judgments about 'what they know and can do' in situations that matter."

I teamed with my classmate, Karen Higgins. She interviewed me and, together, we went back through what I had articulated to her, and we bracketed the information. We discovered that the difficulty of the class assignments and my accomplishment of the assigned coursework gave me the confidence to approach and complete further assignments. I shared with her that I had so many insecurities as a woman in my late 40s believing that I had the intellectual ability to achieve at the doctoral level. We discussed the stereotypical views of women our age—they emerged from a period in time when women became teachers, nurses, librarians, or homemakers. Although this assignment occurred years later, there was still tremendous societal and familial pressure as well as personal guilt over leaving family roles and obligations behind and pursuing personal educational growth. It was a constant struggle not to give it up and slide back into the traditional female roles. The construction and understanding of the experience allowed me to make meaning of what was happening to me as I successfully completed each assignment of the class throughout the semester.

As a music educator at the secondary level, I am very aware of the nearly unparalleled ability of music to express and elicit emotional response. I have witnessed this response to musical performance in my students, parents, and community. I have shed tears at the beauty of my students' musical expression. I am also aware that the arts are in constant danger of eradication in the public schools as the current swing of the educational pendulum calls for greater accountability, standardized testing, and rising test scores. With music, or any emotional response, measurable outcomes seem incompatible and, therefore, must be invalid. Eisner (1999) further offers:

> Each of the forms of representation that exist in our culture—visual forms in art, auditory forms in music, quantitation forms in mathematics, propositional forms in science, choreographic forms in dance, poetic forms in language—are vehicles through which meaning is conceptualized and expressed. A life driven by the pursuit of meaning is enriched when the meanings sought and secured are multiple.

Through the nature of this assignment, I was able to utilize that which was most comfortable to me, a familiar mode of emotional expression that would provide the framework for helping others make meaning of my experience—musical performance.

Qualitative Research Evaluation Presentation: A Vocal Parody on "Nothing" from Chorus Line

Submitted by Denise Baccadutre

December 9, 1999

SOMETHING

When I read my e-mail and learned that Tom Smith was back and was going to teach Qualitative Research, all of a sudden the LLSS class I had enrolled in seemed very uninteresting. So I called Tom up and asked if he thought I was ready for this class. I had d iscovered that many students in my previous two semesters were much more brilliant than I was and some had taken an academic writing class. They were surely leaps and bounds ahead of me. Tom kind of snickered and replied, "There's more to qualitative research than writing. Yes, I think you're ready."

In spite of Tom's confidence in my abilities, I had so many insecurities. But pursuing this degree, taking one course a semester, is really the only thing I ever do for myself.

Sing:

Once a week, for myself, I would wave goodbye to my students, hit the highway, leave it all behind.

Once a week, I would allow myself to feel worthy, myself to feel special, open my mind.

And I dug right down to the bottom of my soul to see what I had inside,

Could I understand what was presented to me? So I tried, I tried. . . .

Speak:

And my students were preparing for All-State, and two District Honor Choirs, and the Winter Concert literature had to be taught, and I got a call asking me to be choral president for the state of New Mexico.

Sing:

But I was learning something, I was feeling something, and Something was Special to me. . . . Could it be happening that I could interpret what the 'other' was telling to me?

Speak:

But I said to myself, "Hey! This is Denise the Insecure fooling herself into believing she understands something."

Sing:

Second month, more advanced and we had to turn in a proposal, focus our research, tell what and why. . . .

Tommie-man, he would say to us, "gotta state the purpose, gotta state the outcome"—I wanted to cry.

But I dug right down to the bottom of my soul to see what I had inside,

Could I represent to him what I wanted to explore—so I tried, I tried. . . .

And I wrote something, I envisioned something, and wrote and re-wrote until I was fried.

I turned it in and Tommie liked it and in my mind I felt suddenly glorified.

Speak:

And then I received an e-mail from Tom stating our second draft of our research must be expanded to at least eight pages—I hyperventilated and whispered—Oh my God!!!!!

Sing:

Went to church, praying, Santa Maria, send me guidance, send me guidance, On my knees.

Went to church, praying Santa Maria, help me feel it, help me know it, Pretty Please?

And a voice from down at the bottom of my soul came up to the top of my head.

And a voice from down at the bottom of my soul, here is what it said:

You are something! You can do something! You can do this, you just need to try.

And when you do it, you'll know you're special—just go to the computer, focus your mind and fly. . . .

Speak:

Well, flying meant many hours of reading, working on the Internet, working on the computer, and rewriting something to submit that would not be an embarrassment. . . .

Sing:

Ernie gave it back to me, and I confess, I hesitantly turned to the back page and nearly cried. . . .

Because he wrote "Emerging beautifully, but still some way to go."

REFERENCES

Eisner, E. (1999, May). The uses and limits of performance assessment. (On-line). Kappan. Available: URL:http://www.pdkintl.org/kappan/keis9905.htm.

9. Ode to Denizen

By M. Cathrene Connery

Sometimes, a learning journey creates movement in people's lives that cannot be expressed in the linear logic of written prose. This poem provides insight into the complexity of a teacher's transformative experience of a graduate class. In her journal she had written: "It has been a long time since I have had a paradigmatic shift like this in such a profound way . . . like a small earthquake or miniature shock of lightning arousing me from my day-to-day automatic pilot semi-slumber."

1st

My
   static
     obscurity
a- stainless- steel- alone
     assigned by
     sharp edged
     numerals,
      bruised
     not so funny bones.

2nd

Two
 his
 his / story?
    Tory, hegemonic
    plot of
     dualistic seesaws
     number battles
     power sought.

III.

You / I / Together
   triads standing strong
     creators
     preservers
     destroyers
    words,
      descriptions,
       songs.

Fourth

We are balanced centers
   body-mind-and-soul
   dance ~ defined ~ e~ motions~
    sensitivity: understanding::
    affect: growth.

Fifth

The promise of a homecoming
   as we slowly top the rise.
   Smoke of distant fires
    clearing in the skies.
Circles of atonement
   no ethical postponement
    for ours is now the moment,

Sixth.

10. Children's Construction of History: A Quilt

By Ann Claunch

This dissertation study by an elementary school teacher sought ways to improve teaching history by understanding how children learned history. She started from the research question "How do 9- and 10-year-olds construct historical time from reading and discussing narrative?" The outcomes of repeated cycles of inquiry were presented pictorially and assembled as a quilt.

SEGMENT ONE

I chose to use a visual representation for two reasons. Representing my thoughts with images forced me to sort my thinking into concise statements and the artistic representation of thought paralleled what I asked elementary students to do in my research. I used the construction of the images as a prewriting activity. In each segment, there are two figures and a triangle. The two figures represent my husband and daughter. Committing to a doctoral program is a paradox; it is a selfish act but cannot be completed alone. My husband and my daughter were my "emotional committee," which I found as vital as my academic committee. The triangle in each segment represented my attempt to continually view my re-

search from three different angles—through the lens of the curriculum, of the teacher, and of the students.

SEGMENT TWO

I have never held the view of my mother's generation on limiting women to certain roles, but as I entered graduate school again, I discovered there was a residue of a "woman's place" ingrained in my psyche. As I considered continuing my education, I had internal and external pressures reminding me that embarking on this journey was not a necessity. My daughter was seven and an only child. I struggled with the balance between the roles of student, mother, wife, and teacher. My husband let me torture myself for a time, knowing this is a natural decision-making process for me, until he intervened. He helped me narrow my hesitations and I discovered my primary reservation was our daughter. He opened my mind to a new perspective by stating, "What better mom could you hope to be, than to show your daughter life's possibilities?" Thank you John.

SEGMENT THREE

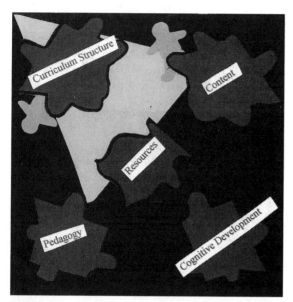

I wanted children to study how history is learned. After teaching for 18 years, I was puzzled how to teach history to 9- and 10-year-olds. The textbooks and the curriculum seem to present isolated facts and events along a timeline, and it was up to the students to piece together the larger pictures over years. The closer I observed and thought about what was actually being learned when I taught from the textbook, the more frustrated I became. I identified that somehow I must match the facts and the events into a complete story to help children understand history. In order to accomplish this I had to mesh together different elements in teaching: the pedagogy, the curriculum, the content, the resources, and the cognitive development of the student. One of the results of my study began with moving from presenting history deductively, large to small to more inductively, small to large.

SEGMENT FOUR

I wanted to provide an entry into the past by moving backwards from the present. I imagined this entry like a curriculum doorway that supported children's experiences and moved them to another place and time. In this segment, I attempted to depict a modern globe and compare it to a T-O map of the early 12th and 13th century when there was thought to be only three continents, Africa, Asia, and Europe.

SEGMENT FIVE

The conceptual plan (Taba, 1969) for my curriculum was my road map. I used the conceptual plan to broaden my thinking for a year-long curriculum plan. It also structured the curriculum for the teacher deductively and for the students inductively. As a teacher, I knew that in order to bring the big picture of history it needed to be developed through description. Stories invite the reader into a mental picture of the setting. I opted to use narrative rather than textbooks in my teaching of history. I wanted to see if it made a difference. Including different narratives, I wanted to create an entry into the past that was relevant to young historians. I wanted the students to be excited about moving from the present into the world of history. The curriculum, the pedagogy, the resources, and my understanding of cognitive development became the passageway to move students mentally into history. My question evolved, "How do 9- and 10-year-olds construct historical time from reading and discussing narrative?"

SEGMENT SIX

History was an interest I developed after obtaining my master's degree and 10 years of teaching. I remembered hating the subject in high school because it was reduced to read these pages, answer the questions, and be prepared for the test on Friday. I learned about skimming and memorizing the bold print words but very little about the content. The history I remembered was about people. The history that was of interest for me was the narratives that were descriptions of how people lived and everyday life in another time. I began to read and think about children's literature as a way to present history. Knowing that it is important to allow

for the voices of history that have traditionally been silenced, I collected books that looked at history from different perspectives. The quilt piece segment has books about WWII that look at the Japanese as heroes, victims, and aggressors.

SEGMENT SEVEN

I had an idea about how to change the curriculum by using narrative, and I had formulated my question. Next I chose my research setting. After four years out of the classroom, working with novice teachers, I did not want to go back to the isolation of one teacher in a classroom so I decided to team teach. I chose someone I had known for 10 years and spent the last four years teaming as a supervisor. We knew each other well. I wanted someone who would tell me what she thought quickly without the dance of politeness. We both believed in the constructivist approach to teaching. We found an opening with a principal that was accepting of my research and team teaching. It was a unique setting because the public school was located in an Air Force Base surrounded by a six-foot chain link fence. Access to the school was through a military gate that required all who entered to show proof of insurance, current registration, and a driver's license. I was interested to see how a traditional military community would react to my "Revisionist" history lessons.

SEGMENT EIGHT

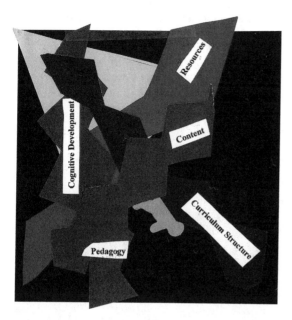

August brought the realities of the classroom and dumped chaos into my research road map. Fissures in my curriculum, my lack of knowledge of the student population, my ability to team with another teacher, and my choice of novels (difficulty level) began to develop. This was not only in teaching history but also in my math, reading, and science. Partly, this was due to being out of the classroom for four years as a supervisor of novice teachers and partly due to trying to layer my research plan onto students I knew very little about.

our time as a community of learners would be better spent on concepts children were ready to learn; geography, alike mapping skills, continents, and states and capitals. She often questioned me if 9- and 10-year-olds were too young to learn history. At times, I agreed with her, but a persistent thought of "How can I present the idea of history better" kept me pursuing my research. The opportunity to articulate my views on teaching and learning were both good and bad. I enjoyed challenging my thinking, but it was emotionally draining having to justify and negotiate every decision in the classroom. Looking back, she was key to my research because she always insisted on my articulating the "why" I thought what I was teaching was important for children to learn.

SEGMENT NINE

Another major chasm in my research was my team teacher. Although we both believed students learned by constructing knowledge, we had a difference about the teacher's role in that learning. I aligned myself with Jerome Bruner and believed that any child can learn any new concept if it is presented in an intellectually honest way. My team teacher held to strong beliefs of not delivering curriculum until it was age appropriate. The agreement was that children constructed their own knowledge but what became an intellectual battleground were what opportunities we provided. After meeting our children, she was firmly convinced that

SEGMENT TEN

During the initial part of the year, I read many historical narratives as a part of the reading aloud section of the day. I chose to do this in order to help students familiarize themselves with a relatively new genre. I immediately noticed a trend in how students scaffold new historical knowledge. The students used the media as their backboard when explaining unfamiliar information. I documented 24 times in a 3-week period where a student referenced something we were reading to a television show or a movie. Popular movies were *Sounder, Gone with the Wind,* Disney's *Pocahontas,* and *Titanic.* I began to wonder what their

Students had a difficult time in organizing time from past (10 years ago) to long ago (400–500 year) and then to the very distant past (1,000–2,000 years ago). Organization by events, thought processes, and articulation were inconsistent. I began to work with the students on passage of time. The class experimented in developing ways that show passages of time and movement through drawings. I did this because history is tied to chronology.

SEGMENT TWELVE

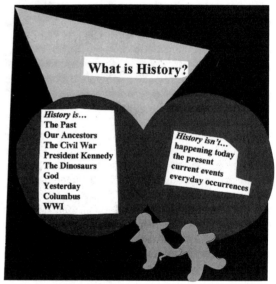

"mind's eye" was seeing as I read the book *Morning Girl* by Michael Dorris (results are in segment seventeen). I began to ask the students to draw as I was reading in an attempt to make comprehension visible.

SEGMENT ELEVEN

I wanted to know what knowledge the students had about history, so I asked them to tell me or illustrate the following question "What is History?" This was prompted by the interest and confusion about the passage of time that I had. The broad categories that I extracted from their responses were: a record of the past, a list of peoples that died a long time ago, and the dinosaurs. I also looked for the binary concepts of what history isn't. The major underlying assumption in the answer to the question was that history happened a long time ago and was not happening now.

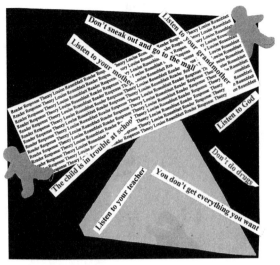

SEGMENT THIRTEEN

Listen to the Mustn'ts is a poem by Shel Silverstein that I read to see how students interpreted texts with multiple meanings and outside the history arena. I knew this was an important mindset of history since there are always multiple truths with any historical event. I read it aloud and asked the students to think about the poem and then asked the students to read the poem silently. The discussion was opened with "Tell me what you read." The 9- and 10-year-olds went into literal interpretation, and I continued, "What does this mean to you?" The literal interpretations of the poem by the students continued. Two aspects of teaching were going on that were frustrating. One, I wanted an answer in the abstract, and the students were entering into the conversation through the concreteness of personal experiences. The second phenomenon was that the open-ended questions I was asking were unsupportive of students that had spent their last years in school believing that reading had a right answer. I needed to listen to what students said, not what I expected them to say. I also need to scaffold my questions when I wanted to elicit abstract responses.

SEGMENT FOURTEEN

Read and Retell. Another "aha" happened during a science lesson when I was exploring a teaching strat-egy known as read and retell. Students would be able to read a crucial paragraph from the text as many times as they needed to reproduce the paragraph in their own words. This is a common strategy used in working with students in a second language. It allows students to be comfortable with the text and then used their own words to reconstruct the meaning. I noticed a trend. Students would read the text, but when they began to reconstruct the paragraph, it was a mixture of what was said in the text and a connection with personal experience.

SEGMENT FIFTEEN

Words≠Action. I continued to note what they were saying about the novels as I read each aloud. I also increased the expectation of drawing as I read. I teased out another insight. When I was reading a historical novel and began a discussion, many times students were able to discuss the novel coherently. At the same time, when I looked at what they drew, it became evident there were discrepancies. This segment shows a drawing of Morning Girl, a character in a book by the same name. It is set in the 1490s. The main character is a Taino Indian. Chapter 14 opens with Morning Girl's mother cooking breakfast and discussing the day's events. When the student

It was at this point that nothing was new in the discovery of how children learned in my research. I knew the information about schema, the importance of relevance in curriculum, and the child development theories, and I was proving them over and over in what I was seeing. I had a paradigm shift in my thinking. Instead of validating all the things that 9- and 10-year-olds could not do, I began to question what they could do. I began to watch for the tools they brought to their historical tool belt of understanding. One of their tools in their tool belt was drawing. Nearly every student doodled and drew while they were thinking. The example I had on the segment was a typical "Spelling Test." Nine- and 10-year-olds used drawing as a way to communicate thought.

referred to this part orally, she said, "Morning Girl is listening as her mother is talking about gathering berries and getting ready for the winter. Her mother is cooking breakfast. Drawing the same scene clearly depicted the kitchen in the present. My next question was how does this impact comprehension of history?

SEGMENT SEVENTEEN

SEGMENT SIXTEEN

I knew that students understand there was a passage of time and certain events came in chronological order. I used this tool of understanding to nudge forward and build a complex, comparative timeline alongside the students as well as at different perspectives in history.

SEGMENT EIGHTEEN

I narrowed what historical time was to the social and cultural aspects of different time periods. I asked the students to concentrate on thinking about the art, the transportation, the architecture, the fashion, the food, and the entertainment of each period we studied. This was a strategy that helped the students to compare their lives to those of another time period.

On-line Resources

9

Introduction

In the past few years, on-line resources to support action research in schools have proliferated. A reasonably superficial search will uncover a vast array of links that provide educational practitioners with access to resources specifically relevant to their work. By judicious selection, action researchers may link to the courses, project descriptions, organizations, resources, listservs, and/or papers most suited to their purposes.

On-line Web Searches

Web searches may be conducted to acquire understanding of action research processes, to acquire data relevant to a particular topic or issue, or to extend a literature review. The Educational Resources Information Center (ERIC) provides a comprehensive database for educational literature, but a broader search may be made using any of the standard search engines like Yahoo, Altavista, and others.

To conduct an on-line web search, researchers should:

- **Carefully Define the Topic:** A succinct definition of a topic aids clarity and precision. It ensures you get the type of information you require. A description that is too general or lengthy will not give sufficient focus to the search.
- **Identify Key Terms:** Key terms identify the type of information required. Select two or three terms that define the nature of the topic. If you were searching for information about the use of phonics in teaching reading, you might use the terms "teaching," "reading," or "phonics."
- **Log-on to Search Function:** Log-on to the ERIC Website (*http://www.accesseric.org*), and click on "Search ERIC Database"; or log-on to a search engine (by clicking on the "search" icon, then selecting the desired search engine).
- **Enter Key Terms:** Enter previously identified key terms.
- **Refine the Search:** Often an initial search will not provide appropriate sources. It may identify many sources only peripherally related to the topic investigated or fail to identify an adequate body of resources. The search may be refined by changing the key terms or by adding another term that locates the topic more precisely. For example, the terms "teaching," "elementary," and

"phonics" may be substituted for the previous key terms. It might also be possible to refine the search by identifying the years to be searched or the type of publication to be included in the search.

- **Evaluate Sources:** Web searches may identify a large array of material; some of which is of questionable value. Researchers should evaluate the quality of material to ensure its adequacy or appropriateness to the study in which they are involved.

Useful Websites

The list in the next section provides but a small sample of Websites giving information about action research. There are some limitations to these materials, insofar as even new sites go temporarily off-line, and some become superseded. In some instances, those authoring the sites have no resources to update the information and they become outdated. Those limitations aside, however, there is a wide range of resources having the potential to greatly enrich an action research project by providing links to practitioners with similar professional or educational interests.

The categories that follow differentiate between types of sites, but these are not mutually exclusive because some sites are linked to others or link to similar sources. A brief search, however, will provide researchers with an understanding of the range of sites relevant to their purposes and contexts. A rather simple, but effective, method of identifying action research sites is to enter "Action Research Schools" in a search engine and review the sites presented. More focused searches using more specific descriptors will reveal sites with more relevant information.

General Website Resources

These Websites are multi-dimensional sites, each providing access or links to a broad range of topics and resources related to action research. They include literature, links, classes, resources, papers, publications, and descriptions of projects.

Action Research: Literature and Websites. A checklist for action research. A definition of action research. *http://www.ched.coventry.ac.uk/Taskforce/actionre.htm.*

Action Research at Queen's University: Provides excellent links to programs, conferences, sites, resources, publications, and student and faculty reports related to action research. *http://educ.queensu.ca/~ar.*

Action Research Network: The Australian Curriculum Studies Association provides a rich body of resources and links for teacher researchers. It includes descriptions of projects in evaluation; civics education; open learning; cross-curricula issues and practices; outcomes-based education; professional development, assessment, and reporting; peace education; self-managing schools; gender issues; early childhood education; education, training, and work for young people; environmental education; technology in education; holistic education; learning how to learn; vocational education; and many more. *http://www. acsa.edu.au/networks/netpages/action_research.htm.*

Action Research Page: A wide range of action research resources, including papers, links, and so on, from the University of Colorado at Denver School of Education. *http://www.cudenver.edu/~mryder/itc/act_res.html.*

Action Research Resources: University of Minnesota. *http://www.extension. umn.edu/~hoefer/educdsgn/actresrc.htm.*

Action Research Resources

Websites in this section provide more specific resources for those engaged in action research studies.

Action Research Resources: An excellent list of links to many good action research sites. *http://www.trinityvt.edu/edsite/action.htm.*

emTech—Action Research: A very comprehensive list of action research resources, including papers, Website links, resources, and project descriptions. *http://www.emtech.net/profdev/action_research.html.*

NSDC Library-Action Research: Papers from the National Staff Development Council on action research in schools. *http://www.nsdc.org/library/action.html.*

/NRM_changelinks/action Research Resources: List links to many useful action research Websites. *http://nrm.massey.ac.nz/changelinks/ar.html.*

Research for Action (RFA): A Philadelphia-based non-profit organization engaged in educational research and reform to improve educational opportunities and outcomes for all students. A rich range of resources. *http://www.researchforaction. org/index.html.*

Action Research Guidelines and Methodology

These sites provide specific guidance to those wishing to extend their knowledge and skills in action research methods.

A Beginner's Guide to Action Research: A very useful and comprehensive guide to action from Bob Dick. *http://ousd.k12.ca.us/netday/links/Action_ Research/begin_guide_action_research.*

Action Research Methodology: An Overview of the Methodological Approach of Action Research. *http://www.web.net/~robrien/papers/arfinal.html.*

Classroom Action Research Overview: Assists the teacher in finding out what's happening in the classroom and uses that information to make wise decisions. Website by Gwynn Mettetal, Division of Education, Indiana University. *http://www.iusb.edu/~gmetteta/Classroom_Action_Research.html.*

Introduction to Action Research: Dorothy Gabel's presidential address to the National Association for Research in Science Teaching (NARST). She suggests that it is through joint research studies that science instruction in the schools will improve, and we need to make a great effort in this regard. *http://www.phy. nau.edu/~danmac/actionrsch.html.*

Teacher Researcher: General Resources

These sites are very specifically oriented toward the teacher researcher. They provide a rich range of resources and descriptions of school-based teacher research projects.

Action Research Overview: League of Professional Schools: Hosted by the University of Georgia, this link provides resources for teacher practitioner researchers to assist them to implement a democratic, student-oriented learning community focused on improving teaching and learning for all. *http://www.coe. uga.edu/lps/action01.htm.*

Education Resources Action Research/Teacher as Researcher: A list of useful sites relevant to teacher researchers. *http://www.mcrel.org/resources/ links/action.asp.*

Links IV: An excellent site for teachers as researchers. Information and sites include: Action research course syllabi; electronic discussions and communities; grants and funding; links and resource pages; global, school-based, and university-based professional organizations; archives of papers, articles, journals, and research reports; and a teacher research bibliography. *http://www.ncte.org/rte/links4.html*

Teacher Research: *http://www.accessexcellence.org/21st/TL/AR/index.html.*

Teacher Research (Action Research Resources): An interesting list of magazine and journal articles. Some of the articles are presented with the full text available on-line. *http://ucerc.edu/teacherresearch/teacherresearch.html.*

What Is Teacher Research?: ERIC digests on this question. *http://www.ed.gov/ databases/ERIC_Digests/ed381530.html.*

Teacher Researcher: Subject Areas

This section provides a non-inclusive listing of Websites available for specific subject areas including science education, early childhood education, ESL, adult education, and educational technology.

Early Childhood Education: Action Research in Early Childhood Education *http://ericps.ed.uiuc.edu/eece/pubs/digests/1996/borgia96.html.*

Elementary Science: Action Research in Elementary School Science. Reports of a number of teacher research projects. Each report provides project introduction, project background, project objectives, project description, staff and support, project results, and references. *http://essc.calumet.purdue.edu/Activity%20 Science%20Research/Reseach%20HP.*

ESL Staff Development: Applied linguistics, computer-assisted language learning, English as a foreign language, English for specific purposes, and ESL in Bilingual Education. *http://www.tesol.org/isaffil/intsec/columns/199904-pa.html.*

Informal, Adult, and Community Education: A select, annotated bibliography covering the nature and use of action research within informal education, adult education, and community education. *http://www.infed.org/research/b-actres.htm.*

Science Education Action Research: Eisenhower National Clearinghouse. Perspectives from teachers' classrooms. Timely ideas and information with daily updates. Complete information about thousands of teaching materials for science education. *http://www.enc.org/.*

Technology: Project Pegasus, Edmonton Public Schools, invites teachers to spread their wings by conducting action research to determine how technology can improve student learning and achievement. The results of their work are summarized at this website. *http://www.epsb.edmonton.ab.ca/pd/pegasus.*

Teacher Education

This section provide sites relevant to teacher education. It includes discussions about and examples of teacher education portfolios and the use of action research in student teaching.

Teacher Education: ERIC citations for portfolios in teacher education. *http://ericae.net/infoguide/PORT_TE.txt.*

Action Research for Schools

School Improvement: Pekin Public Schools District Instructional Leadership Team uses an action research cycle to conduct a two-year action research study related to three aspects of the district strategic plan. *http://www.pekin.net/pekin108/dilt/cycle.html.*

School Renewal: Project description of how Broward County Schools of the South Florida Consortium of Schools are using a school-wide Action Research Process (SAR) as a framework for long-term whole-school renewal. *http://www.fau.edu/coe/sfcel/browsch.htm.*

Videos: School improvement experts Carl Glickman and Emily Calhoun are featured on this series of four videotapes. They demonstrate the use of action research in identifying and solving problems in classrooms and schools. *http://shop.ascd.org.*

Lists and Groups

Action Research Network, Ireland: Provides links to a network of action research contacts in Ireland. *http://www.iol.ie/~rayo/.*

Canterbury Action Research Network: Support network for teachers engaged in action research for curriculum development and school improvement.

Housed at the University of East Anglia in Great Britain, it is an affiliate of the Collaborative Action Research Network. Publishes The Enquirer, an electronic journal. *http://www.canterbury.ac.uk.*

Forum on Action Research: Appalachia Education Laboratory's School Services Center: Resource Center and Action Research Listserv provide a free, facilitated forum for sharing questions and information about action research. *http://www.ael.org/rel/schlserv/actlist.htm.*

On-Line Action Research: Describes a three-year U.S. Department of Education grant that enables The Comprehensive Adult Student Assessment System (CASAS), a non-profit organization, to continue serving as a national resource for action research projects. This involves coordination of a national network of action research practitioners to improve classroom practice and provide an alternative form of staff development. *http://www.scoe.otan.dni.us/casas/16OAR/16_OARMaster.html.*

Papers and Journal Articles: Collections

Suggested Action Research Readings On-line: A list of suggested action research readings identified by the Pathways to Learning in cooperation with the National Network of Regional Educational Laboratories. *http://www.ncrel.org/sdrs/areas/issues/envrnmnt/drugfree/sa3act.htm.*

Papers and Journal Articles: Individual

Bureaucratisation and Professional Development: The Marino Institute of Education Action Research Project. The Clark and Meloy and Darling-Hammond readings discuss the implications of bureaucratization in schools. *http://inset.ul.ie/buro/marino.htm.*

Involving Teachers in Action Research: An Introduction to Action Research: Presidential address by Dorothy Gabel to the National Association for Research in Science Teaching (NARST) in 1995. Talks of the need to make a greater effort to involve teachers in action research. *http://www.phy.nau.edu/~danmac/actionrsch.html.*

Teacher Enhancement: Science: Teacher action research helps improve schools. The site provides access to nine papers included in the publication resulting from a teacher enhancement program for middle-school science teachers in Georgia and Florida. The program concentrated on helping science teachers find ways to solve some common problems. *http://www.middleweb.com/SERVE report.html.*

Social Movement: Action Research and Social Movement: A Challenge for Policy Research. Stephen Kemmis. Deakin University—Geelong. *http://olam.ed.asu.edu/epaa/v1n1.html.*

Projects and Programs

This section provides links that describe specific action research projects in schools and classrooms.

AELaction: Action Research in Schools and Classrooms: Five action research summaries provide a glimpse into how participants select a focus, choose data collection methods, and reflect on findings. *http://www.ael.org/rel/ schlserv/action/classrm.htm.*

On-Line Action Research: The Comprehensive Adult Student Assessment System (CASAS) is a non-profit organization serving as a national resource for action research projects. This involves coordination of a national network of action research practitioners to improve classroom practice and provide an alternative form of staff development. *http://www.scoe.otan.dni.us/casas/16OAR/ 16_OARMaster.html.*

Research for Action/Projects: The Gratz Connection: Research for Action (RFA) is a Philadelphia-based non-profit organization engaged in educational research and reform. It provided a collaborative action research project as a process evaluation of a Philadelphia Department of Education demonstration site for a dropout prevention program. *http://www.researchforaction.org/ projects.html.*

Teacher Action Research: The Action Research "Teachers as Researchers" Program is a successful program started in the 1999–2000 school year. The program awards teachers a stipend for research projects conducted in their schools. *http://www.tec.leon.k12.fl.us/gi/action_research.htm.*

Teachers as Researchers: The Action Research "Teachers as Researchers" Program is a successful program started in the 1999–2000 school year. The program awards teachers a stipend for research projects conducted in their schools. *http://www.tec.leon.k12.fl.us/gi/action_research.htm* .

References

Altheide, D., & Johnson, J. (1998). Criteria for assessing interpretive validity in qualitative research. In N. K. Denzin & Y. S. Lincoln (Eds.), *Collecting and interpreting qualitative materials.* Thousand Oaks, CA: Sage.

Anderson, G., Herr, K., & Nihlen, A. (1994). *Studying your own school: An educator's guide to qualitative research.* Thousand Oaks, CA: Corwin.

Arhar, J., Holly, M. L., & Kasten, W. C. (2000). *Action research for teachers: Traveling the yellow brick road.* Upper Saddle River, NJ: Prentice-Hall.

Arnett, R. (1986). *Communication and community.* Carbondale, IL: Southern Illinois University Press.

Atkinson, P. (1992). *Understanding ethnographic texts.* Newbury Park, CA: Sage.

Atwah, B., Weeks, P., & Kemmis, S. (1998). *Action research in practice: Partnerships for social justice in education.* New York: Routledge.

Baldwin, S. (1997). High school students participation in action research: An ongoing learning process. In E. Stringer and colleagues, *Community-based ethnography: Breaking traditional boundaries of research, teaching and learning.* Mahwah, NJ: Lawrence Erlbaum.

Barbour, S., & Kitzinger, J. (Eds.). (1998). *Developing focus group research: Politics, theory, and practice.* Thousand Oaks, CA: Sage.

Baudrillard, J. (1983). *Simulations.* New York: Foreign Agent Press.

Bell, G., Stakes, R., & Taylor, G. (Eds.). (1994). *Action research, special needs and school development.* London: David Fulton.

Bell, J. (1993). *Doing your research project: A guide for first-time researchers in education and social science.* Buckingham: Open University Press.

Berge, B. M., & Ve, H. (2000). *Action research for gender equity.* Buckingham: Open University Press.

Berger, P., Berger, B., & Kellner, H. (1973). *The homeless mind: Modernization and consciousness.* New York: Random House.

Berger, P., & Luckmann, T. (1967). *The social construction of reality: A treatise in the sociology of knowledge.* Garden City, NY: Anchor.

Berliner, D. (200). Blanket cure won't fix inequalities in education. *Albuquerque Journal,* 5 Feb 2001.

Block, P. (1990). *The empowered manager: Positive political skills at work.* San Francisco: Jossey-Bass.

Boeckh, P. (1968). *On interpretation and criticism* (J. Pritchard, Ed., Trans.). Norman, OK: University of Oklahoma Press.

Bogdan, R., & Biklen, S. (1992). *Qualitative research for education.* Boston: Allyn & Bacon.

Bray, J. L., Smith, L., & Yorks, L. (Eds.). (2000). *Collaborative inquiry in practice: Action, reflection, and making meaning.* Thousand Oaks, CA: Sage.

Brown, R. (1992). Max van Manen and pedagogical human science research. In W. Pinar & W. Reynolds (Eds.), *Understanding curriculum as phenomenological and deconstructed text.* New York: Teachers College Press.

Brown, A., & Dowling, P. (1998). *Doing research/reading research. A mode of interrogation for education.* London: Falmer.

Buber, M. (1958). *I and thou.* New York: Charles Scribner's Sons.

Buber, M. (1969). *A believing humanism.* New York: Simon & Schuster.

Burnaford, G. E., Fischer, J., & Hobson, D., (Eds.). (2001). *Teachers doing research: The power of action through inquiry* (2nd ed.). Mahwah, NJ: Lawrence Erlbaum Associates.

Burns, A. (1999). *Collaborative action research for English language teachers.* Cambridge, UK: Cambridge University Press.

Calhoun, E. (1993). *Action research: Three approaches.* Educational Leadership. October. Washington D.C.: NEA.

Calhoun, E. (1994). *How to use action research in the self-renewing school.* Alexandria, VA: Association for Supervision and Curriculum Development.

Carr, W., & Kemmis, S. (1986). *Becoming critical: Education, knowledge, and action research.* Philadelphia: Falmer Press.

Carson, T., & Sumara, D. (Eds.). (1997). *Action research as a living practice.* New York: Peter Lang.

Chirban, J. (1996). *Interviewing in depth: The interactive-relational approach.* Thousand Oaks, CA: Sage.

Christensen, L. (1997). Philosophical and pedagogical development: An ethnographic process. In E. Stringer and colleagues, *Community-based ethnography: Breaking traditional boundaries of research, teaching and learning.* Mahwah, NJ: Lawrence Erlbaum.

Christiansen, H., Goulet, L., Krentz, C., & Maeers, M. (Eds.). (1997). *Recreating relationships: Collaboration and educational reform.* Albany: SUNY Press.

Claunch, A. (2000). *Understanding teaching history.* Unpublished manuscript, University of New Mexico.

Clifford, J. (1988). *The predicament of culture.* Cambridge, MA: Harvard University Press.

Clifford, J., & Marcus, G. (Eds.). (1986). *Writing culture: The poetics and politics of ethnography.* Berkeley, CA: University of California Press.

Connelly, F., and D. Clandinin (Eds.) (1999). *Shaping a professional identity: Stories of educational practice.* NY: Teachers College Press.

Connery, C. (2003). *Sociocultural semiotic texts of emerging biliterates in non-academic settings.* Ph.D. dissertation. University of New Mexico. Albuquerque, NM.

Cook, T., & Campbell, D. (1979). *Quasi-experimentation: Design and analysis for field settings.* Chicago, IL: Rand McNally.

Coughlan, D., & Brannick, T. (2001). *Doing action research in your own organization.* Thousand Oaks, CA: Sage.

Creswell, J. (2002). *Educational research: Planning, conducting and evaluating quantitative and qualitative research.* Upper Saddle River, NJ: Pearson.

Dadas, M. (1995). *Passionate enquiry and school development: A story about teacher action research.* London: Falmer.

Darling-Hammond, L., & McLauglin, M. (1995). Policies that support professional development in an era of reform. *Phi Delta Kappan, 76*(8), 597–604.

Davies, P., & Gribben, J. (1991). *The matter myth: Beyond chaos and complexity.* London: Penguin.

delaine, M. (2000). *Fieldwork, participation and practice: Ethics and dilemmas in qualitative research.* Thousand Oaks, CA: Sage.

deMarrais, K. B. (Ed.). (1998). *Inside stories: Qualitative research reflections.* Mahwah, NJ: Lawrence Erlbaum Associates.

Denzin, N. K. (1997). *Interpretive ethnography.* Thousand Oaks, CA: Sage.

Denzin, N. K. (1989a). *Interpretive biography.* Thousand Oaks, CA: Sage.

Denzin, N. K. (1989b). *Interpretive interactionism.* Newbury Park, CA: Sage.

Denzin, N. K. (1989c). The Research Act (3rd edition). Upper Saddle River, NJ: Prentice Hall.

Denzin, N. K., & Lincoln, Y. S. (Eds.). (1994). *Handbook of qualitative research.* Thousand Oaks, CA: Sage.

Denzin, N. K., & Lincoln, Y. S. (Eds.). (2000). *Handbook of qualitative research* (2nd ed.). Thousand Oaks, CA: Sage.

Denzin, N. K., & Lincoln, Y. S. (Eds.). (1998a). *Collecting and interpreting qualitative materials.* Thousand Oaks, CA: Sage.

Denzin, N. K., & Lincoln, Y. S. (Eds.). (1998b). *The landscape of qualitative research: Theories and issues.* Thousand Oaks, CA: Sage.

Derrida, J. (1976). *Of grammatology.* Baltimore, MD: Johns Hopkins University Press.

Derrida, J. (1978). *Writing and difference.* Chicago: University of Chicago Press.

Deshler, D. (1990). Conceptual mapping: Drawing charts of the mind. In J. Mezirow & Associates (Eds.), *Fostering critical reflection in adulthood* (pp. 336–353). San Francisco: Jossey-Bass.

Dewey, J. (1916/1966). *Democracy in education.* NY: Macmillan.

Dewey, J. (1930). From absolutism to experimentalism. In G. Adams, and W. Montgomery (Eds.), *Contemporary American philosophy* (pp.13–27). NY: Macmillan.

Edwards, C., Gandini, L., & Forman, G. (1993). *The hundred languages of children: The Reggio Amelia Approach—Advanced Reflections.* Greenwich, CT: Ablex.

Fals-Borda, O., & Rahman, M. (1991). *Action and knowledge: Breaking the monopoly with participatory action research.* New York: Apex.

Feiman-Nemser, S. (2000). *From preparation to practice: Designing a continuum to strengthen and sustain teaching.* Unpublished manuscript, Michigan State University.

Fine, G., & Sandstrom, K. (1988). *Knowing children: Participant observation with minors.* Thousand Oaks, CA: Sage.

Fink, A. (1995). *The survey handbook.* Thousand Oaks, CA: Sage.

Foucault, M. (1972). *The archaeology of knowledge.* New York: Random House.

Foucault, M. (1984). *The Foucault reader* (P. Rabinow, Ed.). Harmondsworth, UK: Penguin.

Friedman, M. (1974). *The hidden human image.* New York: Dell Publishing.

Friedman, M. (1983). *The confirmation of otherness: In family, community, and society.* New York: Pilgrim Press.

Gadamer, H-G. *Dialogue and dialectic: Eight hermeneutical studies on Plato* (P. Smith, Trans.). New Haven: Yale University Press.

Garfinkel, H. (1967). Studies in ethnomethodology. Englewood Cliffs, NJ: Prentice Hall.

Genat, W. (2002). *Aboriginal health workers: Beyond the clinic, beyond the rhetoric.* Unpublished Ph.D. Thesis. Perth, West Australia: University of Western Australia.

Goffman, E. (1961). *Asylums: Essays on the social situation of mental patients and other inmates.* Garden City, NY: Anchor.

Goodenough, W. (1971). *Culture, language and society.* Reading, MA: Addison-Wesley.

Graue, M., & Walsh, D. (1998). *Studying children in context: Theories, methods, and ethics.* Thousand Oaks, CA: Sage.

Greenbaum T. (Ed.). (2000). *Moderating focus groups: A practical guide for group facilitation.* Thousand Oaks, CA: Sage.

Greig, A., & Taylor, J. (1998). Doing research with children. Thousand Oaks, CA: Sage.

Guba, E. G., & Lincoln, Y. S. (1989). *Fourth generation evaluation.* Newbury Park, CA: Sage.

Habermas, J. (1979). *Communication and the evolution of society* (T. McCarthy, Trans.). Boston: Beacon.

Haraway, D. Situated knowledges: The science question in feminism and the privilege of partial perspective. *Feminist Studies, 14*(3), 575–599.

Hawley, W., & Valli, L. (1999). The essentials of effective professional development: A new consensus. In L. Darling-Hammond & G. Sykes (Eds.), *Teaching as the learning profession: A handbook of policy and practice.* San Francisco: Jossey-Bass.

Heath, S. B. (1983). *Ways with words: Language, life and work in communities and classrooms.* Cambridge, UK: Cambridge University Press.

Heidegger, M. (1962) *Being and time* (J. Macquarie & E. Robinson, Trans.). New York: Harper & Row.

Helm, J. (1999). Projects: Exploring children's interests. *Scholastic Early Childhood Today.* NY: Scholastic.

Henderson, J., Hawthorne, R., & Stollenwerk, D. (2000). *Transformative curriculum leadership* (2nd ed.). Upper Saddle River, NJ: Merrill Prentice Hall.

Heron, J. (1996). *Co-operative inquiry: Research into the human condition.* London: Sage.

Hollingsworth, S. (Ed.). (1997). *International action research: A casebook for educational reform.* London: Falmer.

Holstein, J., & Gubrium, J. (1995). *The active interview.* Thousand Oaks, CA: Sage.

Horowitz, I. (1970). Sociological snoopers and journalistic moralizers. *Transaction, 7,* 4–8.

Huffman, J. (1997). *Beyond Tqm: Tools and techniques for high performance improvement.* Sunnyvale, CA: Lanchester Press.

Husserl, E. (1976). *Logical investigations* (J. Findlay, Trans.). New York: The Humanities Press.

Huyssens, A. (1986). *After the great divide: Modernism, mass culture, postmodernism.* Bloomington: Indiana University Press.

Johnson, B. (2001). Toward a new classification of non-experimental quantitative research. *Educational Researcher, 30* (2).

Johnson, G. (1995). *Fire in the mind: Science, faith and the search for order.* New York: Vintage Books.

Keck, L. (2000). *Children's experience of art in the classroom.* Unpublished manuscript, University of New Mexico at Albuquerque.

Kelly, A., & Sewell, S. (1988). *With head, heart, and hand.* Brisbane, Australia: Boolarong.

Kemmis, S., & McTaggart, R. (1988). *The action research planner.* Geelong, Australia: Deakin University Press.

Kickett, D., McCauley, D., & Stringer, E. (1986). *Community development processes: An introductory handbook.* Perth, Australia: Curtin University of Technology.

Kincheloe, J., & McClaren, P. (1994). Rethinking critical theory and qualitative research. In N. Denzin & Y. Lincoln (Eds.), *Handbook of qualitative research,* 138–157. Thousand Oaks, CA: Sage.

Kozol, J. (1991). *Savage inequalities: Children in America's schools.* New York: Crown.

Krueger, R. (1994). *Focus groups: A practical guide for applied research* (2nd ed.). Thousand Oaks, CA: Sage.

Krueger, R. (1997a). *Moderating focus groups.* Thousand Oaks, CA: Sage.

Krueger, R. (1997b). *Developing questions for focus groups.* Thousand Oaks, CA: Sage.

Krueger, R. A., & Casey, M. A. (2000). *Focus groups: A practical guide for applied research* (3rd ed.). Newbury Park: Sage.

Kvale, S. (1996). *Interviews: An introduction to qualitative research interviewing.* Thousand Oaks, CA: Sage.

Lather, P. (1993). Fertile obsession: Validity after poststructuralism. *Sociological Quarterly, 35.*

Lewin, G., & Lewin, K. (1942). Democracy and the school. *Understanding the Child, 10,* 7–11.

Lewin, K. (1938). Experiments on autocratic and democratic principles. *Social Frontier, 4,* 316–319.

Lewin, K. (1946). Action research and minority problems. *Journal of Social Issues, 2*(4), 34–46.

Lewin, K. (1948). *Resolving Social Conflicts.* New York: Harper.

Lincoln, Y. and E. Guba (1985). *Naturalistic Inquiry.* Newbury Park, CA: Sage.

Lyotard, J-F. (1984). *The postmodern condition: A report on knowledge.* Minneapolis: University of Minnesota Press.

Little, J. (1993). Teacher professional development in a climate of educational reform. Educational evaluation and policy analysis, 15, 129-151.

Makay, J. (1972). *The rhetorical dialogue.* Dubuque, IA: William C. Brown.

Malaguzzi, L. (1995). *The fountains: The unheard voice of children.* Reggio Amelia, Italy: Reggio Children.

Marcus, G. (1986). *Anthropology as cultural critique: An experimental moment in the human sciences.* Chicago: University of Chicago Press.

Marcus, G. (1998). *Ethnography through thick and thin.* Princeton, NJ: Princeton University Press.

Marshall, C., & Rossman, G. (1999). *Designing qualitative research* (3rd ed.). Thousand Oaks, CA: Sage.

McCaleb, S. (1997). *Building communities of learners: A collaboration among teachers, students, families and community.* Mahwah, NJ: Lawrence Erlbaum.

McCracken, G. (1988). *The long interview.* Thousand Oaks, CA: Sage.

McLean, J. (1995). *Improving education through action research: A guide for administrators and teachers.* Thousand Oaks, CA: Corwin.

McDiarmid, G. (1994). *Realizing new learnings for all students: A framework for professional development of Kentucky teachers.* East Lansing, MI: National center for research on teaching.

McEwan, P. (2000). The potential impact of large-scale voucher programs. *Review of Educational Research, 70* (2), 103–149.

McNiff, J. (1995). *Action research principles and practice.* New York: Routledge.

McNiff, J., Lomax, P., & Whitehead, J. (1996). *You and your action research project.* Bournemouth, UK: Hyde.

McTaggart, R. (Ed.). (1997). *Participatory action research: International contexts and consequences.* Albany, NY: SUNY Press.

Mead, G. (1934). *Mind, self and society.* Chicago: University of Chicago Press.

Meerdink, J. (1999). Driving a car for the first time: Teachers, caregivers and a child-driven approach. *Early Childhood Matters: The Bulletin of the Bernard Van Leer Foundation,* Feb. 1999 (91).

Merchant, B., & Willis, A. I. (Eds.). (2001). *Multiple and intersecting identities in qualitative research.* Mahwah, NJ: Lawrence Erlbaum Associates.

Meriam-Webster Online Dictionary (2001).

Milgram, S. (1963). Behavioral study of obedience. *Journal of Abnormal and Social Psychology, 67,* 371–378.

Mills, C. W. (1959). *The sociological imagination.* New York: Oxford.

Mills, G. (2000). *Action research: A guide for the teacher researcher.* Columbus, OH: Merrill/Prentice Hall.

Morgan, D. (1997a). *Planning focus groups.* Thousand Oaks, CA: Sage.

Morgan, D. (1997b). *The focus group guidebook.* Thousand Oaks, CA: Sage.

Morgan, D., & Krueger, R. (1997). The focus group kit: Volumes 1–6. Thousand Oaks, CA: Sage.

Mueller-Vollmer, K. (Ed.). (1985). *The hermeneutics reader.* New York: Continuum.

National Board for Professional Teaching Standards. (1994). *What teachers should know and be able to do.* Detroit: NBPTS.

National Commission on Teaching and America's Future. (1996). *What matters most: Teaching for America's future.* New York: National Commission on Teaching and America's Future.

Nietszche, F. (1979). *On truth and lies in a nonmoral sense. Philosophy and truth: Selections from Nietzsche's notebooks in the early 1870's.* Atlantic City, NJ: Humanities Press.

Noffke, S. (1997). Professional, personal and political dimensions of action research. *Review of Educational Research, 22.* Washington, D.C.: AERA.

Noffke, S., & Stevenson, R. (Eds.). (1995). *Educational action research: Becoming practically critical.* New York: Teachers College Press.

Olesen, V. (1994). Feminist models of qualitative research. In N. Denzin and Y. Lincoln (Eds.), *The handbook of qualitative research.* Thousand Oaks, CA: Sage.

Oliva, P. (2001). *Developing the curriculum* (5th ed.). New York: Longman.

Oppenheim, A. (1966). *Questionnaire design and attitude measurement.* London: Heinemann.

Persig, R. (1974). *Zen and the art of motorcycle maintenance.* New York: Bantam.

Petty, R. (1997). Everything is different now: Surviving ethnographic research. In E. Stringer and colleagues, *Community-based ethnography: Breaking traditional boundaries of research, teaching and learning.* Mahwah, NJ: Lawrence Erlbaum.

Pratiss, J. (Ed.). (1985). *Reflections: The anthropological muse.* Washington, DC: American Anthropological Association.

Punch, M., (1994). Politics and ethics in qualitative research. In N. Denzin, and Y. Lincoln (Eds.), *Handbook of qualitative research.* Thousand Oaks, CA: Sage.

Rabinow, P., & Sullivan, W. (Eds.). (1987). *Interpretive social science: A second look* (2nd ed.). Berkeley: University of California Press.

Reason, P., & Bradbury, H. (2001). *Handbook of action research.* Thousand Oaks, CA: Sage.

Rorty, R. (1989). *Contingency, irony and solidarity.* Cambridge UK: Cambridge University Press.

Rosenau, P. (1992). *Postmodernism and the social sciences: Insights, inroads and intrusions.* Princeton, NJ: Princeton University Press.

Rossi, P. (1997). Having an experience in five act: Multiple literacies through young children's opera. *Language Arts, 74,* No. 5, Sept., 352-367.

Rossi, P. (2000). *Let the data sing: Enlarging understanding through evocative textual forms.* Presentation to the American Educational Research Association national conference, New Orleans, LA.

Rubin, H., & Rubin, I. (1995). *Qualitative interviewing: The art of hearing data.* Thousand Oaks, CA: Sage.

Scheurich, J. (1992). *The paradigmatic transgressions of validity.* Unpublished manuscript. Quoted in N. Denzin & Y. Lincoln, *Handbook of qualitative research.* Thousand Oaks, CA: Sage.

Schmuck, R. (1997). *Practical action research for change.* Arlington Heights, IL: IRI/Skylight Training and Publishing.

Schouten, D., & Watling, R. (1997). *Media action projects: A model for integrating video in project-based education, training and community development.* Nottingham, UK: University of Nottingham Urban Programme Research Group.

Scott, A. (2000). Speaking out: *Middle school students exploration of harassment.* Unpublished paper, University of New Mexico at Albuquerque.

Scriven, M. (1981a). *The logic of evaluation.* Inverness, CA: Edgepress.

Scriven, M. (1981b). Summative teacher evaluation. In J. Millan (Ed.), *Handbook of teacher evaluation.* Beverley Hills, CA: Sage.

Selekman, M. (1997). *Solution-focused therapy with children.* New York: Guilford Press.

Senge, P., et. al. (1994). *The fifth discipline fieldbook.* Garden City, NY: Doubleday.

Sieber, J. (1992). *Planning ethically responsible research.* Newbury Park, CA: Sage.

Silverman, D. (2000). *Doing qualitative research. A practical handbook.* Thousand Oaks, CA: Sage.

Spradley, J. (1979a). *The ethnographic interview.* New York: Holt, Rinehart & Winston.

Spradley, J. (1979b). *Participant observation.* New York: Holt, Rinehart & Winston.

Spradley, J., & McCurdy, D. (1972). *The cultural experience: Ethnography in complex society.* Prospect Heights, IL: Waveland Press.

Stein, M., M. Smith and E. Silver (1999). The development of professional developers: Learning to assist teachers in new settings in new ways. *Harvard Educational Review,* Vol 69, No.3, Fall.

Stringer, E. (1997). *Community based ethnography: Breaking traditional boundaries of research, teaching and learning.* Mahwah, NJ: Lawrence Erlbaum.

Stringer, E. (1999). *Action Research* (2nd ed.). Thousand Oaks, CA: Sage.

Stringer, E., Genat, W., & Associates. (1998). *The double helix of action research.* Qualitative Research in Education Conference, Athens, GA.

Tennant, G. (2001). *Six sigma: SPC and TQM in manufacturing and services.* Brookfield, VT: Gower Publishing.

Trinh, T. (1991). *When the moon waxes red: Representation, gender and cultural politics.* New York: Routledge.

Tyler, R. (1949). *Basic principles of curriculum and instruction.* Chicago: University of Chicago Press.

Van Manen, M. (1979). The phenomenology of pedagogic observation. *Canadian Journal of Education, 4*(1), 5–16.

Van Manen, M. (1982). Phenomenological pedagogy. *Curriculum Inquiry, 12*(3), 283–299.

Van Manen, M. (1984). Practising phenomenological writing. *Phenomenology and pedagogy, 2*(1), 36–39.

Van Manen, M. (1988). The relation between research and pedagogy. In W. F. Pinar (Ed.), *Contemporary curriculum discourses* (pp. 437–452). Scottsdale, AZ: Gorsuch Scarisbrick.

Van Manen, M. (1990). *Researching lived experience: Human science for an action sensitive pedagogy.* London, Ontario: Althouse Press.

Wadsworth, Y. (1997). *Everyday evaluation on the run* (2nd ed.). St. Leonards, NSW: Allen and Unwin.

Wallace, M. (1998). *Action research for language teachers.* Cambridge, UK: Cambridge University Press.

Weis, L., & Fine, M. (2000). *Speed bumps: A student-friendly guide to qualitative research.* New York, NY: Teachers College Press.

Wells, G., Bernard, L., Gianotti, M., Keating, C., Konjevic, C., Kowal, M., Mayer, C., Moscoe, T., Orzechowska, E., Smieja, A., & Swartz, L. (1994). *Changing schools from within: Creating communities of inquiry.* Toronto: OISE Press.

Wiggington, E. (1985). *Sometimes a shining moment: The Foxfire experience.* Garden City, NY: Doubleday.

Wolcott, H. (1994). *Transforming qualitative data: Description, analysis and interpretation.* Thousand Oaks, CA: Sage.

Young, S. (1999). *Negotiating racial boundaries and organizational borders: An interpretive study of a cross cultural training programme.* Unpublished Ph.D. Thesis. Perth, Western Australia: University of Western Australia.

Youngman, M. (1982). Designing and analyzing questionnaires. In J. Bell (Ed.), *Conducting small-scale investigations in educational management.* London: Harper & Row.

Index